UNDERSTANDING ENTOMOLOGY

UNDERSTANDING
ENTOMOLOGY

By

Dr. M. Prakash

Dept. of Zoology
M.M.H. Post Graduate College
Ghaziabad (U.P.)
(India)

DISCOVERY PUBLISHING HOUSE PVT. LTD.
NEW DELHI-110 002

Reprinted - 2019

First Published - 2010

ISBN: 978-81-8356-518-9

Understanding Entomology

Published by:

DISCOVERY PUBLISHING HOUSE PVT. LTD.

4383/4B, Ansari Road, Darya Ganj

New Delhi-110 002 (India)

Phone: +91-11-23279245, 23253475; 43596065

E-mail: discoverybooksindia@gmail.com

discoverypublishinghouse@gmail.com

web: www.discoverypublishinggroup.com

Printed at:

Infinity Imaging Systems

Delhi

Preface

The present title "Understanding Entomology" has been written for those students interested in careers in diverse fields of biological sciences. It provides a structured approach to learning by covering all the important topics in a uniform, systematic format. The book has been comprehensively designed incorporating recent advances in this fast moving field. It also provides accessible information on molecular biology in compact form for undergraduate students in biology and related life sciences. It is intelligible to the educated layman, though it deals with some complex ideas. It is an adequate text for all the requirements of students in this area. In addition, busy lecturers who require a quick reference compendium will find it useful, particularly for tutional planning. Simple, yet hopefully clear figures and tables are provided throughout the book.

The over-riding goal of this book, and indeed of the whole *Understanding series,* is to present the essential information concering molecular biology in a compact, readily accessible form which leads itself to student learning and revision. The convergence of various approaches has generated a rich panorama of detail, the significance of which we are still attempting to unraval. The present text has been written as an introduction to this rapidly growing field.

To make the work more comprehensive and informative, the author has consulted many authoritative books, research journals, abstracts, monographs etc., so there can be no claim to originality except in the manner of treatment.

The author expresses his thanks to his friends and colleagues whose continue inspirations have initiated him to bring out this book.

The author expresses his gratitude to Mr. Wasan and staff of M/s Discovery Publishing House Pvt. Ltd. for their whole hearted cooperation in the publication of this book.

In the mean time, the author will remain sincerely responsible for any shortcomings of the book and be grateful to the readers for their suggestions and constructive criticism for the continuous betterment of the book. He takes this opportunity to appeal to the readers to send their suggestions straightaway to his Publisher.

Author

Contents

1

INTRODUCTION

One of the most striking observations made by travellers (or by visitors to zoos and botanic gardens) is that different plants and animals live in different countries. This is more than a matter of differing climates and ecologies: for example, Australia has suitable trees but no woodpeckers, tropical rain forests without monkeys, and prairie grasslands without native ungulates.

Non-American deserts lack cacti but have a range of ecological analogues including succulent euphorbs. Biogeography is the study of the distributions and the past historical and current ecological explanations for these distributions. Insects, no less than plants and vertebrates, show patterns of restriction to one geographical area (endemism) and entomologists have been and remain amongst the most prominent biogeographers.

Our ideas on the relationship between the size of an area, the number of species supported, and species turnover in ecological time (island biogeography), have come from the study of insects on islands, both oceanic and as habitats isolated in metaphorical 'oceans' of unsuitable habitat. Entomologists were prominent amongst the scientists studying dispersal between areas, across land bridges and corridors, with carabidologists especially prominent.

When the paradigm shifted to interpretation of biogeography within a framework of mobile continents, much of the early biological evidence for the break-up of the once-united southern continental land mass (Gondwana) came from entomologists studying the distribution and evolutionary relationships of organisms shared exclusively between the southern parts of the modern-day continents.

Amongst this cohort, those studying aquatic insects were especially prominent, perhaps because the adult stages are so ephemeral, and the immature stages so tied to freshwater habitats, that long-distance trans-oceanic dispersal seemed an unlikely explanation for the observed disjunct distributions.

Stoneflies, mayflies, dragonflies and aquatic flies including midges (Chironomidae) all show southern hemisphere disjunct associations, even at low taxonomic level. Such studies have implied quite great ages of many of these groups—their current distribution suggests that their direct ancestors must have been subject to Upper Jurassic-Cretaceous earth history events and thus the groups must have been around for well over 140 million years.

Such time-scales do appear to be confirmed by increasing amounts of fossil material, and by some estimations of the purported clock-like acquisition of mutations in molecules. On the finer scale, insect studies have played a major role in understanding the role of geography in processes of species formation and maintenance of local differentiation.

Naturally, the genus *Drosophila* figures prominently, with the Hawaiian radiation having provided valuable data. Studies of parapatric speciation-divergence of spatially separated populations that share a boundary-have involved detailed understanding of orthopteran, especially grasshopper, genetics and microdistributions.

Experimental evidence for sympatric speciation derives principally from tephritid fruitfly research. The range modelling analyses outlined elsewhere in this book exemplify some potential uses of ecological biogeographic rationales to the shallower (recent historical) environmental or climatic distributioninfluencing events.

Entomologists using these tools to interpret recent fossil material from lake sediments have played a vital role in recognizing how some insect distributions changed to track past environmental change, and have been able to provide estimates of past climate fluctuations.

Strong biogeographic patterns in the modern fauna are becoming more difficult to recognize and interpret, as humans have been responsible for the expansion of ranges of certain species and the loss of much endemism such that many of our most familiar insects are *cosmopolitan* (i.e. virtually worldwide) in distribution.

There are at least five explanations for this expansion of so many insects of previously restricted distribution:

- human-loving (anthropophilic) insects, such as many cockroaches, silverfish and houseflies, accompany humans virtually everywhere;

- humans create disturbed habitats wherever they live, and some *synanthropic* (humanassociated) insects act rather like weedy plants and are able to take advantage of disturbed conditions better than native species can (synanthropy is a weaker association with humans than anthropophily);
- insect (and other arthropod) external parasites (*ectoparasites*) and internal parasites (*endoparasites*) of humans and domesticated animals are often cosmopolitan;
- humans rely on agriculture and horticulture, with a few food crops cultivated very widely; plantfeeding (*phytophagous*) insects associated with plant species that were once localized but now disseminated by humans, can follow the introduced plants and may cause damage wherever the host plants grow: many insects have been distributed in this way;
- insects have expanded their ranges by deliberate *anthropogenic* (aided by humans) introduction of selected species as *biological control* agents to control pest plants and animals, including other insects.

Attempts are made to restrict the shipment of agricultural, horticultural, forestry and veterinary pests through quarantine regulations, but much of the mixing of insect faunas took place before effective measures were implemented.

Thus pest insects tend to be identical throughout climatically similar parts of the world, meaning that applied entomologists must take a worldwide perspective in their studies.

NAMING AND CLASSIFICATION OF INSECTS

The formal naming of insects follows the rules of ***nomenclature*** developed for all animals (plants have a slightly different system). *Formal* scientific names are required for unambiguous communication between all scientists, no matter what their native language amongst the thousands used worldwide.

Vernacular (common) names cannot fulfil this need: the same insects may even have different vernacular names amongst peoples that speak the same language. For instance, the British refer to '*ladybirds*' whereas the same coccinellid beetles are 'ladybugs' to Americans. Many insects have no vernacular name, or one common name is given to many species as if only one is involved.

These difficulties are addressed by the *Linnaean* system, in which every species described is given two names. The first is the *generic* (genus) name, used for a usually broader grouping than the second name, which is the *specific* (species) name. These latinized names are always used together and are italicized, as in this book.

The combination of the generic and specific names provides a unique name for every organism. Thus the name *Aeries aegypti* is recognized by any medical entomologist, anywhere, whatever the local name (and there are many) for this disease-transmitting mosquito. In scientific publications, the species name often is followed by the name of the original describer of the species and perhaps also the year in which the name was published legally.

In this textbook we do not follow this practice but, when particular insects are discussed, we give the order and family names to which the species belongs. In publications, after first citation of the combination of generic and species names in the text, it is common practice in subsequent citations to abbreviate the genus to the initial letter only (e.g. *A. aegypti*).

However, where this might be ambiguous, such as for the two mosquito genera *Aeries* and *Anopheles*, the initial two letters *Ae.* and *An.* are used. Various taxonomically defined groups, also called *taxa* (singular: *taxon*), are recognized amongst the insects. As for all other organisms, the basic biological taxon, lying above the individual and population, is the species, which is both the fundamental nomenclatural unit in taxonomy and, arguably, a unit of evolution.

Multi-species studies allow recognition of genera, which are more or less discrete higher groups. In similar manner, genera can be grouped into tribes, tribes into subfamilies, and subfamilies into families. The families of insects are placed in relatively large but easily recognized groups called *orders*.

This hierarchy of *ranks* (or categories) thus extends from the species level through a series of 'higher' levels of greater and greater inclusivity until all true insects are included in one class, the Insecta. There are standard suffixes for certain ranks in the taxonomic hierarchy, so that the rank of some group names can be recognized by inspection of the ending.

According to the classification system used, some 26-29 orders of Insecta may be recognized. Differences arise principally because there are no hardand-fast rules for deciding the taxonomic ranks cited above. There is only a general agreement that groups should be monophyletic, comprising all the descendants of a common ancestor. Orders have been recognized rather arbitrarily in the past two centuries, and the most that can be said is that presently constituted orders contain similar insects sharing major differences from other insect groups.

Over time, a relatively stable classification system has developed, but there remain differences of opinion as to the boundaries around groups, with 'splitters' recognizing a greater number of groups and 'lumpers' favouring broader categories.

Table 1.1: Taxonomic categories (obligatory categories are shown in bold).

Taxonomic category	*Standard suffix*
Order	
Suborder	
Superfamily	-oidea
Family	-idae
Subfamily	-inae
Tribe	-ini
Genus	
Subgenus	
Species	

For example, some American taxonomists group ('lump') the alderflies, dobsonflies, snakeflies and lacewings into one order, the Neuroptera, whereas others, including ourselves, 'split' the group and recognize three separate (but related) orders, Megaloptera, Raphidioptera and a more narrowly defined Neuroptera.

The order Hemiptera sometimes is split into two orders, Homoptera and Heteroptera, but the homopteran grouping now is considered to be invalid (non-monophyletic) and a new classification for these bugs is used. In this book we recognize 29 orders for which the physical characteristics and biologies of their constituent taxa are described, and their relationships considered.

Amongst these orders, we distinguish the '*major*' orders containing a relatively large number of species and including the Coleoptera, Diptera, Lepidoptera, Hymenoptera and Hemiptera -and the remaining 'minor' orders.

Furthermore, the minor orders often have homogeneous ecologies, which can be summarized conveniently in a single descriptive-ecological box following the appropriate ecologically based chapter.

INSECTS AS FOOD

Insects as Human Food: Entomophagy

In this final introductory section, the increasingly *popular* study of insects as human food is reviewed. Probably 1000 or more species of insects in more than 370 genera and 90 families are or have been used for food somewhere in the world, especially in central and southern Africa, Asia, Australia and Latin America.

However, western society has largely overlooked entomological cuisine. Insects are high in protein, energy, and various vitamins and minerals: they can form 5-10% of the annual animal protein consumed by some indigenous peoples.

Food insects generally feed on either living or dead plant matter and chemically protected species are avoided. Termites, crickets, grasshoppers, locusts, beetles, ants, bee brood and moth larvae are the most frequently consumed insects. The typical 'western' repugnance of entomophagy is cultural rather than scientific or rational.

After all, other invertebrates such as certain crustaceans and molluscs are favoured culinary items. Objections to eating insects cannot be justified on the grounds of taste or food value. Many are reported to have a nutty flavour and studies report favourably on the nutritional content of insects, although their aminoacid composition is not ideal and needs to be balanced with suitable plant protein.

Table elsewhere in this chapter presents the nutritional values obtained from analyses conducted on samples of four species of insects cooked according to traditional methods in central Angola, Africa. The insects concerned are: reproductive individuals of a termite, *Macrotermes subhyalinus* (Isoptera: Termitidae), which are de-winged and fried in palm oil; the large caterpillars of two species of moth, *Imbrasia ertli* and *Usta terpsichore* (Lepidoptera: Saturniidae), which are de-gutted and cooked in water, roasted or sun-dried; and the larvae of the palm weevil, *Rhynchophorus phoenicis* (Coleoptera: Curculionidae), which are slit open and then fried whole in oil.

Mature larvae of *Rhynchophorus* species have been appreciated by people in tropical areas of Africa, Asia and the Neotropics for centuries.

These fat, legless grubs, often called palmworms, provide one of the richest sources of animal fat with substantial amounts of riboflavin, thiamine, zinc and iron.

Primitive cultivation systems, involving the cutting down of palm trees to provide suitable food for the weevils, are known from Brazil,

Table 1.2: Proximate, mineral and vitamin analyses of four edible Angolan insects (percentages of daily human dietary requirements/ 100 g of insects consumed).

Requirement per capita (reference Nutrient	*Macrotermes subhyalinus* person)	*Rhynchophorus Imbrasia ertli* (Termitidae)	*Usta terpsichore* (Saturniidae)	*phoenicis* (Saturniidae)	(Curculionidae)
Energy	2850 kcal	21.5	13.2	13.0	19.7
Protein	37g	38.4	26.3	76.3	18.1
Calcium	1g	4.0	5.0	35.5	18.6
Phosphorus	1g	43.8	54.6	69.5	31.4
Magnesium	400mg	104.2	57.8	13.5	7.5
Iron	18 mg	41.7	10.6	197.2	72.8
Copper	2 mg	680.0	70.0	120.0	70.0
Zinc	15 mg			153.3	158.0
Thiamine	1.5 mg	8.7		244.7	201.3
Riboflavin	1.7mg	67.4		112.2	131.7
Niacin	20 mg	47.7		26.0	38.9

Colombia, Paraguay and Venezuela. In plantations, however, palmworms are regarded as pests because they can seriously damage living coconut and oil palm trees. In central Africa, the people of southern Zaire (the present Democratic Republic of Congo) eat caterpillars belonging to a few dozen species.

The calorific value of these caterpillars is high, with their protein content ranging from 45 to 80%, and they are a rich source of iron. Where there is chronic or seasonal shortage of vertebrate protein reserves elsewhere in sub-Saharan Africa, insect alternatives are often used or even preferred. For instance, caterpillars are the most important source of animal protein in some areas of the Northern Province of Zambia.

The edible caterpillars of the emperor moth *Imbrasia belina* (Saturniidae), locally called mumpa, are much prized as food. People travel hundreds of kilometres to pick mumpa, which provides a highly lucrative market. The caterpillars contain 60-70% protein on a dry-matter basis, and offset malnutrition caused by protein deficiency. Mumpa are fried fresh or they are boiled and sun-dried prior to storage.

Further south, in Botswana, Namibia, South Africa and Zimbabwe, the caterpillars of the same emperor moth *I. belina*, here called phane (but often referred to as mopane or mophane worms, a tautology), also are widely utilized. Caterpillars are usually de-gutted, boiled, salted

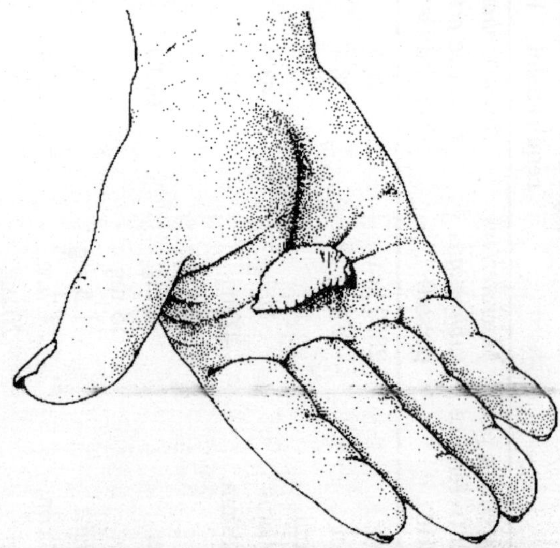

Figure 1.1: A mature larva of the palm weevil, Rhynchophorus phoenicis (Coleoptera: Curculionidae)—a traditional food item in central Angola, Africa.

and then dried; after processing they contain about 50% protein and 15% fat -approximately twice the values for cooked beef.

The Pedi people of northern Transvaal are reported to prefer phane to beef. There are concerns, however, that the phane may be over-exploited unless harvesting can be controlled at sustainable levels. In the Philippines, June beetles (melolonthine scarabs), weaver ants (*Oecophylla smaragdina*), mole crickets and locusts are eaten in some regions. Locusts form an important dietary supplement during outbreaks, which apparently have become less common since the widespread use of insecticides.

Various species of grasshoppers and locusts were eaten commonly by native tribes in western North America prior to the arrival of Europeans. The number and identity of species used have been poorly documented, but species of *Melanoplus* were consumed.

Harvesting involved driving grasshoppers into a pit in the ground by fire or advancing people, or herding them into a bed of coals. Today people in central America, especially Mexico, still harvest, sell, cook and consume grasshoppers. Australian Aborigines use (or once used) a wide range of insect foods, especially moth larvae.

The caterpillars of wood or ghost moths (Cossidae and Hepialidae) are called witchety grubs, from an Aboriginal word 'witjuti' for the *Acacia* species (wattles), whose roots and stems the grubs feed on.

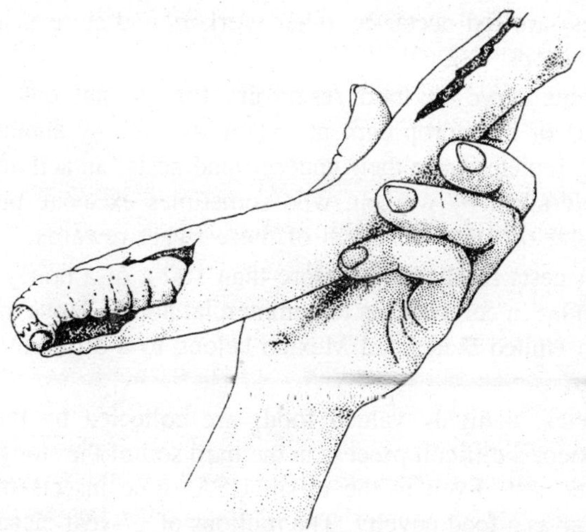

Figure 1.2: A delicacy of the Australian Aborigines-a witchety (or witjuti) grub, a caterpillar of a wood moth (Lepidoptera: Cossidae), that feeds on the roots and stems of witjuti bushes (certain Acacia *species).*

Witchety grubs are regarded as a delicacy and they contain 7-9% protein, 14-38% fat and 7-16% sugars, as well as being good sources of iron and calcium.

Adults of the bogong moth, *Agrotis infusa* (Noctuidae), once formed another famous Aboriginal food, being collected in their millions from aestivating sites in narrow caves and crevices on mountain summits in southeastern Australia. Moths cooked in hot ashes provided a rich source of dietary fat.

Aboriginal people living in central and northern Australia eat the contents of the apple-sized galls of *Cystococcus porniformis* (Hemiptera: Eriococcidae), commonly called bush coconuts or bloodwood apples. These galls occur only on bloodwood eucalypts (*Corymbia* spp.) and can be very abundant after a favourable growing season.

Each mature gall contains a single adult female, up to 4cm long, which is attached by her mouth area to the base of the inner gall and has her abdomen plugging a hole in the gall apex. The inner wall of the gall is lined with white edible flesh, about 1 cm thick, which serves as the feeding site for the male offspring of the female.

Aborigines relish the watery female insect and her nutty-flavoured nymphs, and also scrape out and consume the white coconut-like flesh of the inner gall. A favourite source of sugar for Australian aboriginals living in arid regions is from species of *Melophorus* and *Cainponotus* (Formicidae), popularly known as honeypot ants. Specialized workers (called repletes) are fed nectar by other workers and store it in their huge distended crops.

The repletes serve as food reservoirs for the ant colony and regurgitate part of their crop contents when solicited by another ant. Aborigines dig repletes from their underground nests, an activity most frequently undertaken by women, who sometimes excavate pits to a depth of a metre or more in search of these sweet rewards.

Individual nests rarely supply more than 100 g of a honey that is essentially similar in composition to commercial honey. Honeypot ants in the western United States and Mexico belong to a different genus, *Myrmecocystus*.

The repletes, a highly valued food, are collected by the rural people of Mexico, a difficult process in the hard soil of the stony ridges where the ants nest. Even in the urban USA some insects may yet become popular as a food novelty. The millions of 17-year cicadas that periodically plague cities such as Chicago are edible.

Newly hatched cicadas, called tenerals, are best for eating because their soft body cuticle means that they can be consumed without first removing the legs and wings. These tasty morsels can be marinated or dipped in batter and then deep-fried, boiled and spiced, roasted and ground, or stir-fried with favourite seasonings.

Large-scale harvest or mass production of insects for human consumption brings some practical and other problems. The small size of most insects presents difficulties in collection or rearing and in processing for sale.

The unpredictability of many wild populations needs to be overcome by the development of culture techniques, especially as overharvesting from the wild could threaten the viability of some insect populations. Another problem is that not all insect species are safe to eat. Warningly coloured insects are often distasteful or toxic and some people can develop allergies to insect material.

However, several advantages derive from eating insects. The encouragement of entomophagy in many rural societies, particularly those with a history of insect use, may help diversify peoples' diets. By incorporating mass harvesting of pest insects into control programmes, the use of pesticides can be reduced.

Furthermore, if carefully regulated, cultivating insects for protein should be less environmentally damaging than cattle ranching, which devastates forests and native grasslands. Insect farming (the rearing of minilivestock) is compatible with low-input, sustainable agriculture, and most insects have a high food conversion efficiency compared with conventional meat animals.

Insects as Feed for Domesticated Animals

If you do not relish the prospect of eating insects yourself, then perhaps the concept of insects as a protein source for domesticated animals is more acceptable. The nutritive value of insects as feed for fish, poultry, pigs and farm-grown mink certainly is recognized in China, where feeding trials have shown that insect-derived diets can be cost-effective alternatives to more conventional fishmeal diets.

The insects involved are primarily the larvae and pupae of houseflies (*Musca domestics*), the pupae of silkworms (*Bombyx mori*) and the larvae of mealworms (*Tenebrio molitor*). The same or related insects are being used or investigated elsewhere, particularly as poultry or fish feedstock.

Silkworm pupae, a byproduct of the silk industry, can be used as a highprotein supplement for chickens. In India, poultry are fed the meal that remains after the oil has been extracted from the pupae. Fly larvae fed to chickens can recycle animal manure, and the development of a range of insect recycling systems for converting organic wastes into feed supplements is inevitable, given that most organic substances are fed on by one or more insect species.

Clearly insects can form part of the nutritional base of people and their domesticated animals. Further research is needed and a database with accurate identifications is required to handle biological information. We must know which species we are dealing with in order to make use of information gathered elsewhere on the same or related insects.

Data on the nutritional value, seasonal occurrence, host plants or other dietary needs, and rearing or collecting methods must be collated for all actual or potential food insects. Opportunities for insect food enterprises are numerous, given the immense diversity of insects.

2

Social Insects

The study of insect social behaviours is a favourite entomological topic and there is a voluminous literature, ranging from the popular to the highly theoretical. The proliferation of some insects, notably the ants and termites, is attributed to the major change from a solitary lifestyle to a social one.

Social insects are ecologically successful and have important effects on human life. Leaf-cutter ants (*Atta spp.*) are the major herbivores in the Neotropics, and in southwestern US deserts, harvester ants take as many seeds as do mammals. Termites turn over as much or more soil than earthworms in many regions.

The numerical dominance of social insects can be astonishing, with a Japanese supercolony of *Formica* ycssensis estimated at 306 million workers and over I million queens dispersed over 2.7km^2 amongst 45000 interconnected nests. In west African savanna, densities of up to 20 million resident ants per hectare have been estimated, and single nomadic colonies of driver ants (*Dorylits* sp.) may attain 20 million workers.

Estimates of the value of honey bees in commercial honey production, as well as in pollination of agricultural and horticultural crops, run into hundreds of millions of dollars per annum in the USA alone. Social insects clearly affect our lives. A broad definition of social behaviour could include all insects that interact in any way with other members of their species.

However, entomologists limit sociality to a more restricted range of *cooperative* behaviours. Amongst the social insects, we can recognize *eusocial* (*'true social'*) insects, which co-operate in reproduction and have division of reproductive effort, and subsocial (*'below social'*) *insects*, which have less strongly developed social habits, falling short of extensive co-operation and reproductive partitioning. Solitary insects exhibit no social behaviours.

Eusociality is defined by three traits:

- Division of labour, with a caste *system* involving sterile individuals assisting those that reproduce.
- Co-operation among colony members in tending the young.
- Overlap of generations capable of contributing to colony functioning.

Eusociality is restricted to all ants and termites and some bees and wasps, such as the vespine paper wasps depicted in the vignette of this chapter. Subsociality is a more widespread phenomenon, known to have arisen independently in 13 orders of insects, including some cockroaches, embiids, thysanopterans, hemipterans, beetles and hymenopterans.

As insect lifestyles become better known, forms of subsociality may be found in yet more orders. The term 'presociality' often is used for social behaviours that do not fulfil the strict definition of eusociality. However, the implication that presociality is an evolutionary precursor to eusociality is not always correct and the term is best avoided.

In this chapter we discuss subsociality prior to detailed treatment of eusociality in bees, wasps, ants and termites. We conclude with some ideas concerning the origins and success of eusociality.

SUBSOCIALITY IN INSECTS

Aggregation

Non-reproductive aggregations of insects, such as the gregarious overwintering of monarch butterflies at specific sites in Mexico and California, are social interactions. Many tropical butterflies form roosting aggregations, particularly in *aposematic* species (distasteful and with warning signals including colour and/or odour).

Aposematic phytophagous insects often form conspicuous feeding aggregations, sometimes using pheromones to lure conspecific individuals to a favourable site. A solitary aposematic insect runs a greater risk of being encountered by a naive predator (and being eaten by it) than if it is a member of a conspicuous group.

Belonging to a conspicuous social grouping, either of the same or several species, provides benefits by the sharing of protective warning colouration and the education of local predators.

Parental Care as a Social Behaviour

Parental care may be considered to be a social behaviour, although few insects, if any, show a complete lack of parental care: eggs are not deposited randomly. Females select an appropriate oviposition site, affording protection to the eggs and ensuring an appropriate food resource for the hatching offspring.

The ovipositing female may protect the eggs in an ootheca, or deposit them directly into suitable substrate with her ovipositor, or modify the environment, as in nest construction.

Parental care conventionally is seen as postoviposition and/or posthatching attention, involving providing and protecting food resources for the young. A convenient basis for discussing parental care is to distinguish between care with and without nest construction.

Parental Care Without Nesting

For most insects, the highest mortality occurs in the egg and first instar, and many insects tend these stages until the more mature larvae or nymphs can better fend for themselves. The orders of insects in which tending of eggs and young is most frequent are the *Blattodea*, *Orthoptera* and *Dermaptera* (the orthopteroid orders), *Embiidina*, *Psocoptera*, *Thysanoptera*, *Hemiptera*, *Coleoptera* and *Hymenoptera*.

There has been a tendency to assume that subsociality in orthopteroids is a precursor of Isoptera eusociality, as the eusocial termites are related to cockroaches. The phylogenetic position and social behaviour, including parental care, of the subsocial cockroach *Cryptocercus*, has provoked much speculation on the origin of sociality. Egg and early-instar attendance is predominantly a female role, yet paternal guarding is known in some Hemiptera, notably amongst some tropical assassin bugs (Reduviidae) and giant water bugs (Belostomatidae).

The female belostomatid oviposits onto the dorsum of the male, which receives eggs in small batches after each copulation. The male may even accept eggs from more than one female. The male either swims close to the oxygenated surface of the water, or makes deliberate ventilatory movements that create an oxygenated current over the eggs, which die if unattended.

There is no tending of belostomatid nymphs, unlike many other hemipterans in which the female (or in some reduviids, the male) often guards at least the early-instar nymphs. In these species, experimental removal of the tending adult leads to increased losses of eggs and nymphs as a result of parasitization and/or predation. Other functions of parental care include keeping the eggs free from fungi, maintaining appropriate conditions for egg development, herding the young and sometimes actually feeding them.

In an unusual case, certain treehoppers (Hemiptera: Membracidae) have 'delegated' parental care of their young to ants. Ants obtain honeydew from treehoppers, which are protected from their natural enemies by the presence of the ants. In the presence of protective ants, brooding females prematurely may cease to tend a first brood and raise a second one.

Another species of membracid will abandon its eggs in the absence of ants and seek a larger treehopper aggregation, where ants are in attendance, before laying another batch of eggs. Many wood-mining beetles show advanced subsocial care that verges on the nesting described in the following section and on eusociality.

For instance, all Passalidae (Coleoptera) live in communities of larvae and adults, with the adults chewing dead wood to form a substrate for the larvae to feed upon. Some ambrosia beetles (Platypodidae) prepare galleries for their offspring, where the larvae feed on cultivated fungus and are defended by a male that guards the tunnel entrance. Whether or not these feeding galleries are called nests is a matter of semantics.

Parental Care with Wolitary Nesting

Nesting is a social behaviour in which the parents use a structure (pre-existing or newly constructed) in which to lay their eggs, and to which the parent(s) bring food supplies for the young. Nesting, as thus defined, is seen in only five insect orders, of which the nests of eusocial Hymenoptera and the prodigious mounds of the eusocial termites will be discussed later in this chapter.

Nest-builders amongst the subsocial Orthoptera, Dermaptera, Coleoptera and subsocial Hymenoptera are discussed below. Earwigs of both sexes overwinter in a nest. In spring, the male is ejected when the mother starts to tend the eggs. In some species mother earwigs forage and provide food for the young nymphs. Mole crickets and other ground-nesting crickets exhibit somewhat similar behaviour.

A greater range of nesting behaviours is seen in the beetles, particularly in the dung beetles (Scarabaeidae) and carrion beetles (Silphidae). Here the food source is shortlived, scattered, but nutrient-rich dung (and carrion) that attracts so many insects that competition is great. Dung beetles that locate a fresh source remove it from danger of usurpation and desiccation by rapid burial.

Some scarabs roll the dung away from its source, others coat the dung with clay. Both sexes co-operate, but the female is mostly responsible for burrowing and preparation of the larval food source. Eggs are laid on the buried dung and in some species no further interest is taken.

However, in others parental care is well developed, commonly with maternal attention to fungus reduction, and paternal defence to remove or exclude ants. Amongst the Hymenoptera, subsocial nesting is restricted to some aculeate Apocrita, namely within the superfamilies Chrysidoidea, Vespoidea and Apoidea; these wasps and bees are the most prolific and diverse nest builders amongst the insects.

Excepting bees, nearly all these insects are parasitoids, in which adults attack and immobilize arthropod prey upon which the young feed. Wasps demonstrate a series of increasingly complex prey handling and nesting strategies, from using the prey's own burrow (e.g. many Pompilidae), to building a simple burrow after prey-capture (a few Sphecidae), to construction of a burrow (which can be termed a nest) prior to prey-capture (most Sphecidae).

In bees and masarine wasps, pollen replaces arthropod prey as the food source that is collected and stored for the larvae. Nest complexity in the aculeates ranges from a single burrow provisioned with one food item for one developing egg, to linearly or radially arranged multicellular nests.

The primitive nest site was probably a pre-existing burrow, with the construction medium later being soil or sand. Further specializations involved the use of plant material-stems, rotten wood, and even solid wood by carpenter bees (Xylocopini)-and free-standing constructions of chewed vegetation (Megachilinae), mud (Eumeninae) and saliva (Colletinae).

In some subsocial nesters, many individuals of one species may aggregate, building their nests close together as in mason wasps (Eumeninae).

Parental Care with Communal Nesting

When favourable conditions for nest construction are scarce and scattered throughout the environment, communal nesting may occur. Even under apparently favourable conditions, many subsocial and all eusocial hymenopterans share nests.

Communal nesting may stem from daughters choosing to nest in their natal nest, giving enhanced utilization of nesting resources and mutual defence against parasites. However, communal nesting in subsocial species allows 'antisocial' or selfish behaviour, with nest and prey usurpation apparently a frequent occurrence, so that extended time defending the nest against others of the same species may be required.

Furthermore, the same cues that lead the wasps and bees to communal nesting sites easily can direct specialized nest parasites to the location. Examples of communal nesting in subsocial species are known or presumed in the Sphecidae, Halictinae, Megachilinae and Andreninae. After oviposition, female bees and wasps remain in their nests, often until the next generation emerges as adults.

They generally guard, but they also may remove faeces and generally maintain nest hygiene. The supply of provisions to the nest may be through mass provisioning, as in many communal sphecids and subsocial bees, or replenishment, as seen in the many vespid wasps that return with new prey as their larvae develop.

Subsocial Aphids and Thrips

Certain aphids belonging to the subfamilies Pemphiginae and Hormaphidinae (Hemiptera: Aphididae) have a sacrificial sterile soldier caste, consisting of some first- or second-instar nymphs that exhibit aggressive behaviour and never develop into adults.

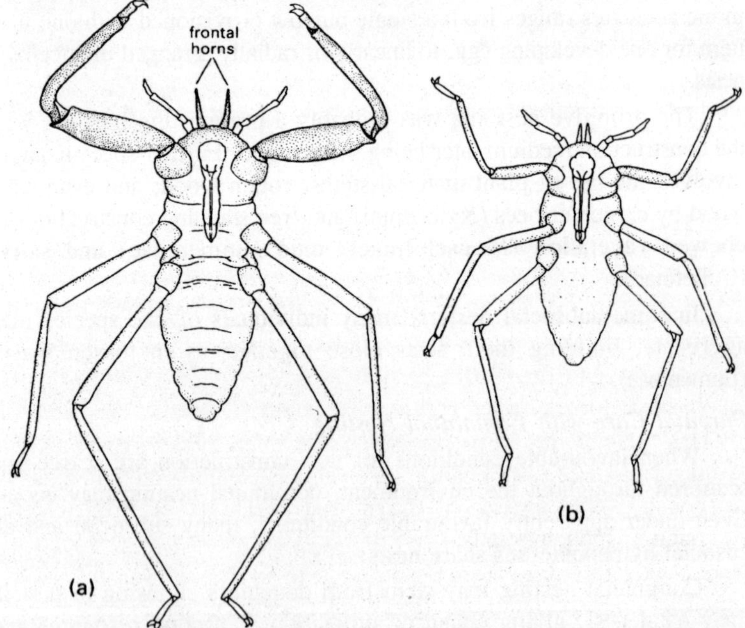

Figure 2.1: First-instar nymphs of the subsocial aphid Pseudoregina alexanderi (Hemiptera: Hormaphidinae): (a) pseudoscorpion-like soldier; (b) normal nymph.

A similar phenomenon occurs in other related aphid species, but in this case all nymphs become temporary soldiers, which later moult into normal, nonaggressive individuals that reproduce. Soldiers are pseudoscorpion-like, as a result of body sclerotization and enlarged anterior legs, and will attack intruders using either their frontal horns (anterior cuticular projections) or feeding stylets (mouthparts) as piercing weapons.

These modified individuals may defend good feeding sites against competitors or defend their colony against predators. As the offspring are produced by parthenogenesis, soldiers and normal nymphs from the same mother aphid should be genetically identical, favouring the evolution of these non-reproductive and apparently altruistic soldiers (as a result of increased inclusive fitness via kin selection).

This unusual aphid polymorphism has led some researchers to claim that the Hemiptera is a third insect order displaying eusociality. Although these few aphid species clearly have a reproductive division of labour, they do not appear to fulfil the other attributes of eusocial insects, as overlap of generations capable of contributing to colony labour is equivocal and tending of offspring does not occur.

Here we consider these aphids to exhibit subsocial behaviour. A range of subsocial behaviours is seen in a few species of several genera of thrips (*Thysanoptera*: *Phlaeothripidae*). At least in the gall thrips, the level of sociality appears to be similar to that of the aphids discussed above. Thrips sociality is well developed in a bark-dwelling species of *Anactinothrips from* Panama, in which thrips live communally, cooperate in brood care and forage with their young in a highly co-ordinated fashion. However, this species has no obvious non-reproductive females and all adults may disappear before the young are fully grown.

Evolution of subsocial behaviours in *Anactinothrips* may bring advantages to the young in group foraging, as feeding sites, although stable over time, are patchy and difficult to locate. In several species of Australian gall thrips, females show polymorphic wing reduction associated in some species with very enlarged fore legs.

This 'soldier' morph is more frequent amongst the first young to develop, which are differentially involved in defending the gall against intrusion by other species of thrips, and appear to be incapable of dispersing or inducing galls.

As most thrips probably have a haplodiploid sex determination system, gall foundation by a single female, polymorphic offspring and establishment of multiple generations, self-sacrificing defence by some individuals should be favoured by the high relatedness of the offspring.

However, it seems that soldiers are defending their siblings, and any offspring, but not their mother, as there is little generational overlap. There is no definitive evidence that soldiers are a non-reproductive caste, and thus the case for eusociality is not yet established in thrips. Nonetheless these examples are valuable in showing the circumstances under which co-operation might evolve.

Quasisociality and Semisociality

Division of reproductive labour is restricted to the subsocial aphids amongst the insect groups discussed above: all females of all the other subsocial insects can reproduce. Within the social Hymenoptera, females show variation in fecundity, or reproductive division of labour.

This variation ranges from fully reproductive (the subsocial species described above), through reduced fecundity (many halictine bees), the laying of only male eggs (workers of *Bombes*), sterility (workers of *Aphaenogaster*), to super-reproductives (queens of *Apis*).

This range of female behaviours is reflected in the classification of social behaviours in the Hymenoptera. Thus, in *quasisocial* behaviour, a communal nest consists of members of the same generation all of which assist in brood rearing, and all females are able to lay eggs, even if not necessarily at the same time.

In *semisocial* behaviour, the communal nest similarly contains members of the same generation co-operating in brood care, but there is division of reproductive labour, with some females (queens) laying eggs, whereas their sisters act as workers and rarely lay eggs. This differs from eusociality only in that the workers are sisters to the egg-laying queens, rather than daughters, as is the case in eusociality.

As in primitive eusocial hymenopterans there is no morphological (size or shape) difference between queens and workers. Any or all the subsocial behaviours discussed above may be evolutionary precursors of eusociality. It is clear that solitary nesting is the primitive behaviour, with communal nesting (and additional subsocial behaviours) having arisen independently in many lineages of aculeate hymenopterans.

EUSOCIALITY IN INSECTS

Eusocial insects have a division of labour in their colonies, involving a caste system comprising a restricted reproductive group of one or several *queens*, aided by *workers*-sterile individuals that assist the reproducers-and in termites and many ants, an additional defensive *soldier* group. There may be further division into subcastes that perform specific tasks. At their most specialized, members of some castes, such as queens and soldiers, may lack the ability to feed themselves.

The tasks of workers therefore include bringing food to these individuals as well as to the brood-the developing offspring. The primary differentiation is female from male. In eusocial Hymenoptera, which are *haplodiploid* in sex determination, queens control the sex of their offspring. Releasing stored sperm fertilizes haploid eggs, which develop into diploid female offspring, whereas unfertilized eggs produce male offspring.

At most times of the year, reproductive females (queens, or *gynes*) are rare compared with sterile female workers. Males do not form castes and may be infrequent and short-lived, dying soon after mating. In termites (Isoptera), males and females may be equally represented, with both sexes contributing to the worker caste.

A single male termite, the king, may permanently attend the gyne. Members of different castes, if derived from a single pair of parents, are close genetically and may be morphologically similar, or, as a result of environmental influence, may be morphologically very different (polymorphic).

Individuals within a caste (or subcaste) often differ behaviourally, in what is termed *polyethism*, either by an individual performing different tasks at different times in its life (age polyethism), or by individuals within a caste specializing on certain tasks during their lives.

The intricacies of social insect caste systems can be considered in terms of the increasing complexity demonstrated in the Hymenoptera, but concluding with the remarkable systems of the termites (Isoptera).

The Primitively Eusocial Hymenopterans

Hymenopterans exhibiting primitive eusociality include polistine vespids (paper wasps of the genus *Polistes*), stenogastrine wasps and even one sphecid. In these wasps, all individuals are morphologically similar and live in colonies that seldom last more than one year.

The colony is often founded by more than one *gyne*, but rapidly becomes *monogynous*, i.e. dominated by one queen with other foundresses either departing the nest or remaining but reverting to a worker-like state. The queen establishes a dominance hierarchy physically by biting, chasing and begging for food, with the winning queen gaining monopoly rights to egg-laying and initiation of cell construction.

Dominance may be incomplete, with non-queens laying some eggs: the dominant queen may eat these eggs or allow them to develop as workers to assist the colony. The first brood of females produced by the

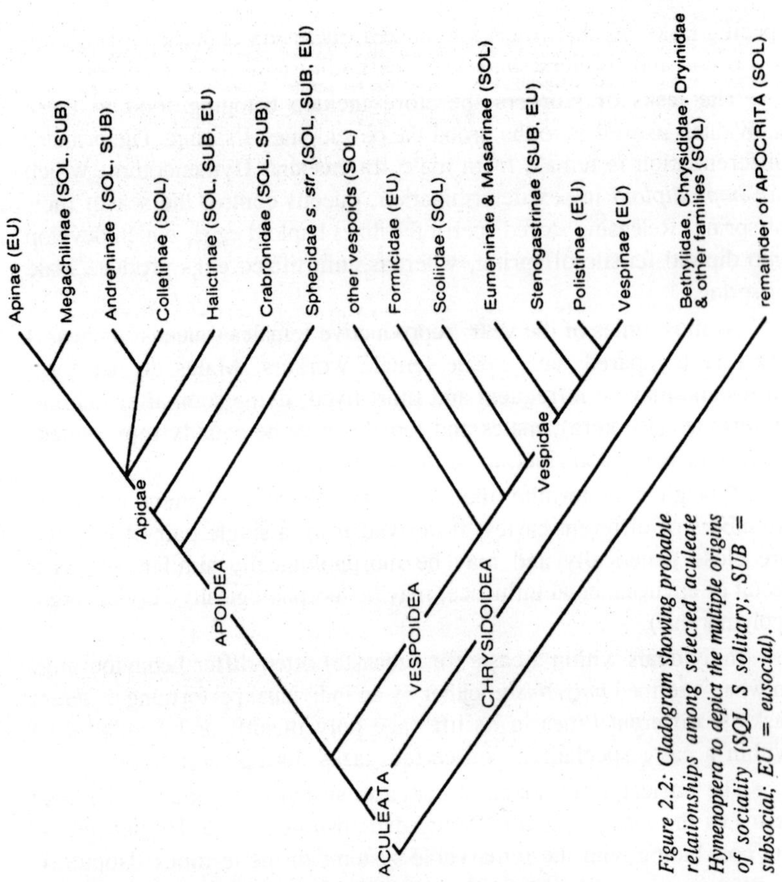

Figure 2.2: Cladogram showing probable relationships among selected aculeate Hymenoptera to depict the multiple origins of sociality (SOL S solitary; SUB = subsocial; EU = eusocial).

colony is of small workers, but subsequent workers increase in size as nutrition improves and as worker assistance in rearing increases.

Sexual retardation in subordinates is reversible: if the queen dies (or is removed experimentally) either a subordinate foundress takes over, or if none is present, a high-ranking worker can mate (if males are present) and lay fertile eggs.

Some other species of primitively eusocial wasps are *polygynous*, retaining several functional queens throughout the duration of the colony, whereas others are serially polygynous, with a succession of functional queens. Primitively eusocial bees, such as certain species of Halictinae, have a similar breadth of behaviours.

In female castes, differences in size between queens and workers range from little or none to no overlap in their sizes. Bumble bees

(Apidae: *Bombus* spp.) found colonies through a single gyne, often after a fight to the death between gynes vying for a nest site. The first brood consists only of workers that are dominated by the queen physically, by aggression and by eating of any worker eggs, and by means of pheromones that modify the behaviour of the workers.

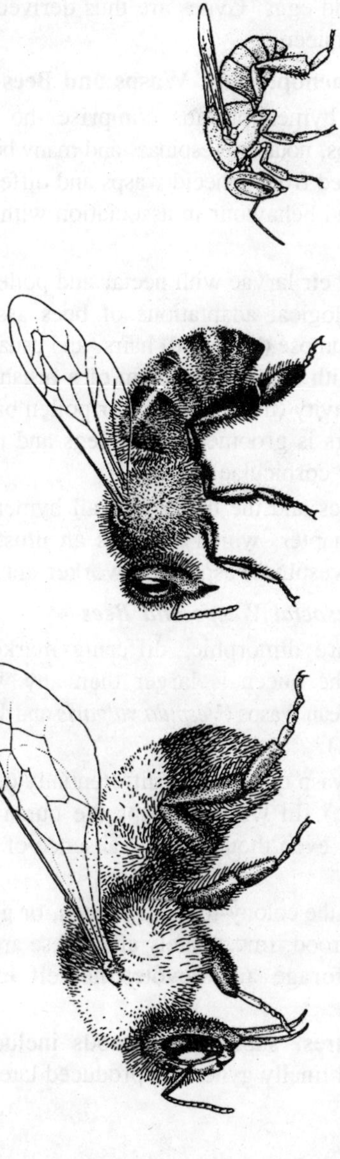

Figure 2.3: Worker bees from three eusocial genera, from left, Boinhis, Apis and Trigona (Apidae: Apinae) superficially resemble each other in morphology, but they differ in size and ecology, including their pollination preferences.

In the absence of the queen, or late in the season as the queen's physical and chemical influence wanes, workers can undergo ovarian development. The queen eventually fails to maintain dominance over those workers that have commenced ovarian development, and the queen either is killed or driven from the nest.

When this happens workers are unmated, but they can produce male offspring from their haploid eggs. Gynes are thus derived solely from the fertilized eggs of the queen.

Specialized Eusocial Hymenopterans: Wasps and Bees

The highly eusocial hymenopterans comprise the ants (family Formicidae) and some wasps, notably Vespinae, and many bees, including the Apinae. Bees are derived from sphecid wasps and differ from wasps in anatomy, physiology and behaviour in association with their dietary specialization.

Most bees provision their larvae with nectar and pollen rather than animal material. Morphological adaptations of bees associated with pollen collection include plumose (branched) hairs, and usually a widened hind basitarsus adorned with hairs in the form of a brush (*scopa*) or a fringe surrounding a concavity (the *corbicula*, or pollen basket). Pollen collected on the body hairs is groomed by the legs and transferred to the mouthparts, scopae or corbiculae.

The diagnostic features and the biology of all hymenopterans are dealt elsewhere in this chapter, which includes an illustration of the morphology of a worker vespine wasp and a worker ant.

Colony and Castes in Eusocial Wasps and Bees

The female castes are dimorphic, differing markedly in their appearance. Generally, the queen is larger than any worker, as in vespines, such as the European wasps (*Vespula vulgaris* and *V. germanica*), and honey bees (*Apis spp.*).

The typical eusocial wasp queen has a differentially (allometrically) enlarged gaster (abdomen). In worker wasps the bursa copulatrix is small, preventing mating, even though in the absence of a queen their ovaries will develop.

In the vespine wasps, the colony-founding queen, or gyne, produces only workers in the first brood. Immediately after these are hatched, the queen wasp ceases to forage and devotes herself exclusively to reproduction.

As the colony matures, subsequent broods include increasing proportions of males, and finally gynes are produced late in the season

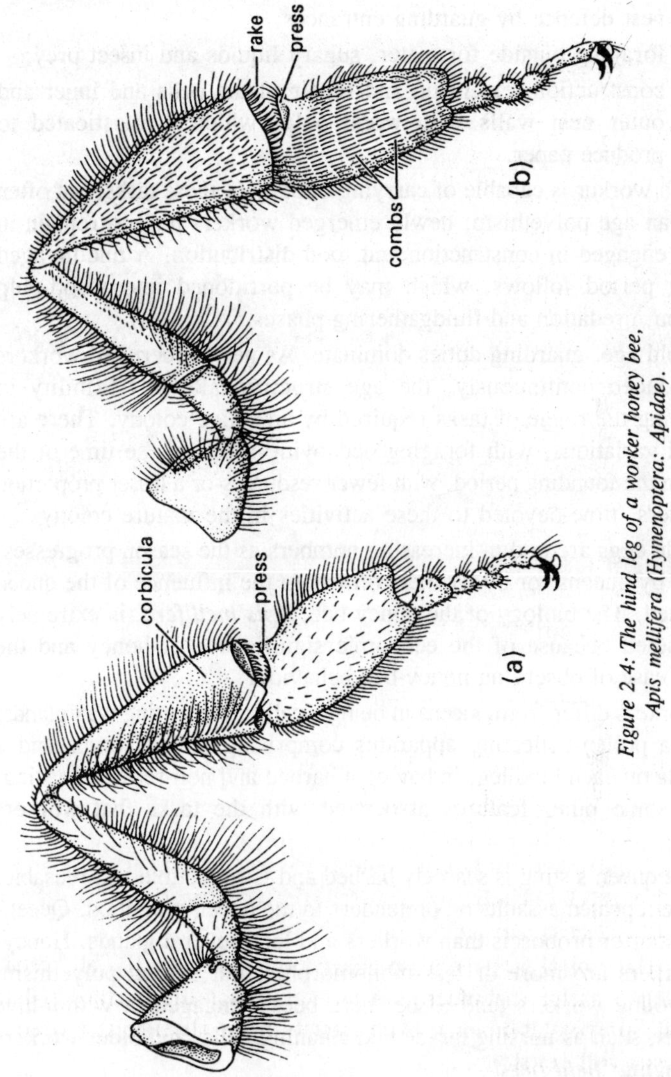

Figure 2.4: The hind leg of a worker honey bee, Apis mellifera (Hymenoptera: Apidae).

from larger cells than those from which workers are produced.

The tasks of vespine workers include:

- distribution of protein-rich food to larvae and carbohydrate-rich food to adult wasps;
- cleaning cells and disposal of dead larvae;
- ventilation and air-conditioning of the nest by wing-fanning;

- nest defence by guarding entrances;
- foraging outside for water, sugary liquids and insect prey;
- construction, extension and repair of the cells and inner and outer nest walls with wood pulp, which is masticated to produce paper.

Each worker is capable of carrying out any of these tasks, but often there is an age polyethism: newly emerged workers tend to remain in the nest engaged in construction and food distribution. A middle-aged foraging period follows, which may be partitioned into wood-pulp collection, predation and fluidgathering phases.

In old age, guarding duties dominate. As newly recruited workers are produced continuously, the age structure allows flexibility in performing the range of tasks required by an active colony. There are seasonal variations, with foraging occupying much of the time of the colony in the founding period, with fewer resources-or a lesser proportion of workers' time-devoted to these activities in the mature colony.

Male eggs are laid in increasing numbers as the season progresses, perhaps by queens, or by workers on whom the influence of the queen has waned. The biology of the honey bee, *Apis mellifera*, is extremely well studied because of the economic significance of honey and the relative ease of observing honey-bee behaviour.

Workers differ from queens in being smaller, possessing wax glands, having a pollen-collecting apparatus comprising pollen combs and a corbicula on each hind leg, in having a barbed and non-retractible sting, and in some other features associated with the tasks that workers perform.

The queen's sting is scarcely barbed and is retractible and reusable, allowing repeated assaults on pretenders to the queen's position. Queens have a shorter proboscis than workers and lack several glands. Honey-bee workers are more or less monomorphic, but exhibit polyethism. Thus, young workers tend to be 'hive bees', engaged in within-hive activities, such as nursing larvae and cleaning cells, and older workers are foraging '*field bees*'.

Seasonal changes are evident, such as the 8-9-month longevity of winter bees, compared with the 4-6 weeks of summer workers. Juvenile hormone (JH) is involved in these behavioural changes, with levels of J H rising from winter to spring, and also in the change from hive bees to field bees. Honey-bee worker activities correlate with seasons, notably in the energy expenditure involved in thermoregulation of the hive.

Caste differentiation in honey bees, as in eusocial hymenopterans generally, is largely trophogenic, i.e. determined by the quantity and quality of the larval diet. In species that provision each cell with enough food to allow the egg to develop to the pupa and adult without further replenishment, differences in the food quantity and quality provided to each cell determine how the larva will develop.

In honey bees, although cells are constructed according to the type of caste that is to develop within them, the caste is determined neither by the egg laid by the queen, nor by the cell itself, but by food supplied by workers to the developing larva. The type of cell guides the queen as to whether to lay fertilized or unfertilized eggs, and identifies to the worker which type of rearing (principally food) to be supplied to the occupant.

Food given to future queens is known as '*royal jelly*' and differs from worker food in having a high sugar content and being composed predominantly of mandibular gland products, namely pantothenic acid and biopterin. Eggs and larvae up to 3 days old can differentiate into queens or workers according to upbringing.

However, by the third day a potential queen has been fed royal jelly at up to 10 times the rate of less rich food supplied to a future worker. At this stage, if a future queen is transferred to a worker cell for further development, she will become an intercaste, a worker-like queen.

The opposite transfer, of a threeday-old larva reared as a worker into a queen cell, gives rise to a queen-like worker, still retaining the pollen baskets, barbed stings and mandibles of a worker. After four days of appropriate feeding, the castes are fully differentiated and transfers between cell types result in either retention of the early determined outcome or failure to develop. Trophogenic effects cannot always be separated from endocrine effects, as nutritional status is linked to corpora allata activity.

It is clear that JH levels correlate with polymorphic caste differentiation in eusocial insects. However, there seems to be much specific and temporal variation in JH titres and no common pattern of control is *yet* evident. The queen maintains control over the workers' reproduction principally through pheromones.

The mandibular glands of queens produce a compound identified as (E)-9-oxodec-2-enoic acid (9-ODA), but the intact queen inhibits worker ovarian development more effectively than this active compound. A second pheromone has been found in the gaster of the queen, and this, together with a second component of the mandibular gland, effectively

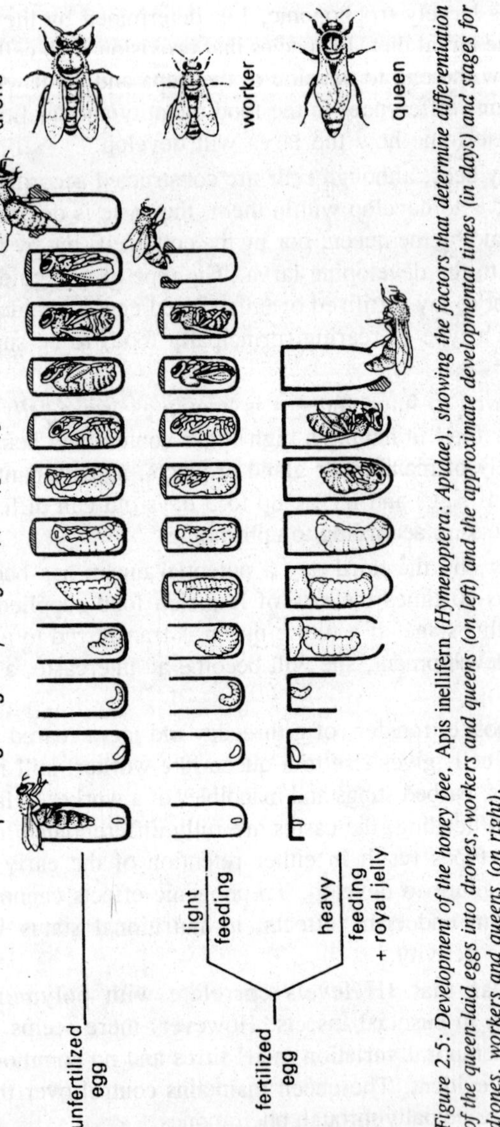

Figure 2.5: Development of the honey bee, Apis inellifern *(Hymenoptera: Apidae), showing the factors that determine differentiation of the queen-laid eggs into drones, workers and queens (on left) and the approximate developmental times (in days) and stages for drones, workers and queens (on right).*

inhibits ovarian development. Queen recognition by the rest of the colony involves a pheromone disseminated by attendant workers that contact the queen and then move about the colony as messenger bees. Also, as the queen moves around on the comb whilst ovipositing into the cells, she leaves a trail of *footprint pheromone*.

Production of queens takes place in cells that are distant from the effects of the queen's pheromonal control, as occurs when nests become very large. Should the queen die, the volatile pheromone signal dissipates rapidly, and the workers become aware of the absence. Honey bees have very strongly developed chemical communication, with specific pheromones associated with mating, alarm and orientation as well as colony recognition and regulation.

Physical threats are rare, and are used only by young gynes towards workers. Males, termed *drones*, are produced throughout the life of the honey-bee colony, either by the queen or perhaps by workers with developed ovaries. Males contribute little to the colony, living only to mate: their genitalia are ripped out after copulation and they die.

Nest Construction in Eusocial Wasps

The founding of a new colony of eusocial vespid wasps takes place in spring, following the emergence of an overwintering queen. After her departure from the natal colony the previous autumn, the new queen mates, but her ovarioles remain undeveloped during the temperature-induced winter quiescence (facultative diapause).

As spring temperatures rise, queens leave hibernation and feed on nectar or sap, and the ovarioles grow. The resting site, which may be shared by several overwintering queens, is not a prospective site for foundation of the new colony.

Each queen scouts individually for a suitable cavity and fighting may occur if sites are scarce. Nest construction begins with the use of the mandibles to scrape wood fibres from sound or, more rarely, rotten wood. The wasp returns to the nest site using visual cues, carrying the wood pulp masticated with water and saliva in the mandibles.

This pulpy paper is applied to the underside of a selected support at the top of the cavity. From this initial buttress, the pulp is formed into a descending pillar, upon which is suspended ultimately the embryonic colony of 20-40 cells.

The first two cells, rounded in cross-section, are attached and then an umbrella-like envelope is formed over the cells. The envelope is elevated by about the width of the queen's body above the cells, allowing the queen to rest there, curled around the pillar.

The developing colony grows by the addition of further cells, now hexagonal in cross-section and wider at the open end, and by either extension of the envelope or construction of a new one. The queen forages only for building material at the start of nest construction. As

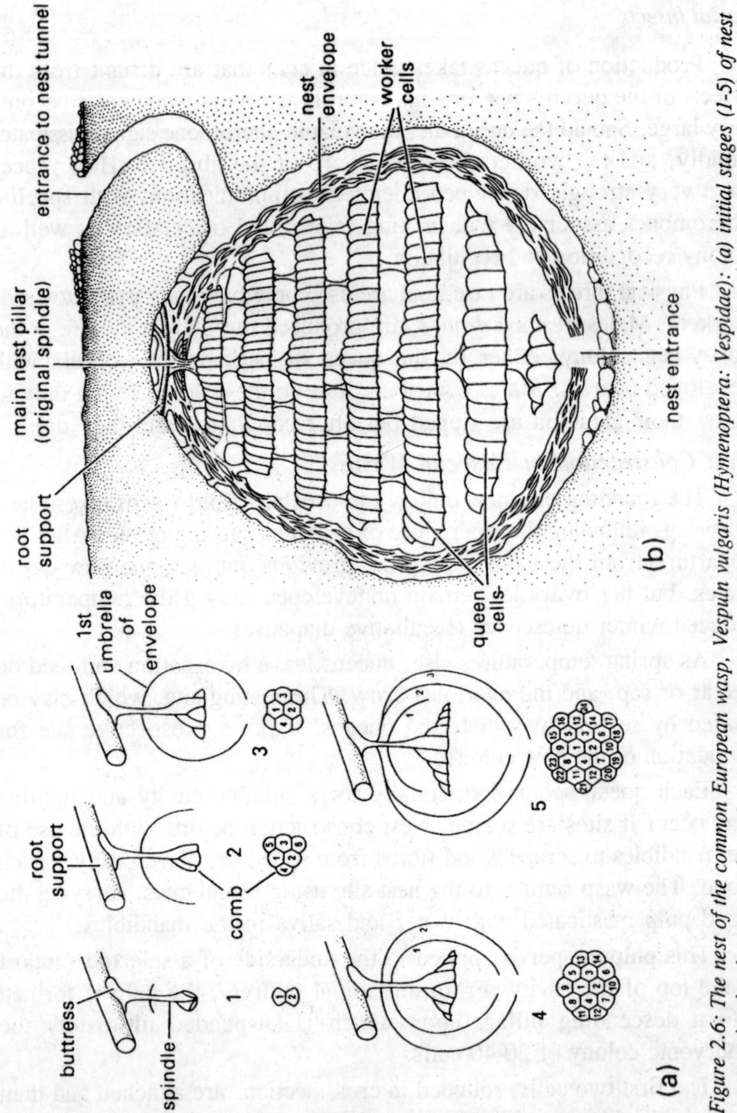

Figure 2.6: The nest of the common European wasp, Vespuln vulgaris (Hymenoptera: Vespidae): (a) initial stages (1-5) of nest construction by the queen (the embryonic phase of the colony's life); (b) a mature nest.

the larvae develop from the first cells, both liquid and insect prey are sought to nourish the developing larvae, although wood pulp continues to be collected for further cell construction.

This first embryonic phase of the life of the colony ceases as the first workers emerge. As the colony grows, further pillars are added, providing support to more lateral areas where brood-filled cells are aligned in *combs* (series of adjoining cells aligned in parallel rows). The early cells and envelopes become overgrown, and their materials may be reused in later construction.

In a subterranean nest, the occupants may have to excavate soil and even small stones to allow colony expansion, resulting in a mature nest, which may contain as many as 12000 cells. The colony has some independence from external temperature, as thoracic heating through wing beating and larval feeding can raise temperature, and high temperature can be lowered by directional fanning or by evaporation of liquid applied to the pupal cells.

At the end of the season, males and gynes (potential queens) are produced and are fed with larval saliva and prey brought into the nest by workers. As the old queen fails and dies, and gynes emerge from the nest, the colony declines rapidly and the nest is destroyed as workers fight and larvae are neglected. Potential queens and males mate away from the nest, and the mated female seeks a suitable overwintering site.

Nesting in Honey Bees

In honey bees, initiation of new colonies is triggered when the old one becomes too crowded. When a bee colony becomes too large and the population density too high, a founder queen, accompanied by a swarm of workers, seeks a new nest site. As workers cannot survive for long on the honey reserves carried in their stomachs, the need to find a suitable site is imperative.

Scouts may have started the search several days before formation of the swarm: when a suitable cavity is found, the scout returns to the cluster and communicates the direction and quality of the site by a dance.

Optimally, a new site should be beyond the foraging territory of the old nest, but not so distant that energy is expended in long-distance flight. Bees from temperate areas select enclosed nest sites in cavities of about 40 litres in volume, whereas more tropical bees choose smaller cavities or nest outside.

Following consensus over the nest site, workers start building a nest using wax. Wax is unique to social bees and is produced by workers that metabolize honey in fat cells located close to the wax glands. These are modified epidermal cells that lie beneath wax mirrors (overlapping plates) ventrally on the 4th to 7th abdominal segments.

Flakes of wax are extruded beneath each wax mirror and protrude slightly from each segment of a worker actively producing wax. Wax is quite malleable at the ambient nest temperature of 35°C, and it is manipulated for cell construction by mixing with saliva. At nest foundation, workers already may have wax protruding from the abdominal wax glands. They start to construct combs of back-to-back hexagonal cells in a parallel series, or comb.

Combs are separated from one another by pillars and bridges of wax. A thick cell base of wax is extended into a thin-walled cell of remarkably constant dimensions, despite a series of workers being involved in construction. In contrast to other social insects such as the vespids described above, cells do not hang downwards but are angled at about 13° above the horizontal, thereby preventing loss of honey.

The precise orientation of the cells and comb derives from the bees' ability to detect gravity through the proprioceptor hair plates at the base of their necks. Although removal of the hair plates prevents cell construction, worker bees transported in the 1984 Challenger space shuttle flight could construct serviceable cells under conditions of weightlessness.

Unlike most other bees, honey bees do not chew up and reuse wax: once a cell is constructed it is permanently part of the nest, and cells are reused after the brood has emerged or the food contents have been used. Cell sizes vary, with small cells used to rear workers, and larger ones for drones.

Later in the life of the nest, elongate conical cells in which queens are reared are constructed at the bottom and sides of the nest. The brood develops and pollen is stored in lower and more central cells, whereas honey is stored in upper and peripheral cells. Honey is formed by workers primarily from nectar taken from flowers, but it can also be derived from extrafloral nectaries or insect-produced honeydew.

Workers carry nectar to the hive in honey stomachs, from which it may be fed directly to the brood and to other adults. However, most often it is converted to honey by enzymatic digestion of the sugars to simpler forms and reduction of the water content by evaporation before storage in wax-sealed cells until required to feed adults or larvae.

It has been calculated that in 66000 bee-hours of labour, 1 kg of beeswax can be formed into 77000 cells, which can support the weight of 22kg of honey. An average colony requires about 60-80 kg of honey per annum. When the lower temperatures of a temperate winter arrive, honey bees do not hibernate (unlike wasps). Colonies are active through the winter, but foraging is curtailed and no brood is reared.

Stored honey is used as an energy source to allow activity and heat generation within the nest. As external temperatures drop, the workers cluster together, heads inwards, forming an inactive layer of bees on the outside, and warmer, more active, feeding bees on the inside. Despite the prodigious stores of honey and pollen, mortality may be high in extreme cold, or if winter is prolonged.

Beehives are artificial constructions that resemble feral honey-bee nests in some dimensions, notably the distance between the combs. When given wooden frames separated by an invariable natural spacing interval of 9.6 mm (3/8 inch) honey bees construct their combs within the frame without formation of the internal waxen bridges needed to separate the combs of a feral nest.

This width between combs is approximately the space required for bees to move unimpeded on both combs. The ability to remove frames allows the apiculturalist (beekeeper) to examine and remove the honey, and replace the frames in the hive. The ease of construction allows the building of several ranks of boxes.

The hives can be transported to suitable locations without damaging the combs. Although the apiculture industry has developed through commercial production of honey, lack of native pollinators in monocultural agricultural systems has led to increasing reliance on the mobility of hive bees to ensure the pollination of crops as diverse as canola, nuts, soybeans, fruits, clover, alfalfa and other fodder crops.

In the USA alone, the 1990 value of the pollination duties provided by over one million bee colonies available for pollinator rental is estimated to be well in excess of US$ 10 million. Yield losses of over 90% of fruit, seed and nut crops would occur without honey-bee pollination. The role of the many species of eusocial native bees is little recognized, but may be important in areas of natural vegetation.

Specialized Hymenopterans: Ants

Ants (Formicidae) form a well-defined, highly specialized group within the superfamily Vespoidea. The morphology of a worker ant of *Formica* is illustrated elsewhere in this chapter.

Colony and Castes in Ants

All ants are social and their species are polymorphic. There are two major female castes, the reproductive queen and the workers, usually with complete dimorphism between them. Many ants have monomorphic workers, but others have distinct subcastes called, according to their size, *minor*, *media* or major workers.

Although workers may form clearly different morphs, there is more often a gradient in size. Workers are never winged, but wings are present in queens, which shed them after mating, and in most males, which die after mating. Winged individuals are called alates. Polymorphism in ants is accompanied by polyethism, with the queen's role restricted to oviposition, and the workers performing all other tasks.

If workers are monomorphic, there may be temporal or age polyethism, with young workers undertaking internal nurse duties and older ones foraging outside the nest. If workers are polymorphic, the subcaste with the largest individuals, the major workers, usually has a defensive or soldier role. The workers of certain ants, such as the fire ants (*Solenopsis*), have reduced ovaries and are irreversibly sterile.

In others, workers have functional ovaries and may produce some or all of the male off spring by laying haploid (unfertilized) eggs. In some species, when the queen is removed, the colony continues to produce gynes from fertilized eggs previously laid by the queen, and males from eggs laid by workers.

The inhibition by the queen of her daughter workers is quite striking in the African weaver ant, *Oecophylla longinoda*. A mature colony of up to half a million workers, distributed amongst as many as 17 nests, is completely prevented from reproduction by a single queen. Workers, however, do produce male offspring in nests that lie outside the influence (or territory) of the queen.

Queens prevent the production of reproductive eggs by workers, but may allow the laying of specialized trophic eggs that are fed to the queen and/or larvae. By this means the queen not only prevents any reproductive competition, but directs much of the protein in the colony towards her own offspring. Caste differentiation is largely trophogenic (dietdetermined), involving biased allocation of volume and quality of food given to the larvae.

A highprotein diet promotes differentiation of gyne/queen and a less rich, more dilute diet leads to differentiation of workers. The queen generally inhibits the development of gynes indirectly by modifying the feeding behaviour of workers towards female larvae, which have the potential to differentiate as either gynes or workers.

In *Myrmica*, large, slowly developing larvae will become gynes, so stimulation of rapid development and early metamorphosis of small larvae, or food deprivation and irritating of large larvae by biting to accelerate development, both induce differentiation as workers. When queen influence wanes, either through the increased size of the colony, or because the inhibitory pheromone is impeded in its circulation throughout the colony, gynes are produced at some distance from the queen. There is also a role for juvenile hormone (JH) in caste differentiation. JH tends to induce queen development during egg and larval stages, and induces production of major workers from already differentiated workers.

According to a seasonal cycle, ant gynes mature to winged reproductives, or alates, and remain in the nest in a sexually inactive state until external conditions are suitable for departing the nest. At the appropriate time they make their nuptial flight, mate and attempt to found a new colony.

Nesting in Ants

The subterranean soil nests of *Myrmica* and the mounds of plant debris of *Formica* are typical temperate ant nests. Colonies are founded when a mated queen sheds her wings and overwinters, sealed into a newly dug nest that she will never leave. In spring, the queen lays some eggs and feeds the hatched larvae by *stomodeal* or oral trophallaxis, i.e. regurgitation of liquid food from her internal food reserves.

Colonies develop slowly whilst worker numbers build up, and a nest may be many years old before alates are produced. Colony foundation by more than one queen, known as *pleometrosis*, appears to be fairly widespread, and the digging of the initial nest may be shared, as in the honeypot ant *Myrinecocystus inimicus*.

In this species and others, multi-queen nests may persist as polygynous colonies, but monogyny commonly arises through dominance of a single queen, usually following rearing of the first brood of workers. Polygynous nests often are associated with opportunistic use of ephemeral resources, or persistent but patchy resources.

Amongst the best known complex nest constructions of ants are the woven nests of *Oecophylla* species. These African and Asian/Australian weaver ants have extended territories that workers continually explore for any leaf that can be bent. A remarkable collaborative construction effort follows, in which leaves are manipulated into a tentshape by linear ranks of workers, often involving '*living chains*' of ants that bridge wide gaps between the leaf edges.

Another group of workers take larvae from existing nests and carry them held delicately between their mandibles to the construction site. There, larvae are induced to produce silk threads from their well-developed silk glands and a nest is woven linking the framework of leaves. Living plant tissues provide a location for nests of ants such as

Pseudomyrnex ferruginea, which nests in the expanded thorns of the Central American bull'shorn acacia trees. Cases such as these demonstrate mutualism involving plant defence, as discussed elsewhere in this chapter, with plants benefiting from the ants deterring phytophagous animals.

Foraging efficiency of ants can be very high. A typical mature colony of European red ants (*Formica polyctena*) is estimated to harvest about 1 kg of arthropod food per day. The legionary, or army, and driver ants are popularly known for their voracious predatory activities. These ants, which predominantly belong to the subfamilies Ecitoninae and Dorylinae, alternate cyclically between sedentary (statary) and migratory or nomadic phases.

In the latter phase, a nightly *bivouac* is formed, which often is no more than an exposed cluster of the entire colony. Each morning, the millions-strong colony moves *in tote*, bearing the larvae. The advancing edge of this massive group raids and forages on a wide range of terrestrial arthropods, and group predation allows even large prey items to be overcome.

After some two weeks of nomadism, a statary period commences, during which the queen lays 100000300000 eggs in a statary bivouac. This is more sheltered than a typical overnight bivouac, perhaps within an old ants' nest, or beneath a log. The eggs hatch after some three weeks and during this period, the larvae of the previous oviposition period complete their development to emerge as new workers, which stimulates the next migratory period.

Not all ants are predatory: certain ants are specialist harvesters of grain and seeds (*myrmecochory*) and others feed almost exclusively on insect-produced honeydew. One of the most extraordinary examples is seen in the honeypot ants.

Workers of these species return to the nest with crops filled with honeydew, which is fed by oral trophallaxis to selected workers called *repletes*. The abdomen of repletes are so distensible that they become virtually immobile '*honey pots*', which act as food reserves for all in the nest.

Isoptera (Termites)

All termites (Isoptera) are eusocial. Their diagnostic features and biology are summarized elsewhere in this chapter.

Colony and Castes in Termites

In contrast to the adult and female-only castes of holometabolous

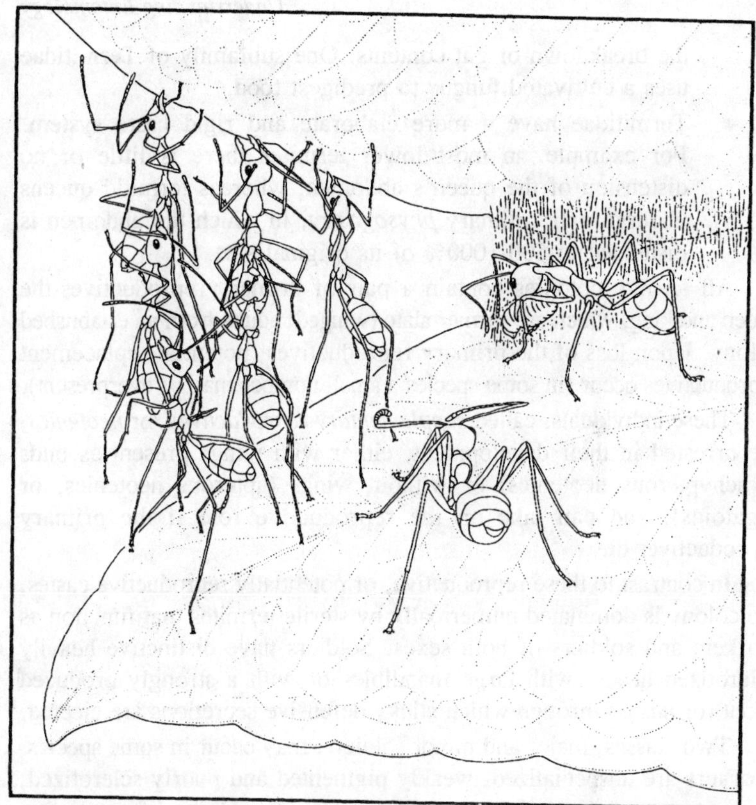

Figure 2.7: Weaver ants of Oecophylla making a nest by pulling together leaves and binding them with silk produced by larvae that are held in the mandilbles of worker ants.

eusocial Hymenoptera, the castes of the hemimetabolous Isoptera involve immature stages and equal representation of the sexes. However, before castes are discussed further, terms for termite immature stages must be clarified.

Termitologists refer to the developmental instars of reproductives as nymphs, more properly called brachypterous nymphs, and the instars of sterile lineages as larvae, although strictly the latter are apterous nymphs. The termites may be divided into two groups -the 'lower' and 'higher' termites. The species-rich higher termites (*Termitidae*), differ from lower termites in the following manner:

- Members of the Termitidae lack the symbiotic flagellates found in the hindgut of lower termites; these protists (protozoa) secrete enzymes (including cellulases) that may contribute to the breakdown of gut contents. One subfamily of Termitidae uses a cultivated fungus to predigest food.

- Termitidae have a more elaborate and rigid caste system. For example, in most lower termites there is little or no distension of the queen's abdomen, whereas termitid queens undergo extraordinary *physogastry*, in which the abdomen is distended to 500-1000% of its original size.

All termite colonies contain a pair of primary reproductives-the queen and king, which are former alate (winged) adults from an established colony. Upon loss of the primary reproductives, potential replacement reproductives occur (in some species a small number may be everpresent).

These individuals, called *supplementary reproductives*, or *neotenics*, are arrested in their development, either with wings present as buds (brachypterous neotenics) or without wings (apterous neotenics, or ergatoids), and can take on the reproductive role if the primary reproductives die.

In contrast to these reproductive, or potentially reproductive castes, the colony is dominated numerically by sterile termites that function as workers and soldiers of both sexes. Soldiers have distinctive heavily sclerotized heads, with large mandibles or with a strongly produced snout (or *nasus*) through which sticky defensive secretions are ejected.

Two classes, major and minor soldiers, may occur in some species. Workers are unspecialized, weakly pigmented and poorly sclerotized, giving rise to the popular name of '*white ants*'. Caste differentiation pathways are portrayed best in the more rigid system of the higher termites (Termitidae), which can then be contrasted with the greater plasticity of the lower termites.

In *Nasutitermes exitiosus* (Termitidae: subfamily Nasutitermitinae), two different developmental pathways exist; one leads to reproductives and the other (which is further subdivided) gives rise to sterile castes. This differentiation may occur as early as the first larval stage, although some castes may not be morphologically recognizable until later moults.

The reproductive pathway is relatively constant between termite taxa and is typically exopterygote, giving rise to alates-the winged reproductives that leave the colony, mate, disperse and found new colonies. In *N. exitiosus* no neotenics are formed; replacement for lost primary reproductives comes from amongst alates retained in the colony. Other *Nasutitermes* show great developmental plasticity.

The sterile (neuter) lineages are complex and variable between different termite species. In *N. exitiosus*, two categories of second-

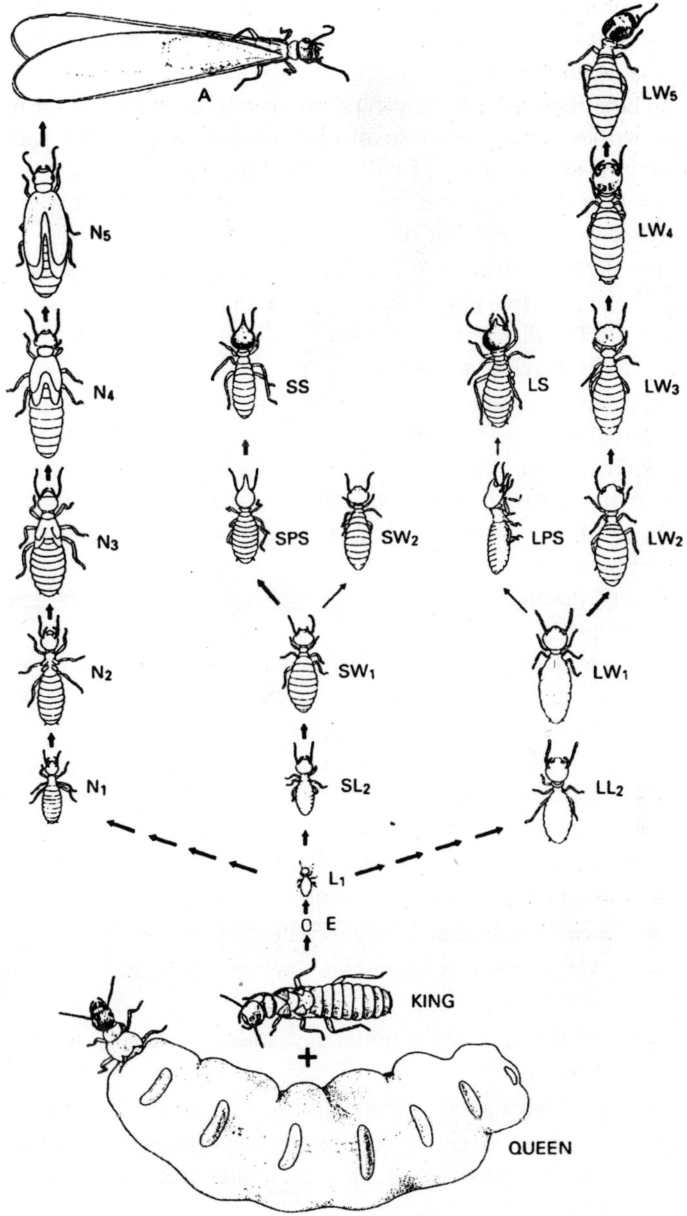

Figure 2.8: Developmental pathways of the termite Nasutitermes exitiosus (Isoptera: Termitidae). Heavy arrows indicate the main lines of development, light arrows the minor lines.

instar larvae can be recognized according to size differences probably relating to sexual dimorphism, although which sex belongs to which size category is unclear.

In both lineages a subsequent moult produces a third-instar nymph of the worker caste, either small or large according to the pathway. These third-instar workers have the potential (*competency*) to develop into a soldier (via an intervening *presoldier* instar) or remain as workers through a variable number of further moults.

The sterile pathway of *N. exitiosus* involves larger workers continuing to grow at successive moults, whereas the small worker ceases to moult beyond the fourth instar. Those that moult to become presoldiers and then soldiers develop no further.

The lower termites are more flexible, exhibiting more routes to differentiation. Lower termites have no true worker caste, but employ a functionally equivalent 'child-labour' *pseudergate* caste composed of either nymphs whose wing buds have been eliminated (regressed) by moulting or, less frequently, brachypterous nymphs or even undifferentiated larvae.

Unlike the 'true' workers of the higher termites, pseudergates are developmentally plastic and retain the capacity to differentiate into other castes by moulting. In lower termites, differentiation of nymphs from larvae, and reproductives from pseudergates may not be possible until a relatively late instar is reached.

If there is sexual dimorphism in the sterile line, the larger workers are often male, but workers may be monomorphic. This may be through the absence of sexual dimorphism, or more rarely, because only one sex is represented. Moults in species of lower termites may give:

- morphological change within a caste;
- no morphological advance (stationary moult);
- change to a new caste (such as a pseudergate to a reproductive);
- saltation to a new morphology, missing a normal intermediate instar;
- supplementation, adding an instar to the normal route;
- reversion to an earlier morphology (such as a pseudergate from a reproductive), or a presoldier from any nymph, late-instar larva or pseudergate.

Instar determination is impossibly difficult in the light of these moulting potentialities. The only inevitability is that a presoldier must moult to a soldier. Certain unusual termites lack soldiers. Even the universal presence of only one pair of reproductives has exceptions; multiple primary queens cohabit in some colonies of some Termitidae.

Individuals in a termite colony are derived from one pair of parents. Therefore genetic differences existing between castes either must be sex-related or due to differential expression of the genes. Gene expression is under complex multiple and synergistic influences entailing hormones (including neurohormones), external environmental factors and interactions between colony members.

Termite colonies are very structured and have high homeostasy-caste proportions are restored rapidly after experimental or natural disturbance, by recruitment of individuals of appropriate castes and elimination of individuals excess to colony needs. Homeostasis is controlled by several pheromones that act specifically upon the corpora allata and more generally on the rest of the endocrine system.

In the well-studied *Kalotermes*, primary reproductives inhibit differentiation of supplementary reproductives and alate nymphs. Presoldier formation is inhibited by soldiers, but stimulated through pheromones produced by reproductives. Pheromones that inhibit reproduction are produced inside the body by reproductives and disseminated to pseudergates by *proctodeal* trophallaxis, i.e. by feeding on anal excretions.

Transfer of pheromones to the rest of the colony is by oral trophallaxis. This was demonstrated experimentally in a *Knlotermes* colony by removing reproductives and dividing the colony into two halves with a membrane. Reproductives were reintroduced, orientated within the membrane such that their abdomens were directed into one half of the colony, their heads into the other.

Only in the 'head-end' part of the colony did pseudergates differentiate as reproductives: inhibition continued at the 'abdomen-end'. Painting the protruding abdomen with varnish eliminated any cuticular chemical messengers but failed to remove the inhibition on pseudergate development.

In constrast, when the anus was blocked, pseudergates became reproductive, thereby verifying anal transfer. The inhibitory pheromones produced by both queen and king have complementary or synergistic effects: a female pheromone stimulates the male to release inhibitory pheromone, whereas the male pheromone has a lesser stimulatory effect on the female.

Production of primary and supplementary reproductives involves removal of these pheromonal inhibitors produced by functioning reproductives. Increasing recognition of the role of juvenile hormone (JH) in caste differentiation comes from observations such as the differentiation of pseudergates into soldiers after injection or topical application of JH or implantation of the corpora allata of reproductives.

Some of the effects of pheromones on colony composition may be due to JH production by the primary reproductives. Caste determination in Termitidae originates as early as the egg, during maturation in the ovary of the queen. As the queen grows, the corpora allata undergoes hypertrophy and may attain a size 150 times greater than the gland of the alate.

The JH content of eggs also varies, and it is possible that a high JH level in the egg causes differentiation to follow the sterile lineage. This route is enforced if the larvae are fed proctodeal foods (or trophic eggs) that are high in JH, whereas a low level of JH in the egg allows differentiation along the reproductive pathway.

In higher and lower termites, worker and soldier differentiation from the third-instar larva is under further hormonal control, as demonstrated by the induction of individuals of these castes by JH application.

Nesting in Termites

In the warmer parts of the temperate northern hemisphere, drywood termites are most familiar because of the structural damage that they cause to timber in buildings. Termites are pests of drywood and dampwood

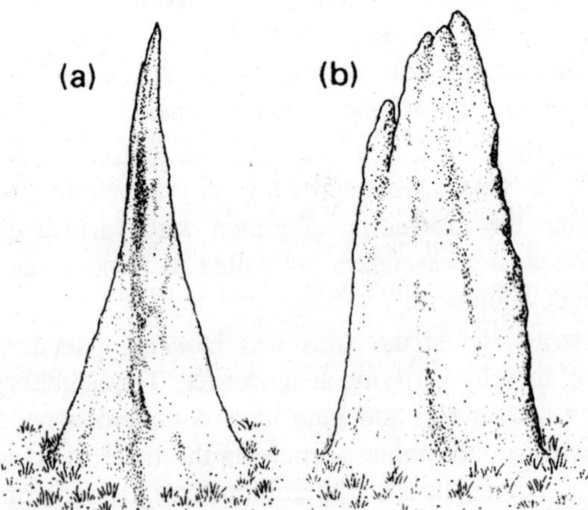

Figure 2.9: The 'magnetic' mound of the debris-feeding termite Amiternues meridionalis (Isoptera: Termitidae) showing: (a) the north-south view, and (b) the east-west view.

in the subtropics and tropics, but in these regions termites may be more familiar through their spectacular mound nests.

In the timber pests, colony size may be no greater than a few hundred termites, whereas in the mound formers, several million individuals may be involved. In all cases, a new nest is founded by a male and female following the nuptial flight of alates. A small cavity is excavated into which the pair seal themselves.

Copulation takes place in this royal cell, and egg-laying commences. The first offspring are workers, which are fed on regurgitated wood or other plant matter, primed with gut symbionts, until they are old enough to feed themselves and enlarge the nest.

Early in the life of the colony, production is directed towards workers, with later production of soldiers to defend the colony. As the colony matures, but perhaps not until it is 5-10 years old, production of reproductives commences. This involves differentiation of alate sexual forms at the appropriate season for swarming and foundation of new colonies.

Tropical termites are able to use virtually all cellulose-rich food sources, from grass tussocks and fungi to living and dead trees, above and below the ground. Workers radiate from the mound, often in subterranean tunnels, less often in above-ground, pheromone-marked trails, in search of materials.

In the subfamily Macrotermitinae (Termitidae), fungi are raised in combs of termite faeces within the mound, and the complete culture of fungus and excreta is eaten by the colony. These fungus-tending termites form the largest termite colonies known, with estimated millions of inhabitants in some East African species.

The giant mounds of tropical termites mostly belong to species in the Termitidae. As the colony grows through production of workers, the mound is enlarged by layers of soil and termite faeces until mounds as much as a century old attain massive dimensions.

Diverse mound architectures characterize different termite species; for example, the 'magnetic mounds' of *Amitermes ineridionalis* in northern Australia have a narrow north-south and broad east-west orientation, like a compass.

Orientation relates to thermoregulation, as the broad face of the mound receives maximum exposure to the warming of the early and late sun, with the narrowest face presented to the high and hot midday sun. Aspect is not the only means of temperature regulation: intricate internal design, especially in fungus-farming *Macrotermes* species, allows

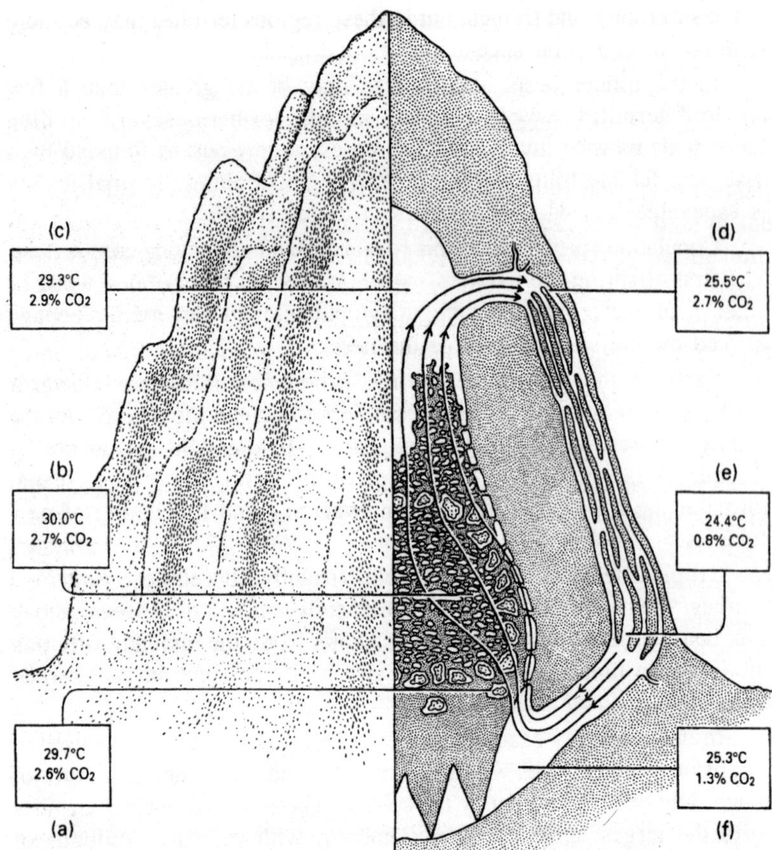

Figure 2.10: Section through the mound nest of the African fungus-farming termite Macrotermes natalensis (Isoptera: Termitidae) showing how air circulating in a series of passageways maintains favourable culture conditions for the fungus at the bottom of the nest (a) and for the termite brood (b). Measurements of temperature and carbon dioxide are shown in the boxes for the following locations: (a) the fungus combs; (b) the brood chambers; (c) the attic; (d) the upper part of a ridge channel; (e) the lower part of a ridge channel; and (f) the cellar.

circulation of air to give microclimatic control of temperature and carbon dioxide.

INQUILINES AND PARASITES OF SOCIAL INSECTS

The abodes of social insects provide many other insects with a hospitable place for their development. The term *inquiline* refers to an organism that shares a home of another. This covers a vast range of organisms that have some kind of obligate relationship with another organism, in this case a social insect.

Complex classification schemes involve categorization of the insect host and the known or presumed ecological relationship between inquiline and host (e.g. myrmecophile, termitoxene). However, two alternative divisions appropriate to this discussion involve the degree of integration of the inquiline lifestyle with that of the host.

Thus integrated inquilines are incorporated into their hosts' social lives by behavioural modification of both parties, whereas non-integrated inquilines are adapted ecologically to the nest, but do not interact socially with the host.

Predatory inquilines may negatively affect the host, whereas other inquilines may merely shelter within the nest, or give benefit, such as by feeding on nest debris. Integration may be achieved by mimicking the chemical cues used by the host in social communication (such as pheromones), or by tactile signalling that releases social behavioural responses, or both.

The term Wasmannian *mimicry* is used to cover some or all of the chemical or tactile mimetic features that allow the mimic to be accepted by a social insect, but the distinction from other forms of mimicry is not always obvious. Wasmannian mimicry may, but need not, include imitation of the body form.

Conversely, mimicry of a social insect does not necessarily imply inquilinism-the ant mimics shown in Figure elsewhere in this chapter are not symbionts, but apparently gain some protection from their natural enemies as a result of their ant-like appearance. The breaking of the social insect chemical code occurs through the ability of an inquiline to produce appeasement and/or adoption chemicals-the messengers that social insects use to recognize one another and to distinguish themselves from intruders.

Many staphylinid beetles are able to do this, as, for example, *Atemeles pubicollis*, which lives as a larva in the nest of the European ant, *Formica rufa*. The staphylinid larva produces a glandular secretion that induces brood-tending ants to groom the alien. Food is obtained by adoption of the begging posture of an ant larva, in which the larva rears up and contacts the adult ant mouthparts, provoking a release of regurgitated food.

The diet of the staphylinid is supplemented by predation on larvae of ants and of their own species. Pupation and adult eclosion take place in the *Formica rufa* nest. However, this species of ant ceases activity in winter and during this period the staphylinid seeks alternative shelter. Adult beetles leave the wooded *Formica* habitat and migrate to the more open grassland habitat of *Myrmica* ants. When *a Myrmica* ant is encountered, secretions from the 'appeasement glands' are offered that suppress the aggression of the ant, and then the products of glands on the lateral abdomen attract the ant.

Feeding on these secretions appears to facilitate ·adoption', as the ant subsequently carries the beetle back to its nest, where the immature adult overwinters as a tolerated food-thief. In spring, the reproductively mature adult beetle departs for the woods to seek out a *Formica* nest for oviposition. Amongst the inquilines of termites, many show convergence in shape in terms of physogastry (dilation of the abdomen), seen also in queen termites.

In the curious case of flies of *Termitoxenia* and relatives (Diptera; Phoridae), the physogastric females from termite nests were the only stage known for so long that published speculation was rife that neither larvae nor males existed. It was suggested that the females hatched directly from huge eggs, were brachypterous throughout their lives (hitching a ride on termites for dispersal), and, uniquely amongst the endopterygotes, the flies were believed to be protandrous hermaphrodites, functioning first as males, then as females.

The truth is more prosaic: sexual dimorphism in the group is so great that wild caught, flying males had been unrecognized and placed in a different taxonomic group. The females are winged, but shed all but the stumps of the anterior veins after mating, before entering the termitarium. Although the eggs are large, larval stages are present, but very short lived.

As the postmated female is *stenogastrous* (with a small abdomen), physogastry develops whilst in the termitarium. Thus *Termitoxenia* is only a rather unconventional fly, well adapted to the rigours of life in a termite nest, where its eggs are treated by the termites as their own, and with attenuation of the vulnerable larval stage, rather than the possessor of a unique suite of life-history features. Inquilinism is not restricted to non-social insects that abuse the hospitality of social insects.

Even amongst the social Hymenoptera some ants may live as temporary or even permanent social parasites in the nests of other species. A reproductive female inquiline gains access to a host nest and usually kills the resident queen.

In some cases, the intruder queen produces workers, which eventually take over the nest. In others, the inquiline usurper produces only males and reproductives-the worker caste is eliminated and the nest survives only until the workers of the host species die off. In a further twist of the complex social lives of ants, some species are slave-makers; they capture pupae from the nests of other species and return them to their own nest where they are reared as slave workers.

This phenomenon, known as dulosis, occurs in several inquiline species, all of which found their colonies by parasitism. The phylogenetic relationships between ant hosts and ant inquilines reveals an unexpectedly high proportion of instances in which host and inquiline belong to sister species (i.e. each other's closest relatives), and many more are congeneric close relatives. One possible explanation envisages the situation in which daughter species formed in isolation come into secondary contact after mating barriers have developed.

If no differentiation of colonyidentifying chemicals has taken place, it is possible for one species to invade the colony of the other, undetected, and parasitization is facilitated. Non-integrated inquilines are exemplified by hover flies of the genus *Volucella* (Diptera: Syrphidae), the adults of which are Batesian mimics of either *Polistcs* wasps or of Bombus bees. Female flies appear free to fly in and out of hymenopteran nests, and lay eggs whilst walking over the comb.

Hatching larvae drop to the bottom of the nest where they scavenge on fallen detritus and fallen prey. Another syrphid, *Microdoii*, has a myrmecophilous larva so curious that it was described first as a mollusc, then as a coccoid. It lives unscathed amongst nest debris (and perhaps sometimes as a predator on young ant larvae), but the emerged adult is recognized as an intruder.

Non-integrated inquilines include many predators and parasitoids whose means of circumventing the defences of social insects are largely unknown. Social insects also support a few parasitic arthropods. For example, varroa and tracheal mites (Acari) and the bee louse, *Braula coeca*, all live on honey bees (Apidae: *Apis* spp.). The extent of colony damage caused by the tracheal mite *Acarapis woodi* is controversial, but infestations of *Varroa* are resulting in serious declines in honey-bee populations in most parts of the world.

Varroa mites feed externally on the bee brood leading to deformation and death of the bees. Low levels of mite infestation are difficult to detect and it can take several years for a mite population to build to a level that causes extensive damage to the hive. Some Apis species, such as *A. cerana*, appear more resistant to varroa but interpretation is complicated by the existence of a sibling species complex of varroa mites with distinct biogeographic and virulence patterning. This suggests that great care should be taken to avoid promiscuous mixing of different bee and mite genotypes.

EVOLUTION OF EUSOCIALITY

At first impression the complex social systems of hymenopterans and termites bear a close resemblance and it is tempting to suggest a common origin. However, examination of the phylogeny presented elsewhere in this chapter shows that these two orders, and the social aphids and thrips, are distantly related and a single evolutionary origin is inconceivable.

Thus we will examine the possible routes for the origin of eusociality in Hymenoptera and Isoptera separately.

The Origins of Eusociality in Hymenoptera

According to estimates derived from the proposed phylogeny of the Hymenoptera, eusociality has arisen independently in wasps, bees and ants with multiple origins within wasps and bees. Comparisons of life histories between living species with different degrees of social behaviour allow extrapolation to possible historical pathways from solitariness to sociality.

Three possible routes have been suggested and in each case, communal living is seen to provide benefits through sharing the costs of nest construction and defence of offspring. The first suggestion envisages a monogynous (single queen) subsocial system with eusociality developing through the queen remaining associated with her offspring through increased maternal longevity.

In the second scenario, involving semisociality and perhaps applicable only to certain bees, several unrelated females of the same generation associate and establish a colonial nest in which there is some reproductive division of labour, with an association that lasts only for one generation.

The third scenario involves elements of the previous two, with a communal group comprising related females (rather than unrelated) and multiple queens (in a polygynous system), within which there is increasing reproductive division. The association of queens and daughters arises through increased longevity. These life-history-based scenarios must be considered in relation to genetic theories concerning eusociality, notably concerning the origins and maintenance by selection of altruism (or self-sacrifice in reproduction).

Ever since Darwin, there has been debate about altruism-why should some individuals (sterile workers) sacrifice their reproductive potential for the benefit of others? Four proposals for the origins of the extreme reproductive sacrifice seen in eusociality are discussed below.

Three proposals are partially or completely compatible with one another, but *group selection*, the first considered, seems incompatible. In this case, selection is argued to operate at the level of the group: an efficient colony with an altruistic division of reproductive labour will survive and produce more offspring compared with one in which rampant individual self-interest leads to anarchy.

Although this scenario aids in understanding the maintenance of eusociality once it is established, it contributes little if anything to explaining the origin(s) of reproductive sacrifice in non-eusocial or subsocial insects. The concept of group selection operating on pre-eusocial colonies runs counter to the view that selection operates on the genome, and hence the origin of altruistic individual sterility is difficult to accept under group selection.

It is amongst the remaining three proposals, namely kin selection, maternal manipulation and mutualism, that the origins of eusociality are more usually sought. The first, kin selection, stems from recognition that classical or Darwinian fitness-the direct genetic contribution to the gene pool by an individual through its offspring-is only part of the contribution to an individual's total, or inclusive, or *extended, fitness*. An additional indirect contribution, termed the *kinship component*, must be included.

This is the contribution to the gene pool made by an individual that assists and enhances the reproductive success of its kin. Kin are individuals with similar or identical genotypes derived from the relatedness of their parents. In the Hymenoptera, kin relatedness is enhanced by the haplodiploid sex determination system. In this system, males are haploid so that sperm (produced by mitosis) contains 100% of the paternal genes. In contrast, the egg (produced by meiosis) is diploid, containing only half the maternal genes.

Thus daughter offspring, produced from fertilized eggs, share all their father's genes, but only half of their mother's genes. Because of this, full sisters (i.e. those with the same father) share on average three-quarters of their genes.

Therefore sisters share more genes with each other than they would with their own female offspring (50%). Under these conditions, the inclusive fitness of a sterile female (worker) is greater than its classical fitness. As selection operating on an individual should maximize its inclusive fitness, a worker should invest in the survival of her sisters, the queen's offspring, rather than in the production of her own female young. However, there are some difficulties with a haplodiploid explanation alone for the origin of eusociality, as altruism does not arise solely from relatedness.

Although haplodiploidy is universal in hymenopterans and the resultant close relatedness has encouraged repeated eusociality, eusociality is not universal in the Hymenoptera. Furthermore, in other haplodiploid insects such as thrips, eusociality does not occur, although there may be social behaviour.

Other factors involved in promoting eusociality are recognized in Hamilton's rule, which emphasizes the ratio of costs and benefits of altruistic behaviour as well as relatedness. The conditions under which selection will favour altruism can be expressed as follows:

$$rB - C > 0$$

where *r* is the coefficient of relatedness, B is the benefit gained by the recipient of altruism and C is the cost suffered by the donor of altruism. Thus variations in benefits and costs modify the consequences of a particular degree of relatedness (although these factors are difficult to measure).

Kinship calculations assume that all offspring of a single mother in the colony share an identical father, and this assumption is implicit in the kinship scenario for the origin of eusociality. However, at least in the higher eusocial insects, queens may mate several times with different males. For these eusocial insects, intracolony relatedness will be less than predicted by the model.

However, this difficulty is unrelated to the origins of eusociality, being more concerned with the maintenance of an already existing eusocial system. Once sterile castes have originated (theoretically under conditions of single paternity), the requirement for high relatedness may be relaxed if sterile workers lack any opportunity to reproduce.

Evidently it is the opportunity to help relatives, in combination with high relatedness through haplodiploidy, that predisposes insects to eusociality. There are two further ideas concerning the origins of eusociality. The first involves maternal manipulation of offspring (both behaviourally and genetically), such that by reducing the reproductive potential of some offspring, the fitness of the parent may be maximized through reproductive success being assured to a few select offspring.

The ability of most aculeate females to control the sex of offspring through fertilizing the egg or not, and to vary the size of the offspring through the amount of food supplied, makes maternal manipulation a plausible option for the origin of eusociality. A further well-supported scenario emphasizes the roles of competition and mutualism.

This envisages individuals acting to enhance their own classical fitness with contributions to the fitness of neighbours arising only incidentally. Each individual benefits from colonial life through communal defence by shared vigilance against predators and parasites. Thus mutualism (including the benefits of shared defence and nest construction) and kinship encourage the establishment of group living.

Differential reproduction within a familial-related colony confers significant fitness advantages on all members through their kinship. In conclusion, the three scenarios are not mutually exclusive, but are compatible in combination, with kin selection, female manipulation and mutualism acting in concert to allow evolution of eusociality.

The Vespinae illustrate a trend to eusociality commencing from a solitary existence, with nest-sharing and facultative labour division being a derived condition. Further evolution of eusocial behaviour is envisaged as developing through a dominance hierarchy that arose from female manipulation and reproductive competition among the nest-sharers: the 'winners' are queens and the 'losers' are workers.

From this point onwards, individuals act to maximize their fitness and the caste system becomes more rigid. As the queen and colony acquire greater longevity and the number of generations retained increases, short-term monogynous societies (those with a succession of queens) become long-term, monogynous, matrifilial (mother-daughter) colonies. Exceptionally, a derived polygynous condition may arise in large colonies, and/or in colonies where queen dominance is relaxed.

The Origins of Eusociality in Isoptera

In contrast to the haplodiploidy of Hymenoptera, termite sex is determined universally by an XX-XY chromosome system and thus there is no genetic predisposition toward kinship-based eusociality.

Furthermore, and in contrast to the widespread subsociality seen in hymenopterans, such intermediate stages on the route to termite eusociality are few and uncertain. Subsocial behaviours do occur in the cockroaches, from which the termites appear to be derived and it has been proposed that evolution of eusociality in Isoptera can be deduced from the behaviour of *Cryptocercus-like* cockroaches. Environmental conditions of a nutrient-poor food source and adult longevity appear to induce social living.

Thus a possible scenario for the origin of the termite social system involves the requirement for internal symbiotic organisms to assist in the digestion of the cellulose-rich but nutrient-poor food. The need to transfer symbionts in order to replenish supplies that are lost at each moult encourages unusual levels of intracolony interaction through trophallaxis. Furthermore, transfer of symbionts between members of successive generations requires overlapping generations.

Trophallaxis, slow growth induced by the poor diet, and parental longevity, act together to encourage group cohesion. These factors, together with patchiness of adequate food resources such as rotting logs, can lead to colonial life, but do not readily explain altruistic caste origins.

When an individual gains substantial benefits from successful foundation of a colony, and with a high degree of intracolony relatedness (as is found in some termites), eusociality may arise. However, the origin of eusociality in termites remains much less clear cut than for eusocial hymenopterans.

SUCCESS OF EUSOCIAL INSECTS

As we saw in the introduction, social insects can attain numerical and ecological dominance in some regions. Social insects are most abundant at low latitudes and low elevations, and their activities are most conspicuous either in summer in temperate (or even sub-Arctic and montane) areas, or year-round in subtropical to tropical climates.

As a generalization, the most abundant and dominant social insects are the most derived phylogenetically and have the most complex social organization. Three qualities of social insects are believed to contribute to their competitive advantage, all of which derive from the caste system that allows multiple tasks to be performed.

Firstly, the tasks of foraging, feeding the queen, caring for offspring and maintenance of the nest can be performed simultaneously by different groups rather than sequentially as in solitary insects. Performing tasks in parallel means that one activity does not jeopardize another, thus the nest is not vulnerable to predators or parasites whilst foraging is taking place.

Furthermore, mistakes made by individuals have little or no consequence in parallel operations compared with those performed serially. Secondly, the ability of the colony to marshall all workers can overcome serious difficulties that a solitary insect cannot deal with, such as defence against a much larger or more numerous predator, or construction of a nest under unfavourable conditions.

Thirdly, the specialization of function associated with castes allows some homeostatic regulation, including holding of food reserves in some castes (such as honeypot ants) or in developing larvae, and behavioural control of temperature and other microclimatic conditions within the nest.

The ability to vary the proportion of individuals allocated to a particular caste allows appropriate distribution of community resources according to the differing demands of season and colony age. The widespread use of a variety of pheromones allows a high level of control to be exerted, even over millions of individuals.

However, within this apparently rigid eusocial system, there is scope for a wide variety of different life histories to have evolved, from the nomadic army ants to the parasitic inquilines.

3

PHYTOPHAGOUS INSECTS

Insects and plants share ancient associations that probably date from the Carboniferous. However, fossil evidence suggests that the major taxa of phytophagous (plant-feeding) insects become diverse only later, in the Cretaceous period. At this time angiosperms (flowering plants) dramatically increased in diversity in a radiation that displaced the previously dominant plant groups of the Jurassic period.

Interpreting the early evolution of the angiosperms is contentious, partly because of the paucity of fossilized flowers prior to the period of radiation, and also because of the apparent rapidity of the origin and diversification within the major angiosperm families.

However, according to several hypotheses of their phylogeny, the earliest angiosperms may have been insect-pollinated, perhaps by beetles. Many living representatives of primitive families of beetles feed on fungi, fern spores or pollens of other non-angiosperm taxa such as cycads. As this feeding type preceded the angiosperm radiation, it can be seen as a preadaptation for angiosperm pollination.

The ability of flying insects to transport pollen from flower to flower on different plants is fundamental to cross-pollination. Other than the beetles, the most significant and diverse present-day pollinator taxa belong to three orders-the Diptera (flies), Hymenoptera (wasps and bees) and Lepidoptera (moths and butterflies).

Pollinator taxa within these orders are unrepresented in the fossil record until late in the Cretaceous. Although insects probably pollinated cycads and other primitive plants, insect pollinators may have promoted speciation in angiosperms, through pollinator-mediated isolating mechanisms.

As seen elsewhere in this chapter, many modern-day noninsect hexapods and apterygote insects scavenge in soil and litter, predominantly feeding on decaying plant material. The earliest true insects probably fed similarly.

This manner of feeding certainly brings soil-dwelling insects into contact with plant roots and subterranean storage organs, but specialized use of plant aerial parts by sap sucking, leaf chewing and other forms of phytophagy arose later in the phylogeny of the insects. Feeding on living tissues of higher plants presents problems that are experienced neither by the scavengers living in the soil or litter, nor by predators.

First, a phytophagous insect must be able to gain and retain a hold on the vegetation in order to feed on leaves, stems or flowers. Second, the exposed phytophage may be subject to greater desiccation than an aquatic or litter-dwelling insect.

Third, a diet of plant tissues (excluding seeds) is nutritionally inferior in protein, sterol and vitamin content compared with food of animal or microbial origin. Last, but not least, plants are not passive victims of phytophages, but have evolved a variety of means to deter herbivores.

These include physical defences, such as spines, spicules or sclerophyllous tissue, and/or chemical defences that may repel, poison, reduce food digestibility, or otherwise adversely affect insect behaviour and/or physiology. Despite these barriers, about half of all living insect species are phytophagous, and the exclusively plant-feeding Lepidoptera, Curculionidae (weevils), Chrysomelidae (leaf beetles), Agromyzidae (leafmining flies) and Cynipidae (gall wasps) are very speciose.

Plants represent an abundant resource and insect taxa that can exploit this have flourished in association with plant diversification. This chapter begins with a consideration of the evolutionary interactions among insects and their plant hosts, amongst which a euglossine bee pollinator at work on the flower of a *Stanhopea* orchid, a chrysomelid beetle feeding on the orchid leaf and a pollinating bee fly hovering nearby are illustrated in the chapter vignette.

The vast array of interactions of insects and living plants can be grouped into three categories, defined by the effects of the insects on the plants. Phytophagy (herbivory) includes leaf chewing, sap sucking, seed predation, gall inducing and mining the living tissues of plants. The second category of interactions is important to plant reproduction and involves mobile insects that transport pollen between conspecific plants (pollination) or seeds to suitable germination sites (myrmecochory). These interactions are mutualistic because the insects obtain food or some other resource from the plants that they service.

The third category of insect-plant interaction involves insects that live in specialized plant structures and provide their host with either defence against herbivores or nutrition, or both. Such mutualisms, like the nutrient-producing fly larvae that live unharmed within the pitchers of carnivorous plants, are unusual but provide fascinating opportunities for evolutionary and ecological studies.

There is a vast literature dealing with insect-plant interactions and the interested reader should consult some of the reading listed at the end of this chapter. The chapter concludes with seven taxonomic boxes that summarize the morphology and biology of the primarily phytophagous orders Orthoptera, Phasmatodea, Thysanoptera, Hemiptera, Psocoptera, Coleoptera and Lepidoptera.

COEVOLUTIONARY INTERACTIONS BETWEEN INSECTS AND PLANTS

Reciprocal interactions over evolutionary time between phytophagous insects and their food plants, or between pollinating insects and the plants they pollinate, have been described as *coevolution.* This term, coined by Ehrlich and Raven in 1964 from a study of butterflies and their host plants, was broadly defined and now several modes of coevolution are recognized.

These differ in the emphasis placed on the specificity and reciprocity of the interactions. Specific or pair-wise coevolution refers to the evolution of a trait of one species (such as an insect's ability to detoxify a poison) in response to a trait of another species (such as the elaboration of the poison by the plant), which in turn originally evolved in response to the trait of the first species (i.e. the insect's food preference for that plant).

This is a strict mode of coevolution, as reciprocal interactions between specific pairs of species are postulated. The outcomes of such coevolution may be evolutionary 'arms races' between eater and eaten or convergence of traits in mutualisms so that both members of an interacting pair appear perfectly adapted to each other.

Reciprocal evolution between the interacting species may contribute to at least one of the species becoming subdivided into two or more reproductively isolated populations, thereby acting to generate species diversity. Another mode, diffuse or *guild coevolution*, describes reciprocal evolutionary change among groups, rather than pairs, of species.

Here the criterion of specificity is relaxed so that a particular trait in one or more species (e.g. of flowering plants) may evolve in response to a trait or suite of traits in several other species (e.g. as in several different, perhaps unrelated, pollinating insects). These are the main modes of coevolution that relate to insect-plant interactions, but clearly they are not mutually exclusive.

The study of such interactions is bedevilled with the problem that unequivocal demonstration of the occurrence of any kind of coevolution is difficult. Evolution takes place over geological time and hence the selection pressures responsible for changes in 'coevolving' taxa can be inferred only retrospectively, principally from correlated traits of interacting organisms.

Specificity of interactions among living taxa can be demonstrated or refuted far more convincingly than can historical reciprocity in the evolution of the traits of these same taxa. For example, by careful observation, a flower bearing its nectar at the bottom of a very deep tube may be shown to be pollinated exclusively by a particular moth species with a very long proboscis, or a hummingbird with a particular length and curvature of its beak.

Specificity of the association between any individual pollinator species and plant is an observable fact, but flower tube depth and mouthpart morphology are mere correlation and only suggestive of coevolution.

PHYTOPHAGY (OR HERBIVORY)

The majority of plant species support complex faunas of herbivores, each of which may be defined in relation to the range of plant taxa used. Thus *monophages* are specialists that feed on one plant taxon, *oligophages* feed on few, and polyphages are generalists that feed on many plant groups.

The adjectives for these feeding categories are *monophagous*, *oligophagous* and *polyphagous*. Gall-inducing cynipid wasps (Hymenoptera) exemplify monophagous insects as nearly all species are host-plant specific; furthermore, all cynipid wasps of the tribe Rhoditini induce their galls only on roses (*Rosa*) and almost all species of Cynipini form their galls only on oaks (*Quercus*).

The monarch or wanderer butterfly, *Danaus plexippus* (Nymphalidae), is an example of an oligophagous insect, with larvae that feed on various milkweeds, predominantly species of *Asclepias*. The Chinese wax scale, *Ceroplastes sinensis* (Hemiptera: Coccidae), is truly polyphagous with its recorded host plants belonging to about 200 species in at least 50 families. Many plants appear to have broad-spectrum defences against a very large suite of enemies, including insect and vertebrate herbivores and pathogens.

These defences, as mentioned above, are primarily physical or chemical in nature and are discussed elsewhere in this chapter in relation to host-plant resistance to insect pests. Spines or pubescence on stems and leaves, silica or sclerenchyma in leaf tissue, or leaf shapes that aid camouflage are amongst the physical attributes of plants that may deter some herbivores.

Furthermore, in addition to the chemicals considered essential to plant function, most plants contain compounds whose role generally is assumed to be defensive, although these chemicals may have, or once may have had, other metabolic functions or simply be metabolic waste products. Such chemicals are often called *secondary plant compounds*, *noxious phytochemicals* or *allelochemicals*.

A huge array exists, including phenolics (such as tannins), terpenoid compounds (essential oils), alkaloids, cyanogenic glycosides and sulphur-containing glucosinolates. The antiherbivore action of many of these compounds has been demonstrated or inferred.

For example, in *Acacia*, the loss of the otherwise widely distributed cyanogenic glycosides in those species that harbour mutualistic stinging ants implies that the secondary plant chemicals do have an antiherbivore function in those many species that lack ant defences. In terms of plant defence, secondary plant compounds may act in one of two ways. At a behavioural level, these chemicals may repel an insect or inhibit feeding and/or oviposition.

At a physiological level, they may poison an insect or reduce the nutritional content of its food. However, the same chemicals that repel some insect species may attract others, either for oviposition or feeding (thus acting as kairomones). Such insects, thus attracted, are said to be adapted to the chemicals of their host plants, either by tolerating, detoxifying or even sequestering them.

An example is the wanderer butterfly, *D. plexippns*, which usually oviposits on milkweed plants, many of which contain toxic cardiac glycosides (cardenolides), which the feeding larva can sequester for use as an antipredator device. Secondary plant compounds have been classified into two broad groups based on their inferred biochemical actions: (i) qualitative or toxic, and (ii) quantitative.

The former are effective poisons in small quantities (e.g. alkaloids, cyanogenic glycosides), whereas the latter act in proportion to their concentration, being more effective in greater amounts (e.g. tannins, resins, silica). However, for insects that are specialized to feed on particular plants containing either group of secondary plant compound, these chemicals actually can act as phagostimulants.

The observation that some kinds of plants are more susceptible to insect attack than others also has been explained by the relative apparency of the plants. Thus large, long-lived, clumped trees are very much more apparent to an insect than small, annual, scattered herbs. Apparent plants tend to have quantitative secondary compounds, with high metabolic costs in their production.

Unapparent plants often have qualitative or toxic secondary compounds, produced at little metabolic cost. Human agriculture often turns unapparent plants into apparent ones, when monocultures of annual plants are cultivated, with corresponding increases in insect damage.

Another consideration is the predictability of resources sought by insects, such as the suggested predictability of the presence of new leaves on a eucalypt or creosote bush in contrast to the erratic spring flush of new leaves on a deciduous tree. However, the question of what is predictability (or apparency) of plants to insects, is essentially untestable.

Furthermore, insects can optimize the use of intermittently abundant resources by synchronizing their life cycles to identical environmental cues as those used by the plant. A third correlate of variation in herbivory rates concerns the nature and quantities of resources (i.e. light, water, nutrients) available to plants. One hypothesis is that insect herbivores feed preferentially on stressed plants (e.g. affected by waterlogging, drought or nutrient deficiency), because stress can alter plant physiology in ways beneficial to insects.

Alternatively, insect herbivores may prefer to feed on vigorously growing plants (or plant parts) in resource-rich habitats. Evidence for and against both is available. Thus gall-forming phylloxera prefers fast-growing meristematic tissue found in rapidly extending shoots of its healthy native vine host.

In apparent contrast, the larva of *Dioryctria albovitella* (the pinyon pine cone and shoot boring moth; Pyralidae) attacks the growing shoots of nutrient-deprived and/or water-stressed pinyon pine (Pin us *edulis*) in preference to adjacent, less-stressed trees.

Experimental alleviation of water stress has been shown to reduce rates of infestation, and enhance pine growth. Examination of a wide range of resource studies leads to the following partial explanation: boring and sucking insects seem to perform better on stressed plants, whereas gallinducers and chewing insects are adversely affected by plant stress.

Additionally, performance of chewers may be reduced more on stressed, slowgrowing plants than on stressed, fast growers. The presence in Australia of a huge radiation of oecophorid moths whose larvae specialize in feeding on fallen Eucalyptus leaves suggests that even welldefended food resources can become available to the specialist herbivore.

Evidently no single hypothesis (model) of herbivory is consistent with all observed patterns of temporal and spatial variation within plant individuals, populations and communities. However, all models of current herbivory theory make two assumptions, both of which are difficult to substantiate. These are:

1. Damage by herbivores is a dominant selective force on plant evolution.
2. Food quality has a dominant influence on the abundance of insects and the damage they cause. Even the substantial evidence that hybrid plants may incur much greater damage from herbivores than either adjacent parental population is not unequivocal evidence of either assumption.

   Selection against hybrids clearly could affect plant evolution; but any such herbivore preference for hybrids would be expected to constrain rather than promote plant genetic diversification. The food quality of hybrids is arguably higher than that of the parental plants, as a result of less efficient chemical defences and/or higher nutritive value of the genetically 'impure' hybrids.

   It remains unclear whether the overall population abundance of herbivores is altered by the presence of hybrids (or by food quality *per se*) or merely is redistributed among the plants available. The role of natural enemies in regulating herbivore populations often is overlooked in studies of insect-plant interactions.

Many studies have demonstrated that phytophagous insects can impair plant growth, both in the short term and the long term. These observations have led to the suggestion that host-specific herbivores may affect the relative abundances of plant species by reducing the competitive abilities of host plants. The occurrence of induced defences supports the idea that it is advantageous for plants to deter herbivores.

In contrast with this view is the controversial hypothesis that 'normal' levels of herbivory may be advantageous or selectively neutral to plants. Some degree of pruning, pollarding or mowing may increase (or at least not reduce) overall plant reproductive success by altering growth form or longevity and thus lifetime seed set.

The important evolutionary factor is lifetime reproductive success, although most assessments of herbivore effects on plants involve only measurements of plant production (biomass, leaf number, etc.). A major problem with all herbivory theories is that they have been founded largely on studies of leafchewing insects, as the damage caused by these insects is easier to measure and factors involved in defoliation are more amenable to experimentation.

The effects of sap-sucking, leaf-mining and gallinducing insects may be as important although, except for some agricultural and horticultural pests such as aphids, they are generally poorly understood.

Leaf Chewing

The damage caused by leaf-chewing insects is readily visible compared, for example, with that of many sap-sucking insects. Furthermore, the insects responsible for leaf tissue loss are usually easier to identify than the small larvae of species that mine or gall plant parts. By far the most diverse groups of leaf-chewing insects are the Lepidoptera and Coleoptera.

Most moth and butterfly caterpillars and many beetle larvae and adults feed on leaves, although plant roots, shoots, stems, flowers or fruits often are eaten as well. Certain Australian adult scarabs, especially species of *Anoplognathus* (Coleoptera: Scarabaeidae; commonly called Christmas beetles), can cause severe defoliation of eucalypt trees.

The most important foliage-eating pests in north temperate forests are lepidopteran larvae, such as those of the gypsy moth, *Lymantria dispar* (Lymantriidae). Other important groups of leaf-chewing insects worldwide are the Orthoptera (most species) and Hymenoptera (most Symphyta).

The stick-insects (Phasmatodea) generally have only minor impact as leaf chewers, although outbreaks of the spurlegged stick-insect,

Didymuria violescens, can result in defoliation of eucalypts in Australia. High levels of herbivory result in economic losses to forest trees and other plants, so reliable and repeatable methods of estimating damage are desirable.

Most methods rely on estimating leaf area lost due to leaf-chewing insects. This can be done directly by measuring damage on foliage, either by monitoring marked branches or by destructively collecting separate samples over time ('spot sampling'), or indirectly by measuring the production of insect frass (faeces).

These sorts of measurements have been undertaken in a number of forest types, from rain forests to xeric (dry) forests, in many countries worldwide. Mostly, the herbivory levels are surprisingly uniform. For temperate forests, most values of proportional leaf area missing range from 3 to 17%, with a mean value of 8.8±5.0% (n = 38) (values from Landsberg & Ohmart, 1989). Data collected from rain forests and mangrove forests reveal similar levels of leaf area loss (range 3-15%, with mean 8.8±3.5%).

However, defoliation levels may be very high and even lead to death of plants during outbreaks, especially of introduced pest species. For some plant taxa, herbivory levels may be high (20-45%) even under natural, non-outbreak conditions. Levels of herbivory, measured as leaf area loss, differ among plant populations or communities for a number of reasons.

The leaves of different plant species vary in their suitability as insect food because of variations in nutrient content, water content, type and concentrations of secondary plant compounds, and degree of sclerophylly (toughness). Such differences may occur because of inherent differences among plant taxa and/or may relate to the maturity and growing conditions of the individual leaves and/or the plants sampled.

Communities in which the majority of the constituent tree species belong to different families (such as in many north temperate forests) may suffer less damage from phytophages than communities that are dominated by one or a few genera (such as Australian eucalypt/acacia forests). In the latter systems, specialist insect species may be able to transfer relatively easily to new, closely-related plant hosts.

Thus favourable conditions may result in considerable insect damage to all or most tree species in a given area. In multigenera tree communities, oligophagous insects are unlikely to switch to species unrelated to their normal hosts. Furthermore, there may be differences in herbivory levels within any given plant population over time as a

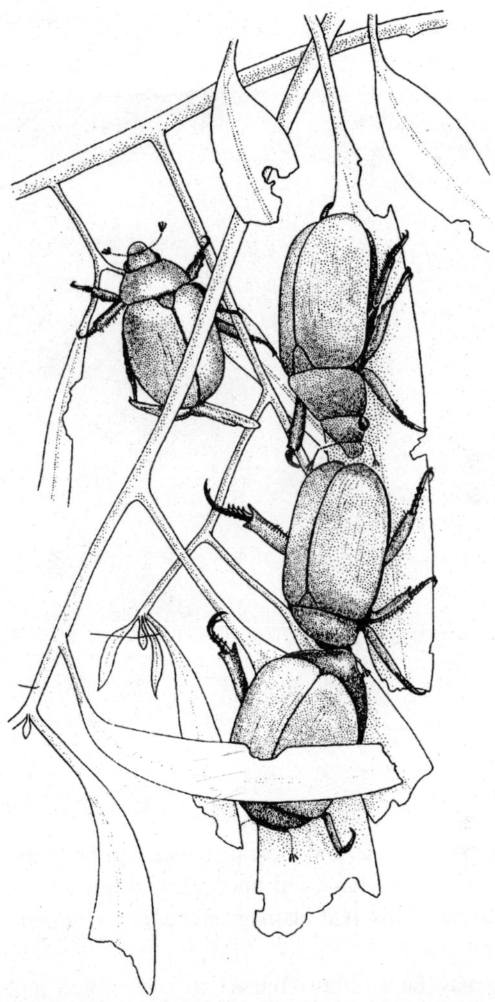

Figure 3.1: Christmas beetles of Anoplognathus (Coleoptera: Scarab-aeidae) on the chewed foliage of a eucalypt tree (Myrtaceae).

result of seasonal and stochastic factors, including variability in weather conditions (which affects both insect and plant growth) or plant defences induced by previous insect damage. Such temporal variation in plant growth and response to insects can strongly influence herbivory estimates that are made over a restricted period.

Plant Mining and Boring

A range of insect larvae reside within and feed on the internal tissues of living plants. *Leaf-mining* species live between the two

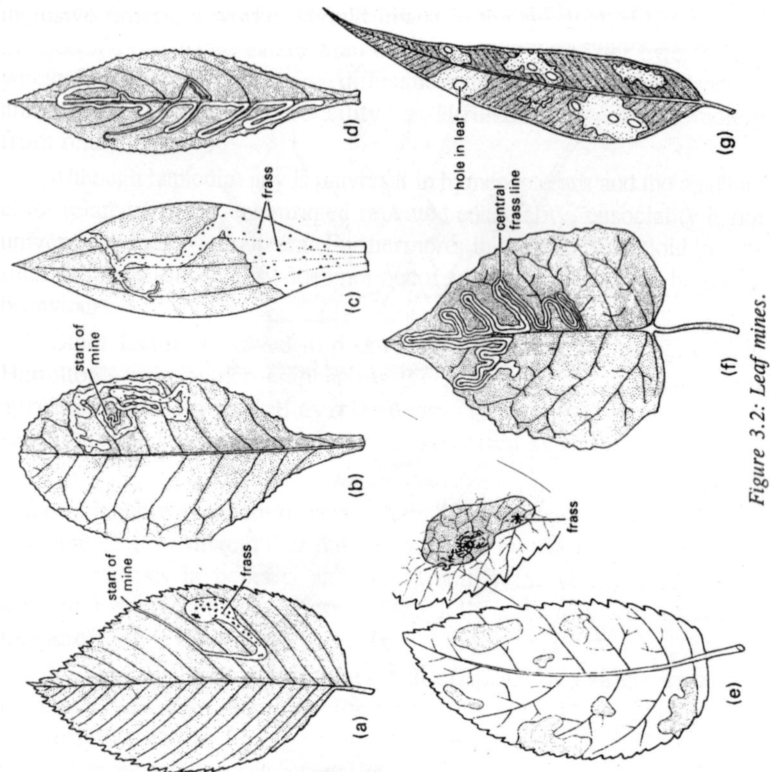

Figure 3.2: Leaf mines.

epidermal layers of a leaf and their presence can be detected externally after the area that they have fed upon dies, often leaving a thin layer of dry epidermis. This leaf damage appears as tunnels, blotches or blisters.

Tunnels may be straight (linear) to convoluted and often widen throughout their course, as a result of larval growth during development. Generally larvae that live in the confined space between the upper and lower leaf epidermis are flattened. Their excretory material, frass, is left in the mine as black or brown pellets or lines.

The leaf-mining habit has evolved independently in only four orders of insects, all of which are holometabolous: the Diptera, Lepidoptera, Coleoptera and Hymenoptera. The commonest types of leaf miners are larval flies and moths. Some of the most prominent leaf mines result from the larval feeding of agromyzid flies.

Agromyzids are virtually ubiquitous; there are about 2500 species, all of which are exclusively phytophagous. Most are leaf miners, although some mine stems and a few occur in roots or flower heads. Some anthomyiids and a few other fly species also mine leaves. Lepidopteran leaf miners mostly belong to the families Gracillariidae, Gelechiidae, Incurvariidae, Lyonetiidae, Nepticulidae and Tisheriidae.

The habits of leaf-mining moth larvae are diverse, with many variations in types of mines, methods of feeding, frass disposal and larval morphology. Generally the larvae are more specialized than those of other leaf-mining orders and are very dissimilar to their non-mining relatives.

A number of moth species have habits that intergrade with gall forming and leaf rolling. Leaf-mining Hymenoptera principally belong to the sawfly superfamily Tenthredinoidea, with most leaf-mining species forming blotch mines. Leaf-mining Coleoptera are represented by species of jewel beetles (Buprestidae), leaf beetles (Chrysomelidae) and weevils (Curculionoidea). Leaf miners can cause economic damage by attacking the foliage of fruit trees, vegetables, ornamental plants and forest trees.

The spinach leaf miner (or mangold fly) *Pegomya hyoscyami* (Diptera: Anthomyiidae), causes commercial damage to the leaves of spinach and beet. The larvae of the birch leaf miner, *Fernusa pusilla* (Hymenoptera: Tenthredinidae), produce blotch mines in birch foliage in northeastern North America, where this sawfly is considered a serious pest.

In Australia, certain eucalypts are prone to the attacks of leaf miners, which can cause unsightly damage. The leaf blister sawflies (Hymenoptera: Pergidae: *Phylacteophaga*) tunnel in and blister the foliage of some species of *Eucalyptus* and related genera of Myrtaceae. The larvae of the jarrah leaf miner, *Perthida glyphopa* (Lepidoptera: Incurvariidae), feed in the leaves of jarrah, *Eucalyptus niarginata*, causing blotch mines and then holes after the larvae have cut leaf discs for their pupal cases.

Jarrah is an important timber tree in Western Australia and the feeding of these leafminers can cause serious leaf damage in vast areas of eucalypt forest. Mining sites are not restricted to leaves, and some insect taxa display a diversity of habits. For example, different species of *Marmara* (Lepidoptera: Gracillariidae) not only mine leaves but some burrow below the surface of stems, or in the joints of cacti, and a few even mine beneath the skin of fruit.

One species that typically mines the cambium of twigs even extends its tunnels into leaves if conditions are crowded. *Stem mining*, or feeding in the superficial layer of twigs, branches or tree trunks, can be distinguished from *stem boring*, in which the insect feeds deep in the plant tissues. Stem boring is just one form of plant *boring*, which includes a broad range of habits that can be subdivided according to the part of the plant eaten and whether the insects are feeding on living or dead and/or decaying plant tissues.

The latter group of saprophytic insects are discussed else where in this chapter and are not dealt with further here. The former group includes larvae that feed in buds, fruits, nuts, seeds, roots, stalks and wood. *Stalk borers*, such as the wheat stem sawflies (Hymenoptera: Cephidae: *Cephus* species) and the European corn borer (Lepidoptera: Pyralidae: *Ostrinia nubilalis*), attack grasses and more succulent plants, whereas *wood borers* feed in the twigs, stems and/or trunks of woody plants where they may eat the bark, phloem, sapwood or heartwood.

The wood-boring habit is typical of many Coleoptera, especially the larvae of jewel beetles (Buprestidae), longicorn (or longhorn) beetles (Cerambycidae) and weevils (Curculionoidea), and some Lepidoptera (e.g. Hepialidae and Cossidae) and Hymenoptera.

The root-boring habit is well developed in the Lepidoptera, but many moth larvae do not differentiate between the wood of trunks, branches or roots. Many species damage plant storage organs by boring into tubers, corms and bulbs. The reproductive output of many plants is reduced or destroyed by the feeding activities of larvae that bore into and eat the tissues of fruits, nuts or seeds. *Fruit borers* include:

- Diptera (especially Tephritidae, such as the apple maggot, *Rhagoletis poinonella*, and the Mediter ranean fruitfly, *Ceratitis capitata*);
- Lepidoptera (e.g. some tortricids such as the oriental fruit moth, *Grapholita molesta*, and the codling moth, *Cydia poinonella*);
- Coleoptera (particularly certain weevils, such as the plum curculio, *Conotrachelus nenuphar*).

Weevil larvae also are common occupants of seeds and nuts and many species are pests of stored grain.

Sap Sucking

The feeding activities of insects that chew or mine leaves and shoots cause obvious damage. In contrast, structural damage caused by sap-sucking insects often is inconspicuous, as the withdrawal of cell contents from plant tissues usually leaves the cell walls intact. Damage to the plant may be difficult to quantify even though the sap-sucker drains plant resources (by removing phloem or xylem contents), causing

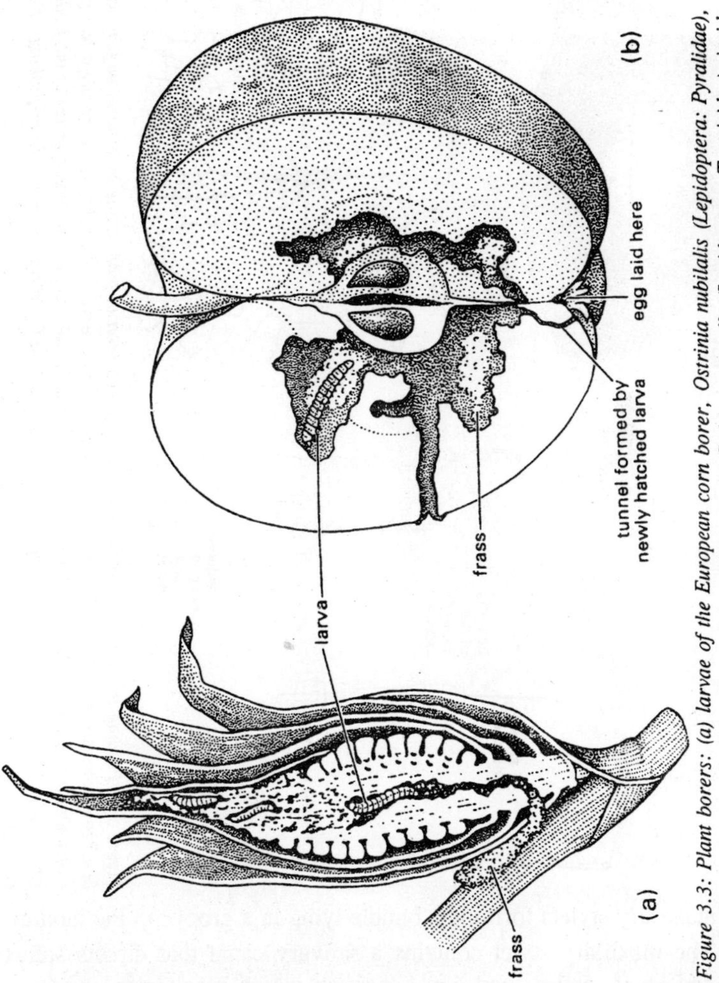

Figure 3.3: Plant borers: (a) larvae of the European corn borer, Ostrinia nubilalis (Lepidoptera: Pyralidae), tunnelling in a corn stalk; (b) a larva of the codling moth, Cyd is pomonella (Lepidoptera: Tortricidae), inside an apple.

loss of condition such as retarded root growth, fewer leaves or less overall biomass accumulation compared with unaffected plants.

These effects may be detectable with confidence only by controlled experiments in which the growth of infested and uninfested plants are compared. Certain sap-sucking insects do cause conspicuous tissue necrosis either by transmitting diseases, especially viral ones, or by injecting toxic saliva, whereas others induce obvious tissue distortion or growth abnormalities called galls.

Most sap-sucking insects belong to the Hemiptera. All hemipterans have long, thread-like mouthparts consisting of appressed mandibular

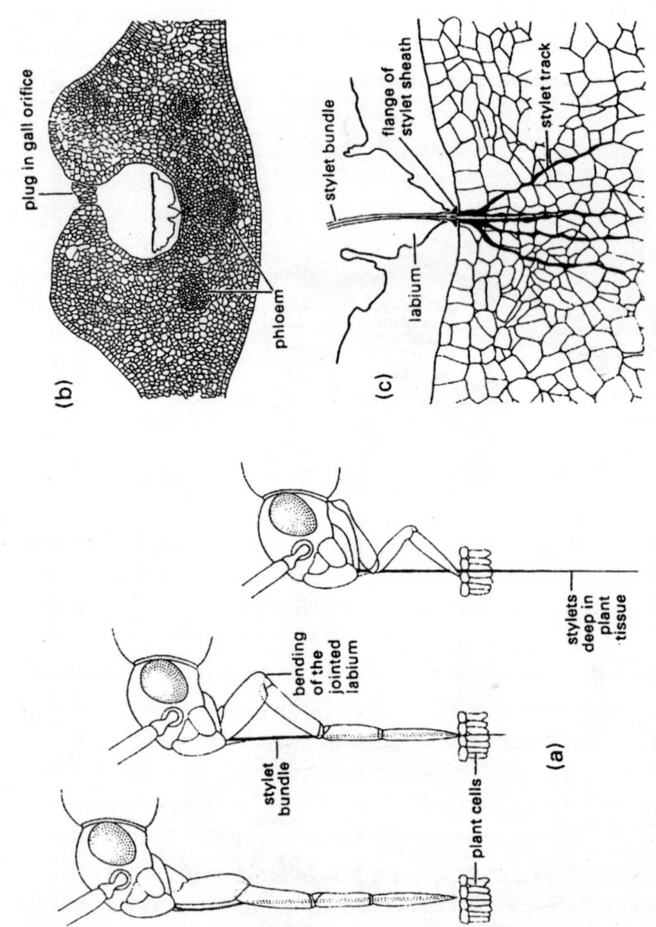

Figure 3.4: Feeding in phytophagous Hemiptera: (a) penetration of plant tissue by a mirid bug showing bending of the labium as the stylets enter the plant; (b) transverse section through a eucalypt leaf gall containing a feeding nymph of a scale insect, Apiomorpha (Eriococcidae); (c) enlargement of the feeding site of (b) showing multiple stylet tracks (formed of solidifying saliva) resulting from probing of the parenchyma.

and maxillary stylets forming a bundle lying in a groove in the labium.

The maxillary stylet contains a salivary canal that directs saliva into the plant, and a food canal through which plant juice or sap is sucked up into the insect's gut. Only the stylets enter the tissues of the host plant. They may penetrate superficially into a leaf or deeply into a plant stem or leaf midrib, following either an intracellular or intercellular path, depending on species.

The feeding site reached by the stylet tips may be in the parenchyma (e.g. some immature scale insects, many Heteroptera), the phloem (e.g. most aphids, mealybugs, soft scales, psyllids and leafhoppers) or the xylem (e.g. spittlebugs and cicadas). In addition to a hydrolysing type of saliva, many species produce a solidifying saliva that forms a sheath around the stylets as they enter and penetrate the plant tissue. .

This sheath can be stained in tissue sections and allows the feeding tracks to be traced to the feeding site. The two feeding strategies of hemipterans, stylet-sheath and macerate-and-flush feeding, are described elsewhere in this chapter, and the gut specializations of hemipterans for dealing with a watery diet are discussed elsewhere in this chapter.

Many species of plant-feeding Hemiptera are considered serious agricultural and horticultural pests. Loss of sap leads to wilting, distortion or stunting of shoots. Movement of the insect between host plants can lead to the efficient transmission of plant viruses and other diseases, especially by aphids and whiteflies.

The sugary excreta (*honeydew*) of phloem-feeding Hemiptera, particularly coccoids, is used by black sooty moulds, which soil leaves and fruits and can impair photosynthesis. Thrips (Thysanoptera) that feed by sucking plant juices penetrate the tissues using their stylets to pierce the epidermis and then rupture individual cells below.

Damaged areas discolour and the leaf, bud, flower or shoot may wither and die. Plant damage typically is concentrated on rapidly growing tissues, so that flowering and leaf flushing may be seriously disrupted. Some thrips inject toxic saliva during feeding or transmit viruses, such as the *Tospovirus* (Bunyaviridae) carried by the pestiferous western flower thrips, *Fraukliniella occiclentalis.*

A few hundred thrips species have been recorded attacking cultivated plants. Outside the Hemiptera and Thysanoptera, the sap-sucking habit is rare in extant insects. Many fossil species, however, had a rostrum with piercingand-sucking mouthparts. Palaeodictyopteroids, for example, probably fed by imbibing juices from plant organs.

Gall Formation

Insect-induced plant galls result from a very specialized type of insect-plant interaction in which the morphology of plant parts is altered, often substantially and characteristically, by the influence of the insect. Generally galls are defined as pathologically developed cells, tissues or organs of plants that have arisen by hypertrophy (increase in cell size) and/or hyperplasia (increase in cell number) as a result of stimulation from foreign organisms.

Some galls are induced by viruses, bacteria, fungi, nematodes and mites, but insects cause many more. The study of plant galls is called *cecidology*, gall-causing animals (insects, mites and nematodes) are *cecidozoa*, and galls induced by cecidozoa are referred to as *zoocecidia*. Cecidogenic insects account for about 2% of all described insect species, with perhaps 13000 species known.

Although galling is a worldwide phenomenon across most plant groups, global survey shows an eco-geographical pattern with gall incidence more frequent in vegetation with a sclerophyllous habit, or at least living on plants in wet-dry seasonal environments. On a world basis, the principal cecidozoa in terms of number of species are representatives of just three orders of insects-the Hemiptera, Diptera and Hymenoptera.

In addition, about 300 species of mostly tropical Thysanoptera (thrips) are associated with galls, although not necessarily as inducers, and some species of Coleoptera (mostly weevils) and microlepidoptera (small moths) induce galls. Most hemipteran galls are elicited by Sternorrhyncha, in particular aphids, coccoids and psyllids; their galls are structurally diverse and those of gall-inducing eriococcids (Coccoidea: Eriococcidae) often exhibit spectacular sexual dimorphism, with galls of female insects much larger and more complex than those of their conspecific males.

Worldwide, there are several hundred gall-inducing coccoid species in about seven families, about 350 gallforming Psylloidea, and perhaps 700 gall-inducing aphid species distributed among the three families, Phylloxeridae, Adelgidae and Aphididae. The Diptera contains the highest number of gallinducing species, perhaps thousands, but the probable number is uncertain because many dipteran gall inducers are poorly known taxonomically.

Most cecidogenic flies belong to one family, the Cecidomyiidae (gall midges), and induce simple or complex galls on leaves, stems, flowers, buds and even roots. The other fly family that includes some important cecidogenic species is the Tephritidae, in which gall inducers mostly affect plant buds, often of the Compositae.

Galling species of both cecidomyiids and tephritids are of actual or potential use for biological control of some weeds. Three superfamilies of wasps contain large numbers of gall-inducing species: Cynipoidea contains the gall wasps (Cynipidae, perhaps 2000 species), which are among the best-known gall insects in Europe and North America, where hundreds of species form often extremely complex galls, especially on oaks and roses; Tenthredinoidea has a number of gall-forming sawflies, such as *Pantania* species (Tethredinidae); and Chalcidoidea includes several families of gall inducers, especially species in the Agaonidae, Eurytomidae and Pteromalidae.

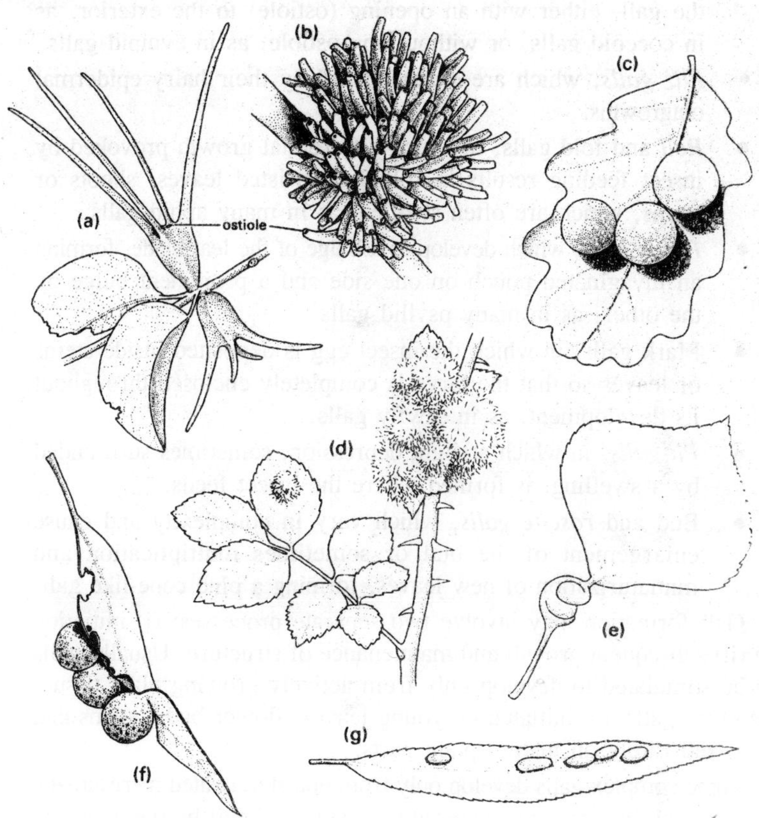

Figure 3.5: A variety of insect-induced galls

There is enormous diversity in the patterns of development, shape and cellular complexity of insect galls. They range from relatively undifferentiated masses of cells ('indeterminate' galls) to highly organized structures with distinct tissue layers ('determinate' galls). Determinate galls usually have a shape that is specific to each insect species.

Cynipids, cecidomyiids and eriococcids form some of the most histologically complex and specialized galls; these galls have distinct tissue layers or types that may bear little resemblance to the plant part from which they are derived.

Among the determinate galls, different shapes correlate with mode of gall formation, which is related to the initial position and feeding method of the insect (as discussed below). Some common types of galls are:

- *Covering galls*, in which the insect becomes enclosed within the gall, either with an opening (ostiole) to the exterior, as in coccoid galls, or without any ostiole, as in cynipid galls.

- *Filz galls*, which are characterized by their hairy epidermal outgrowths.
- *Roll* and fold galls, in which differential growth provoked by insect feeding results in rolled or twisted leaves, shoots or stems, which are often swollen, as in many aphid galls.
- *Pouch galls*, which develop as a bulge of the leaf blade, forming an invaginated pouch on one side and a prominent bulge on the other, as in many psyllid galls.
- Mark galls, in which the insect egg is deposited inside stems or leaves so that the larva is completely enclosed throughout its development, as in sawfly galls.
- *Pit galls*, in which a slight depression, sometimes surrounded by a swelling, is formed where the insect feeds.
- Bud and *rosette galls*, which vary in complexity and cause enlargement of the bud or sometimes multiplication and miniaturization of new leaves, forming a pine cone-like gall.

Gall formation may involve two separate processes: (i) initiation and (ii) subsequent growth and maintenance of structure. Usually galls can be stimulated to develop only from actively growing plant tissue. Therefore galls are initiated on young leaves, flower buds, stems and roots, and rarely on mature plant parts.

Some complex galls develop only from undifferentiated meristematic tissue, which becomes moulded into a distinctive gall by the activities of the insect. Development and growth of insect-induced galls (including, if present, the nutritive cells upon which some insects feed) depend upon continued stimulation of the plant cells by the insect.

Gall growth ceases if the insect dies or reaches maturity. It appears that gall insects, rather than the plants, control most aspects of gall formation, largely via their feeding activities. The mode of feeding differs in different taxa as a consequence of fundamental differences in mouthpart structure.

The larvae of gall-inducing beetles, moths and wasps have biting and chewing mouthparts, whereas larval gall midges and nymphal aphids, coccoids, psyllids and thrips have piercing and sucking mouthparts. Larval gall midges have vestigial mouthparts and largely absorb nourishment by suction.

Thus these different insects mechanically damage and deliver chemicals (or perhaps genetic material) to the plant cells in a variety of ways. Little is known about what stimulates gall induction and growth. Wounding and plant hormones (such as cytokinins) appear important in indeterminate galls, but the stimuli are probably more complex for determinate galls.

Oral secretions, anal excreta and accessory gland secretions have been implicated in different insect-plant interactions that result in determinate galls. The best-studied compounds are the salivary secretions of Hemiptera. Salivary substances, including amino acids, *auxins* (and other plant growth regulators), *phenolic* compounds and phenol oxidases, in various concentrations, may have a role either in gall initiation and growth or in overcoming the defensive necrotic reactions of the plant.

Plant hormones, such as auxins and cytokinins, must be involved in cecidogenesis but it is equivocal whether these hormones are produced by the insect, by the plant as a directed response to the insect, or are incidental to gall induction. In certain complex galls, such as those of eriococcoids and cynipids, it is conceivable that the development of the plant cells is redirected by semiautonomous genetic entities (viruses, plasmids or transposons) transferred from the insect to the plant.

Thus the initiation of such galls may involve the insect acting as a DNA or RNA donor, as in some wasps that parasitize insect hosts. Unfortunately, in comparison with anatomical and physiological studies of galls, genetic investigations are in their infancy.

The gall-inducing habit may have evolved either from plant mining and boring (especially for Lepidoptera, Hymenoptera and certain Diptera) or from sedentary surface feeding (as is likely for Hemiptera, Thysanoptera and cecidomyiid Diptera). It is believed to be beneficial to the insects, rather than a defensive response of the plant to insect attack.

All gall insects derive their food from the tissues of the gall and also some shelter or protection from natural enemies and adverse conditions of temperature or moisture. The relative importance of these environmental factors to the origin of the galling habit is difficult to ascertain because current advantages of gall living may differ from those gained in the early stages of gall evolution.

Clearly most galls are '*sinks*' for plant assimilates-the nutritive cells that line the cavity of wasp and fly galls contain higher concentrations of sugars, protein and lipids than ungalled plant cells. Thus one advantage of feeding on gall rather than normal plant tissue is the availability of high-quality food. Moreover, for sedentary surface feeders, such as aphids, psyllids and coccoids, galls furnish a more protected microenvironment than the normal plant surface. Some cecidozoa may 'escape' from certain parasitoids and predators that are unable to penetrate galls, particularly galls with thick woody walls.

Other natural enemies, however, specialize in feeding on gall-living insects or their galls and sometimes it is difficult to determine which insects were the original inhabitants. Some galls are remarkable for the association of an extremely complex community of species, other than the gall causer, belonging to diverse insect groups.

These other species may be either parasitoids of the gall former (i.e. parasites that cause the eventual death of their host) or inquilines ('guests' of the gall-former) that obtain their nourishment from tissues of the gall. In some cases, gall inquilines cause the original inhabitant to die through abnormal growth of the gall; this may obliterate the cavity in which the gall former lives or prevent emergence from the gall.

If two species are obtained from a single gall or a single type of gall, one of these insects must be a parasitoid, an inquiline or both. There are even cases of hyperparasitism, in which the parasitoids themselves are subject to parasitization.

Seed Predation

Plant seeds usually contain higher levels of nutrients than other tissues, providing for the growth of the seedling. Specialist seed-eating insects use this resource. Notable are many beetles (below), harvester ants (especially species of *Messor*, *Monomorium* and *Pheidole*), which store seeds in underground granaries, bugs (many Coreidae, Lygaeidae, Pentatomidae, Pyrrhocoridae and Scutelleridae) that suck out the contents of developing or mature seeds, and a few moths (such as some Gelechiidae and Oecophoridae).

Harvester ants are ecologically significant seed predators. These are the dominant ants in terms of biomass and/or colony numbers in deserts and dry grasslands in many parts of the world. Usually the species are highly polymorphic, with the larger individuals possessing powerful mandibles capable of cracking open seeds.

Seed fragments are fed to larvae, but probably many harvested seeds escape destruction either by being abandoned in stores or by germinating quickly within the ant nests. Thus seed harvesting by ants, which could be viewed as exclusively detrimental, actually may carry some benefits to the plant through dispersal and provision of local nutrients to the seedling.

An array of beetles (especially bruchine Chrysomelidae and Curculionidae) develop entirely within individual seeds or consume several seeds within one fruit. Some seed beetles (Bruchinae or Bruchidae, according to different texts), particularly those attacking leguminous food plants such as peas and beans, are serious pests.

Species that eat dried seeds are preadapted to be pests of stored products such as pulses and grains. Adult beetles typically oviposit onto the developing ovary or the seeds or fruits, and some larvae then mine through the fruit and/or seed wall or coat. The larvae develop and pupate inside seeds, thus destroying them. Successful development usually occurs only in the final stages of maturity of seeds.

Thus there appears to be a 'window of opportunity' for the larvae; a mature seed may have an impenetrable seed coat but if young seeds are attacked, the plant can abort the infected seed or even the whole fruit or pod if little investment has been made in it.

Aborted seeds and those shed to the ground (whether mature or not) generally are less attractive to seed beetles than those retained on the plant, but evidently stored product pests have no difficulty in developing within cast (i.e. harvested and stored) seeds.

The larvae of the granary weevil, *Sitophilus granarius*, and rice weevil, *S. oryzae*, develop inside dry grains of corn, wheat, rice and other plants. Plant defence against seed predation includes the provision of protective seed coatings or toxic chemicals (allelochemicals), or both.

Another strategy is the synchronous production by a single plant species of an abundance of seeds, often separated by long intervals of time. Seed predators either cannot synchronize their life cycle to the cycle of glut and scarcity, or are overwhelmed and unable to find and consume the total seed production.

Insects as Biological Control Agents for Weeds

Weeds are simply plants that are growing where they are not wanted. Some weed species are of little economic or ecological consequence, whereas the presence of others results in significant losses to agriculture or causes detrimental effects in natural ecosystems.

Most plants are weeds only in areas outside their native distribution, where suitable climatic and edaphic conditions, usually in the absence of natural enemies, favour their growth and survival. Sometimes exotic plants that have become weeds can be controlled by introducing host-specific phytophagous insects from the area of origin of the weed.

This is called classical biological control of weeds and it is analogous

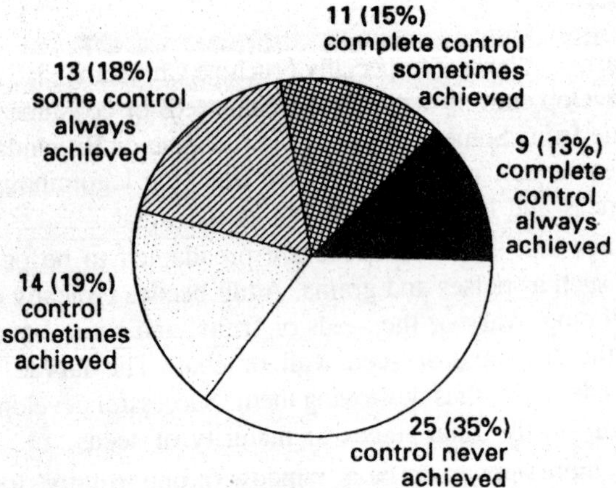

Figure 3.6: Pie chart showing the possible outcomes of releases of alien phytophagous organisms against invasive plants for the biological control of these weeds. The data include 72 weed species that have agents introduced and established long enough to permit control assessment.

to the classical biological control of insect pests. Another form of biological control, called augmentation, involves increasing the natural level of insect enemies of a weed and thus requires mass rearing of insects for inundative release.

This method of controlling weeds is unlikely to be cost-effective for most insect-plant systems. The tissue damage caused by introduced or augmented insect enemies of weeds may limit or reduce vegetative growth, prevent or reduce reproduction, or make the weed less competitive than other plants in the environment.

A classical biological control programme involves a sequence of steps that include biological as well as sociopolitical considerations. Each programme is initiated with a review of available data (including taxonomic and distributional information) on the weed, its plant relatives and any known natural enemies.

This forms the basis for assessment of the nuisance status of the target weed and a strategy for collecting, rearing and testing the utility of potential insect enemies. Regulatory authorities must then approve the proposal to attempt control of the weed. Next, foreign exploration and local surveys must determine the potential control agents attacking the weed both in its native and introduced ranges.

The weed's ecology, especially in relation to its natural enemies, must be studied in its native range. The host specificity of potential control agents must be tested, either inside or outside the country of introduction and, in the former case, always in quarantine.

The results of these tests will determine whether the regulatory authorities approve the importation of the agents for subsequent release or only for further testing, or refuse approval. After importation, there is a period of rearing in quarantine to eliminate any imported diseases or parasitoids, prior to mass rearing in preparation for field release.

Release is dependent on the quarantine procedures being approved by the regulatory authorities. After release, the establishment, spread and effect of the insects on the weed must be monitored. If weed control is attained at the initial release site(s), the spread of the insects is assisted by manual distribution to other sites.

There have been some outstandingly successful cases of deliberately introduced insects controlling invasive weeds. The control of the water weed salvinia by a *Cyrtobagous* weevil (as outlined in Box 10.3), and of prickly pear cacti, *Opuntia* species, by the larvae of the *Cactoblastis* moth are just two examples. On the whole, however, the chances of successful biological control of weeds by released phytophagous organisms are not high and vary in different circumstances, often unpredictably.

Furthermore, biological control systems that are highly successful and appropriate for weed control in one geographical region may be potentially disastrous in another region. For example, in Australia, which has no native cacti, *Cactoblastis* was used safely and effectively to almost completely destroy vast infestations of *Opuntia* cactus.

However, this moth also was introduced into the West Indies and from there spread to Cuba and Florida, where it has led to the extinction of one native cactus species, and it now threatens North America's unique cactidominated ecosystems. In general, perennial weeds of uncultivated areas are well suited to classical biological control, as long-lived plants, which are predictable resources, are generally associated with host-specific insect enemies.

Cultivation, however, can disrupt these insect populations. In contrast, augmentation of insect enemies of a weed may be best suited to annual weeds of cultivated land, where massreared insects could be released to control the plant early in its growing season.

Sometimes it is claimed that highly variable, genetically outcrossed weeds are hard to control and that insects 'newly associated' (in an evolutionary sense) with a weed have greater control potential because of their infliction of greater damage. However, the number of studies for which control assessment is possible are limited and the reasons for variation or failure in control of weeds are diverse.

Currently, prediction of the success or failure of control in terms of weed or phytophage ecology and/or behaviour is unsatisfactory. The interactions of plants, insects and environmental factors are complicated and likely to be case-specific.

In addition to the uncertainty of success of classical biological control programmes, the control of certain weeds can cause potential conflicts of interest. Sometimes not everyone may consider the target weed a weed. For example, in Australia, the introduced *Echium plantagineum* (Boraginaceae) is called 'Paterson's curse' by those who consider it an agricultural weed and 'Salvation Jane' by some pastoralists and beekeepers who regard it as a source of fodder for livestock and nectar for bees.

A second type of conflict may arise if the natural phytophages of the weed are oligophagous rather than monophagous, and thus may feed on a few species other than the target weed. In this case, the introduction of insects that are not strictly host-specific may pose a risk for beneficial and/or native plants in the proposed area of introduction of the control agent(s).

For example, some of the insects that can or have been introduced into Australia as control agents for *E. plantagineum* also feed on other boraginaceous plants. The risks of damage to such non-target species must be assessed carefully prior to releasing foreign insects for the biological control of a weed. Some introduced phytophagous insects may become pests in their new habitat.

INSECTS AND PLANT REPRODUCTIVE BIOLOGY

Insects are intimately associated with plants. Agriculturalists, horticulturalists and gardeners are aware of their role in damage and disease dispersal. However, certain insects are vitally important to many plants, assisting in their reproduction, through pollination, or their dispersal, through spreading their seeds.

Pollination

Sexual reproduction in plants involves *pollination*the transfer of pollen (male germ cells in a protective covering) from the anthers of a flower to the stigma. A pollen tube grows from the stigma down the style to an ovule in the ovary where it fertilizes the egg.

Pollen generally is transferred either by an animal pollinator or by the wind. Transfer may be from anthers to stigma of the same plant (either of the same flower or a different flower) (selfpollination), or between flowers on different plants (with different genotypes) of the same species (crosspollination). Animals, especially insects, pollinate most flowering plants. It is argued that the success of the angiosperms relates to the development of these interactions. The benefits of insect pollination (*entomophily*) over wind pollination (*anemophily*) include:

- increase in pollination efficiency, including reduction of pollen wastage;
- successful pollination under conditions unsuitable for wind pollination;
- maximization of the number of plant species in a given area (as even rare plants can receive conspecific pollen carried into the area by insects). Within-flower self-pollination also brings some of these advantages, but continued selfing induces deleterious homozygosity, and rarely is a dominant fertilization mechanism.

Generally it is advantageous to a plant for its pollinators to be specialist visitors that faithfully pollinate only flowers of one or a few plant species. Pollinator constancy, which may initiate the isolation of small plant populations, is especially prevalent in the Orchidaceae-the most speciose family of vascular plants.

The major *anthophilous* (flower-frequenting) taxa among insects are the beetles (Coleoptera), flies (Diptera), wasps, bees and ants (Hymenoptera), thrips (Thysanoptera), and butterflies and moths (Lepidoptera). These insects visit flowers primarily to obtain nectar and/or pollen, but even some predatory insects may pollinate the flowers that they visit. Nectar primarily consists of a solution of sugars, especially glucose, fructose and sucrose.

Pollen often has a high protein content plus sugar, starch, fat and traces of vitamins and inorganic salts. In the case of a few bizarre interactions, male hymenopterans are attracted neither by pollen nor by nectar but by the resemblance of certain orchid flowers in shape, colour and odour to their conspecific females.

In attempting to mate (pseudocopulate) with the insect-mimicking flower, the male inadvertently pollinates the orchid with pollen that adhered to his body during previous pseudocopulations. Pseudocopulatory pollination is common among Australian thynnine wasps (Tiphiidae), but occurs in a few other wasp groups, some bees and rarely in ants. *Cantharophily* (beetle pollination) may be the oldest form of insect pollination. Beetle-pollinated flowers often are white or dull coloured, strong smelling and regularly bowl- or dish-shaped.

Beetles mostly visit flowers for pollen, although nutritive tissue or

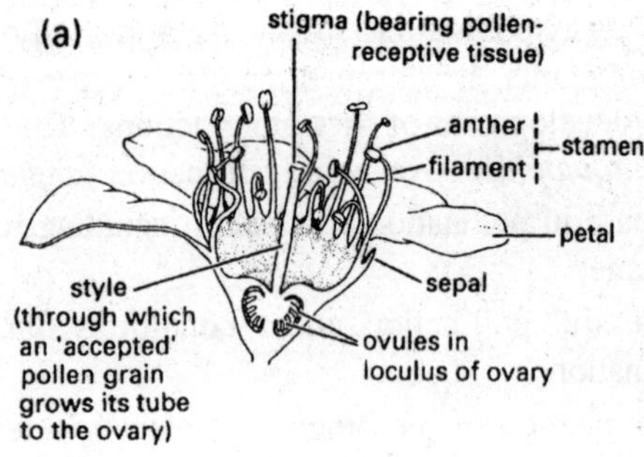

Figure 3.7: Anatomy and pollination of a tea-tree flower, Leptosperinum (Myrtaceae): (a) diagram of a flower showing the parts; (b) a jewel beetle, Stigmodero sp. (Coleoptera: Buprestidae), feeding from a flower.

easily accessible nectar may be utilized, and the plant's ovaries usually are well protected from the biting mouthparts of their pollinators. The major beetle families that commonly or exclusively contain anthophilous species are the Buprestidae, Cantharidae (soldier beetles), Cerambycidae (longicorn or longhorn beetles), Cleridae (checkered beetles), Dermestidae, Lycidae (net-winged beetles), Melyridae (soft-winged flower beetles), Mordellidae (tumbling flower beetles), Nitidulidae (sap beetles) and Scarabaeidae (scarabs).

Myophily (fly pollination) occurs when flies visit flowers to obtain nectar, although hover flies (Syrphidae) feed chiefly on pollen rather than nectar. Fly-pollinated flowers tend to be less showy than other insect-pollinated flowers but may have a strong smell, often malodorous.

Flies generally utilize many different sources of food and thus their pollinating activity is irregular and unreliable. However, their sheer abundance and the presence of some flies throughout the year, mean that they are important pollinators for many plants. Both dipteran suborders contain anthophilous species.

Among the Nematocera, mosquitoes and bibionids are frequent blossom visitors, and predatory midges, principally of *Forcipomyia* species (Ceratopogonidae), are essential pollinators of cocoa flowers. Pollinators are more numerous in the Brachycera, in which at least 30 families are known to contain anthophilous species.

Major pollinator taxa are the Bombyliidae (bee flies), Syrphidae and muscoid families.mMany members of the large order Hymenoptera visit flowers for nectar and/or pollen. The suborder Apocrita, which contains most of the wasps (as well as bees and ants), is more important than the Symphyta (sawflies) in terms of sphecophily (wasp pollination).

Many pollinators are found in the superfamilies Ichneumonoidea and Vespoidea. Fig wasps (Chalcidoidea: Agaonidae) are highly specialized pollinators of the hundreds of species of figs. Ants (Vespoidea: Formicidae) are rather poor pollinators, although *myrmecophily* (ant pollination) is known for a few plant species. Ants are commonly anthophilous (flower loving), but rarely pollinate the plants that they visit.

Two hypotheses, perhaps acting together, have been postulated to explain the paucity of ant pollination. First, ants are flightless, often small and their bodies frequently are smooth, thus they are unlikely to facilitate cross-pollination because the foraging of each worker is confined to one plant, they often avoid contact with the anthers and stigmas, and pollen does not adhere easily to them.

Second, the metapleural glands of ants produce secretions that spread over the integument and inhibit fungi and bacteria, but also can affect pollen viability and germination. Some plants actually have evolved mechanisms to deter ants; however, a few, especially in hot dry habitats, appear to have evolved adaptations to ant pollination.

Generally bees are regarded as the most important group of insect pollinators. They collect nectar and pollen for their brood as well as for their own consumption. There are over 20000 species of bees worldwide and all are anthophilous. Plants that depend on *melittophily* (bee pollination) often have bright (yellow or blue), sweet-smelling flowers with nectar guides-lines (often visible only as UV light) on the petals that direct pollinators to the nectar.

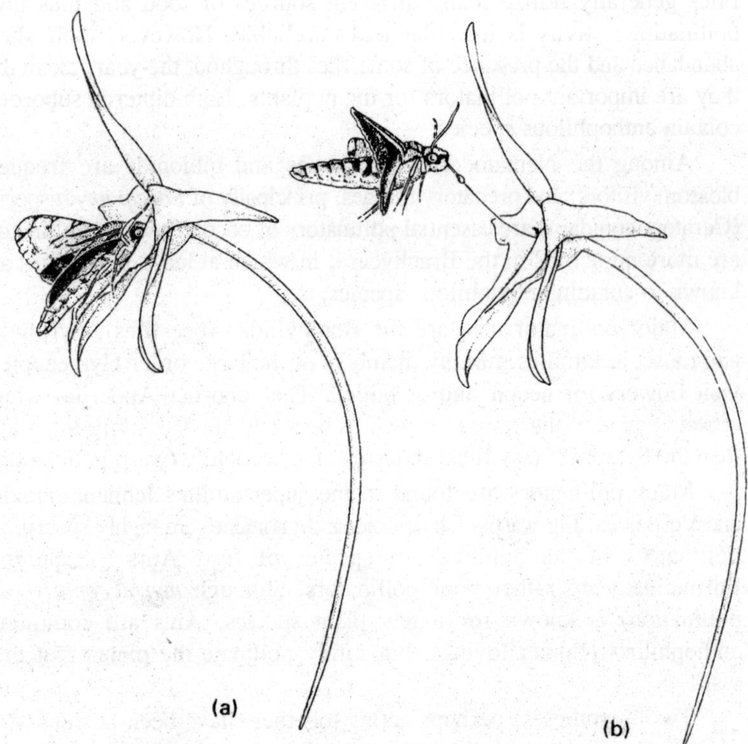

Figure 3.8: A male hawkmoth of Xanthopan morgani praedicta (Lepidoptera: Sphingidae) feeding from the long floral spur of a Malagasy star orchid, Angraecum sesquipedale: (a) full insertion of the moth's proboscis; (b) upward flight during withdrawal of the proboscis with the orchid pollinium attached.

The main bee pollinator worldwide is the honey bee, *Apis mellifera* (Apidae). The pollination services provided by this bee are extremely important for many crop plants, but in natural ecosystems serious problems can be caused. Honey bees compete with native insect pollinators by depleting nectar and pollen supplies and may disrupt pollination by displacing the specialist pollinators of native plant species.

Most members of the Lepidoptera feed from flowers using a long, thin proboscis. In the speciose Ditrysia (the 'higher' Lepidoptera) the proboscis is retractile, allowing feeding and drinking from sources distant from the head. Such a structural innovation may have contributed to the radiation of this successful group, which contains 98% of all lepidopteran species.

Flowers pollinated by butterflies and moths often are regular, tubular and sweet smelling. Phalaenophily (moth pollination) typically is associated with light-coloured, pendant flowers that have nocturnal or crepuscular anthesis (opening of flowers), whereas *psychophily* (butterfly pollination) is typified by red, yellow or blue upright flowers that have diurnal anthesis.

Insect-plant interactions associated with pollination are clearly mutualistic. The plant is fertilized by appropriate pollen, and the insect obtains food (or sometimes fragrances) supplied by the plant, often specifically to attract the pollinator. It is clear that plants may experience strong selection as a result of insects.

In contrast, in most pollination systems, evolution of the pollinators may have been little affected by the plants that they visited. For most insects, any particular plant is just another source of nectar or pollen and even insects that appear to be faithful pollinators over a short observation period may utilize a range of plants in their lifetime.

Nevertheless, symmetrical influences do occur in some insect-plant pollination systems, as evidenced by the specializations of each fig wasp species to the fig species that it pollinates, and by correlations between moth proboscis (tongue) lengths and flower depths for a range of orchids and some other plants.

For example, the Madagasy star orchid, *Angraecum sesquipedale*, has floral spurs that may exceed 30 em in length, and has a pollinator with a tongue length of some 22 cm, a giant hawkmoth, *Xanthopan morgani praedicta* (Sphingidae).

Only this moth can reach the nectar at the apex of the floral spurs and, during the process of pushing its head into the flower, it pollinates the orchid. This is cited often as a spectacular example of a coevolved 'long-tongued' pollinator, whose existence had been predicted by Darwin and Wallace, who knew of the long-spurred flower but not the hawkmoth.

However, the interpretation of this relationship as coevolutionary has been challenged with the suggestion that the long tongue evolved in the nectar-feeding moth to evade (by distance-keeping and feeding in hovering flight) ambushing predators (e.g. spiders) lurking in other less specialized flowers frequented by *X. morgani*.

In this interpretation, pollination of *A. sesquipedale* follows a host-shift of the preadapted pollinator, with only the orchid showing adaptive evolution. The specificity of location of pollinia (pollen masses) on the tongue of X. *inorgani* seems to argue against the pollinator-shift hypothesis, but detailed field study is required to resolve the controversy. Unfortunately, this rare Malagasy insect-plant system is threatened because its natural rain-forest habitat is being destroyed.

Myrmecochory: Seed Dispersal by Ants

Many ants are seed predators that harvest and eat seeds. Seed dispersal may occur when seeds are accidentally lost in transport or seed stores are abandoned. Some plants, however, have very hard seeds that are inedible to ants and yet many ant species actively collect and disperse them, a phenomenon called *myrmecochory*.

These seeds have food bodies, called *elaiosomes*, and special chemical attractants that stimulate ants to collect them. Elaiosomes are seed appendages that vary in size, shape and colour and contain nutritive lipids, proteins and carbohydrates in varying proportions.

These structures have diverse derivations from various ovarian structures in different plant groups. The ants, gripping the elaiosome with their mandibles, carry the entire seed back to their nest, where the elaiosomes are removed and typically fed to the ant larvae.

The hard seeds are then discarded, intact and viable, either in an abandoned gallery of the nest, or close to the nest entrance in a refuse pile. Myrmecochory is a worldwide phenomenon, but is disproportionately prevalent in three plant assemblages: early flowering herbs in the understorey of north temperate mesic forests, perennials in Australian and southern African sclerophyll vegetation, and an eclectic assemblage of tropical plants.

Myrmecochorous plants number more than 1500 species in Australia and about 1300 in South Africa, whereas only about 300 species occur in the rest of the world. They are distributed amongst more than 20 plant families and thus represent an ecological, rather than a phylogenetic, group, although they are predominantly legumes.

This association is of obvious benefit to the ants, for which the

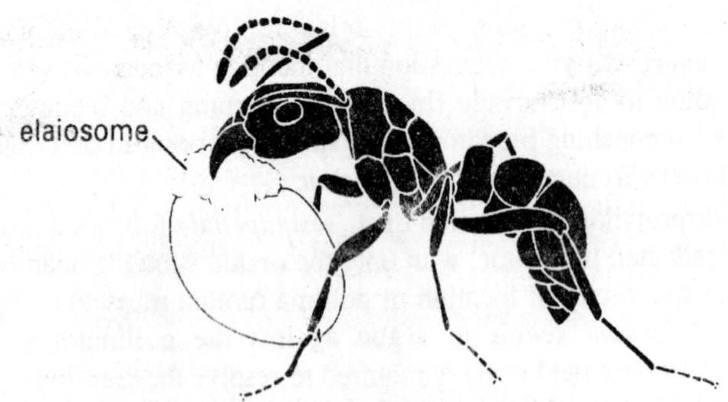

Figure 3.9: An ant of Rh ytidoponera tasnmniensis (Hymenoptera: Formicidae) carrying a seed of Dillwynia jnniperina (Fabaceae) by its elaiosorne (seed appendage).

elaiosomes represent food, and the mere existence of the elaiosomes is evidence that the plants have become adapted for interactions with ants. However, the exact advantages to the plants of this relationship are controversial.

Myrmecochory may reduce intraspecific and/or interspecific competition amongst plants by removing seeds to new sites. Seed removal to underground ant nests may provide protection from fire or seed predators, such as some birds, small mammals and other insects. Alternatively, ant nests may be rich in some or all plant nutrients, making them better microsites for seed germination and seedling establishment.

However, no universal explanation for myrmecochory should be expected, as the relative importance of factors responsible for myrmecochory must vary according to plant species and geographical location. Myrmecochory can be called a mutualism, but specificity and reciprocity do not characterize the association.

There is no evidence that any myrmecochorous plant relies on a single ant species to collect its seeds. Similarly, there is no evidence that any ant species has adapted to collect the seeds of one particular myrmecochorous species. Of course, ants that harvest elaiosome-bearing seeds could be called a guild, and the myrmecochorous plants of similar form and habitat also could represent a guild.

However, it is highly unlikely that myrmecochory represents an outcome of diffuse or guild coevolution, as no reciprocity can be inferred. Elaiosomes are just food items to ants, which display no obvious adaptations to myrmecochory. Thus, this fascinating form of seed dispersal appears to be the result of plant evolution, as a result of selection from ants in general, and not of coevolution of plants and specific ants.

INSECTS THAT LIVE MUULISTICALLY IN SPECIALIZED PLANT STRUCTURES

A great many insects live within plant structures, in bored-out stems, leaf mines or galls, but these insects create their own living spaces by destruction or physiological manipulation. In contrast, some plants have specialized structures or chambers, which house mutualistic insects and form in the absence of these guests. Two types of these special insect-plant interactions are discussed below.

Ant-plant Interactions Involving Domatia

Domatia (little houses) may be hollow stems, tubers, swollen petioles or thorns, which are used by ants either for feeding or as nest sites, or both. True domatia are cavities that form independently of ants, such as in plants grown in glasshouses from which ants are excluded.

It may be difficult to recognize true domatia in the field because ants often take advantage of natural hollows and crevices such as tunnels bored by beetle or moth larvae. Plants with true domatia, called ant plants or *myrmecophytes*, often are trees, shrubs or vines of the secondary regrowth or understorey of tropical lowland rain forest.

Ants benefit from association with myrmecophytes through provision of shelter for their nests and readily available food resources. Food comes either directly from the plant through food bodies or extrafloral

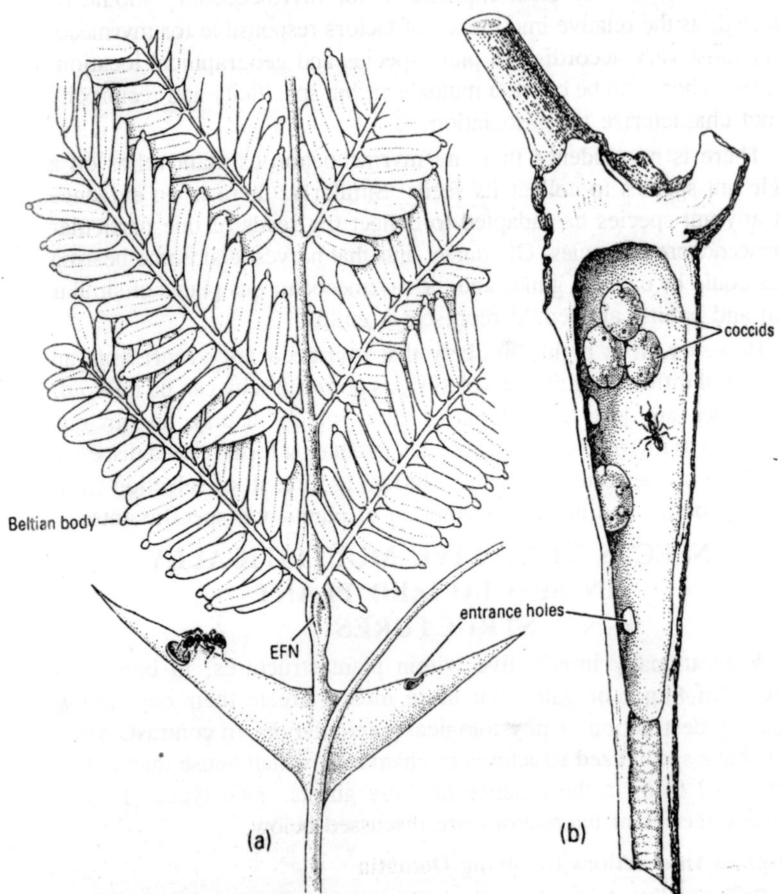

Figure 3.10: Two myrmecophytes showing the domatia (hollow chambers) that house ants and the food resources available to the ants.

nectaries, or indirectly via honeydew-excreting hemipterans living within the domatia.

Food bodies are small nutritive nodules on the foliage or stems of ant plants. Extrafloral nectaries (EFNs) are glands that produce sugary secretions (possibly also containing amino acids) attractive to ants and other insects. Plants with EFNs often occur in temperate areas and lack domatia, for example many Australian *Acacia* species, whereas plants with food bodies nearly always have domatia, and some plants have both EFNs and food bodies.

Many myrmecophytes, however, lack both of the latter structures and instead the ants 'farm' soft scales or mealybugs (Coccoidea: Coccidae or Pseudococcidae) for their honeydew (sugary excreta derived from phloem on which they feed) and possibly cull them to obtain protein. Like EFNs and food bodies, coccoids can draw the ants into a closer relationship with the plant by providing a resource on that plant.

Obviously myrmecophytes receive some benefits from ant occupancy of their domatia. The ants may provide protection from herbivores and plant competitors or supply nutrients to their host plant. Some ants aggressively defend their plant against grazing mammals, remove herbivorous insects and prune or detach other plants, such as epiphytes and vines that grow on their host.

This extremely aggressive tending is demonstrated by ants of *Pseudomyrmex* that protect *Acacia* in tropical America. Rather than protection, some myrmecophytes derive mineral nutrients and nitrogen from ant-colony waste via absorption through the inner surfaces of the domatia.

Such plant 'feeding' by ants, called *myrmecotrophy*, can be documented by following the fate of a radioactive label placed in ant prey. Prey is taken into the domatia, eaten and the remains are discarded in refuse tunnels; the label ends up in the leaves of the plant. Myrmecotrophy occurs in the epiphytic *Myrmecodia* (Rubiaceae), species of which occur in the Malaysian and Australian regions, especially in New Guinea.

The majority of ant-plant associations may be opportunistic and unspecialized, although some tropical and subtropical ants (e.g. some *Pseudomyrmex* and *Azteca* species) are totally dependent on their particular host plants (e.g. *Acacia* or *Triplaris* and *Cecropin* species, respectively) for food and shelter.

Likewise, if deprived of their attendant ants, these myrmecophytes decline. These relationships clearly are obligatorily mutualistic and, no doubt, others remain to be documented.

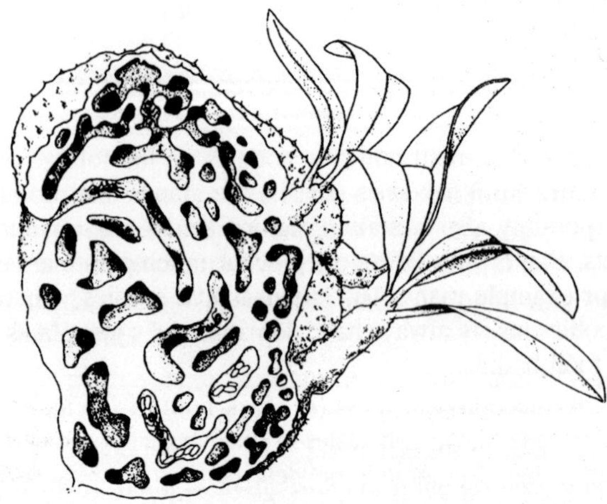

Figure 3.11: A tuber of the epiphytic myrmecophyte, Myrmecodia beccarii (Rubiaceae), cut open to show the chambers inhabited by ants. Ants live in smooth-walled chambers and deposit their refuse in warted tunnels, from which nutrients are absorbed by the plant.

Phytotelmata: Plant-held Water Containers

Many plants support insect communities in structures that retain water. The containers formed by water retained in leaf axils of many bromeliads ('tank-plants'), gingers and teasels, for example, or in rot-holes of trees, appear incidental to the plants.

Others, namely the pitcher plants, have a complex architecture, designed to lure and trap insects, which are digested in the container liquid. The pitcher plants are a convergent grouping of the American Sarraceniaceae, Old World Nepenthaceae and Australian endemic Cephalotaceae.

They generally live in nutrient-poor soils. Odour, colour and nectar entice insects, predominantly ants, into modified leaves-the 'pitchers'. Guard hairs and slippery walls prevent exit and thus the prey cannot escape and drowns in the pitcher liquid, which contains digestive enzymes secreted by the plant.

This apparently inhospitable environment provides the home for a few specialist insects that live above the fluid, and many more living as larvae within. The adults of these insects can move in and out of the pitchers with impunity.

Mosquito and midge larvae are the most common inhabitants, but other fly larvae of more than 12 families have been reported worldwide, and odonates, spiders and even a stem-mining ant occur in southeast

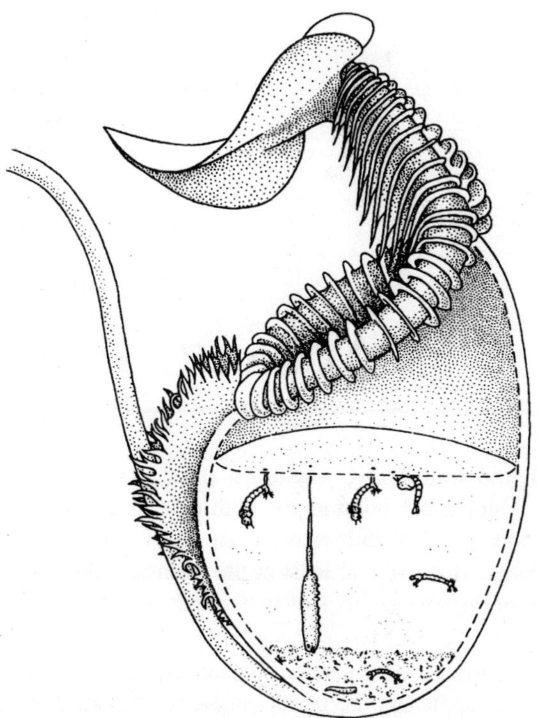

Figure 3.12: A pitcher of Nepenthes *(Nepenthaceae) cut open to show fly inquilines in the fluid: (clockwise from the top left) two mosquito larvae, a mosquito pupa, two chironomid midge larvae, a small maggot and a large rat-tailed maggot.*

Asian pitchers. Many of these insect inquilines live in a mutualistic relationship with the plant, digesting trapped prey and microorganisms and excreting nutrients in a readily available form to the plant.

Another unusual pitcher plant associate is a *Camponotus* ant that nests in the hollow tendrils of the pitcher plant *Nepenthes bicalcarata* in Borneo. The ants feed on large, trapped prey or mosquito larvae, which they haul from the pitchers, and thereby benefit the plant by preventing the accumulation of excess prey, which can lead to putrefaction of pitcher contents.

4

Aquatic Insects

Almost every inland waterbody, whether a river, stream, seepage or lake, supports a biological community within it. The most familiar components of aquatic communities often are the vertebrates, notably fish and amphibians. However, at least at the macroscopic level, invertebrates provide the highest number of individuals and species, biomass and production.

In general, the insects dominate freshwater aquatic systems, where only nematodes can approach the insects in terms of species numbers, biomass and productivity. Crustaceans may be abundant, but rarely diverse in species, in saline (especially temporary) inland waters.

Some representatives of nearly all orders of insects live in water, and there have been many invasions of freshwater from the land. Insects have been almost completely unsuccessful in marine environments, with a few sporadic exceptions such as some water-striders (Hemiptera: Gerridae) and larval dipterans. This chapter surveys the successful insects in aquatic environments and considers the variety of mechanisms they use to obtain scarce oxygen from the water.

Some of their morphological and behavioural modifications to life in water are described, including how they resist water movement, and a classification based on feeding groups is presented. The use of aquatic insects in biological monitoring of water quality is reviewed and the few insects of the marine and intertidal zones are discussed.

Lastly, taxonomic boxes summarize information on mayflies (Ephemeroptera), dragonflies and damselflies (Odonata), stoneflies (Plecoptera), caddisflies (Trichoptera) and other orders of importance in aquatic ecosystems.

TAXONOMIC DISTRIBUTION AND TERMINOLOGY

The orders of insects that are almost exclusively aquatic in their immature stages are the Ephemeroptera, Odonata, Plecoptera and Trichoptera. Amongst the major insect orders, Diptera have many aquatic representatives in the immature stages, and a substantial number of Hemiptera and Coleoptera have at least some aquatic stages, and in the less speciose minor orders two families of Megaloptera and some Neuroptera develop in freshwater.

Some Hymenoptera parasitize aquatic prey but these, together with certain collembolans, orthopteroids and other predominantly terrestrial frequenters of damp places, are considered no further in this chapter. Aquatic entomologists often (correctly) restrict use of the term larva to the immature (i.e. postembryonic and prepupal) stages of holometabolous insects; nymph (or naiad) is used for the preadult hemimetabolous insects, in which the wings develop externally.

However, for the odonates, the terms larva, nymph and naiad have been used interchangeably, perhaps because the sluggish, non-feeding, internally reorganizing, final-instar odonate has been likened to the pupal stage of a holometabolous insect. Although the term 'larva' is being used increasingly for the immature stages of all aquatic insects, here we use the terms in their strict sense, except that immature odonates are referred to as larvae.

Some aquatic adult insects, including notonectid bugs and dytiscid beetles, can use atmospheric oxygen when submerged. Other adult insects are fully aquatic, such as several naucorid bugs and hydrophilid and elmid beetles, which can remain submerged for extended periods and can obtain respiratory oxygen from the water.

However, by far the greatest proportion of the adults of aquatic insects are aerial, and it is only their nymphal or larval (and often pupal) stages that live permanently below the water surface, where oxygen must be obtained whilst out of direct contact with the atmosphere.

The ecological division of life history allows the exploitation of two different habitats, although there are a few insects that remain aquatic throughout their lives. Exceptionally, *Helichus*, a genus of dryopid beetles, has terrestrial larvae and aquatic adults.

THE EVOLUTION OF AQUATIC LIFESTYLES

Hypotheses concerning the origin of wings in insects have different implications regarding the evolution of aquatic lifestyles. The paranotal theory suggests that the 'wings' originated in adults of a terrestrial insect for which immature stages may have been aquatic or terrestrial. Some proponents of the preferred exite-endite theory speculate that the progenitor of the pterygotes had aquatic immature stages.

Support for the latter hypothesis appears to come from the fact that the two extant basal groups of Pterygota (mayflies and odonates) are aquatic, in contrast to the terrestrial apterygotes, but the aquatic habits of Ephemeroptera and Odonata cannot have been primary, as the tracheal system indicates a preceding terrestrial stage.

Whatever the origins of the aquatic mode of life, all proposed phylogenies of the insects demonstrate that it must have been adopted, adopted and lost, and readopted in several lineages, through geological time. The multiple independent adoption of aquatic lifestyles is particularly evident in the Coleoptera and Diptera, with aquatic taxa distributed amongst many families across each of these orders.

In contrast, all species of Ephemeroptera and Plecoptera are aquatic, and in the Odonata the only exceptions to an almost universal aquatic lifestyle are the terrestrial larvae of a few species. Movement from land to water causes physiological problems, the most important of which is the requirement for oxygen. The following section considers the physical properties of oxygen in air and water, and the mechanisms by which aquatic insects obtain an adequate supply.

AQUATIC INSECTS AND THEIR OXYGEN SUPPLIES

The Physical Properties of Oxygen

Oxygen comprises 200 000 ppm (parts per million) of air, but in aqueous solution its concentration is only about 15 ppm in saturated cool water. Anaerobic respiration can provide energy at the cellular level but it is inefficient, providing 19 times less energy per unit of substrate respired than aerobic respiration.

Although insects such as bloodworms (certain chironomid midge larvae) survive extended periods of almost anoxic conditions, most aquatic insects must obtain oxygen from their surroundings in order to function effectively.

The proportions of gases in air and dissolved in water vary according to their solubilities: the amount is inversely proportional to temperature and salinity, and proportional to pressure, decreasing with elevation. In *lentic* (standing) waters, diffusion through water is very slow; it would take years for oxygen to diffuse several metres from the surface in still water. This slow rate, combined with the oxygen demand from microbial breakdown of submerged organic matter, can totally deplete the oxygen on the bottom (*benthic anoxia*).

However, the oxygenation of surface waters by diffusion is enhanced by turbulence, which increases the surface area, forces aeration and mixes the water. If this turbulent mixing is prevented, such as in a deep lake with a small surface area or one with extensive sheltering vegetation or when there is extended ice cover, anoxia can be prolonged or permanent.

Living under these circumstances, benthic insects must tolerate wide annual and seasonal fluctuations in oxygen availability. Oxygen levels in *lotic* (flowing) conditions can reach 15ppm, especially if the water temperature is low. They may even exceed equilibrium concentrations when photosynthesis generates locally abundant oxygen, such as in macrophyte- and algal-rich pools in sunlight.

However, when this vegetation respires at night oxygen is consumed, leading to a decline in dissolved oxygen. In these circumstances it is the diurnal range of oxygen tensions that aquatic insects must cope with.

Gaseous Exchange in Aquatic Insects

The gaseous exchange systems of insects depend upon oxygen diffusion, which is rapid through the air, slow through water and even slower across the cuticle. Although the insect cuticle is extremely impermeable, diffusion across the body surface may suffice for the smallest aquatic insects, such as some early-instar larvae or all instars of some dipteran larvae.

Larger aquatic insects, with respiratory demands equivalent to spiraculate air-breathers, require either augmentation of gaseous-exchange areas or some other means of obtaining increased oxygen, as the reduced surface area to volume ratio precludes dependence upon cutaneous gas exchange. Aquatic insects demonstrate a range of mechanisms to cope with the lower oxygen in aqueous solutions compared with the atmosphere.

As in their air-breathing relatives, aquatic insects may have open tracheal systems with spiracles, either polypneustic (8-10 spiracles opening on the body surface) or oligopneustic (one or two pairs of open, often terminal spiracles), or closed tracheal systems that lack direct external connection.

Oxygen Uptake with a Closed Tracheal System

Simple cutaneous gaseous exchange in a closed tracheal system suffices for only the smallest aquatic insects, such as early-instar caddisflies (Trichoptera). For larger insects, cutaneous exchange can account for a substantial part of oxygen uptake, but other mechanisms are needed. One of the most widespread means of increasing surface area for gaseous exchange is by gillstracheated cuticular lamellar extensions from the body.

These are usually abdominal (ventral, lateral or dorsal) or caudal, but may be located on the mentum, maxillae, neck, at the base of the legs, around the anus in some Plecoptera, or even within the rectum, as in dragonfly larvae. Tracheal gills are found in the immature stages of Odonata, Plecoptera, Trichoptera, aquatic Megaloptera and Neuroptera, some aquatic Coleoptera, a few Diptera and pyralid lepidopterans, and probably reach their greatest morphological diversity in the Ephemeroptera.

In interpreting these structures as gills it is important to demonstrate that they do function in oxygen uptake. In experiments with larvae of *Lestes* (Odonata: Lestidae), the huge caudal gill-like lamellae of some individuals were removed by being broken at the site of natural autotomy.

Both gilled and ungilled individuals were subjected to lowoxygen environments in closed-bottle respirometry, and survivorship was assessed. The three caudal lamellae of this odonate met all criteria for gills, namely:

- large surface area;
- moist and vascular;
- able to be ventilated;
- responsible normally for 20-30% of oxygen uptake.

However, as temperature rose and dissolved oxygen fell, the gills accounted for increased oxygen uptake, until the maximum uptake reached 70%. At this high level, the proportion equalled the proportion of gill surface to total body surface area.

At low temperatures (< 12°C) and with dissolved oxygen at the environmental maximum of 9 ppm, the gills of the lestid accounted for very little oxygen uptake; cuticular uptake was presumed to be dominant. When *Siphlonurus* mayfly nymphs were tested similarly, at 12-13°C the gills accounted for 67% of oxygen uptake, which was proportional to their fraction of total surface area of the body. Another means of extracting dissolved oxygen is through the use of respiratory pigments.

These pigments occur almost universally in vertebrates and they are also found in some invertebrates and even in plants and protists. Amongst the aquatic insects, some larval chironomids (bloodworms) and

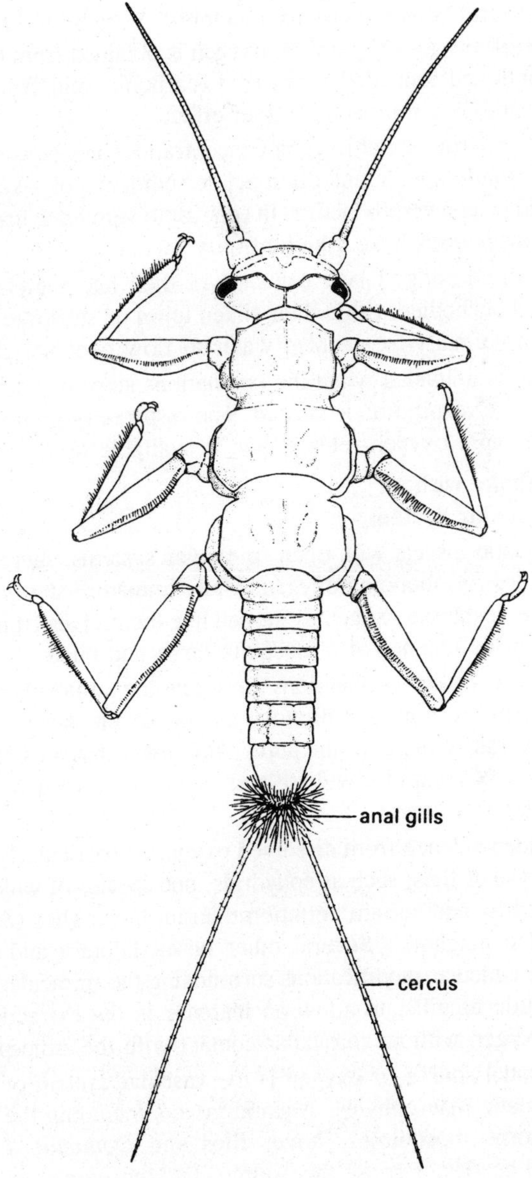

Figure 4.1: A stonefly nymph (Plecoptera: Gripopterygidae) showing filamentous anal gills.

a few notonectid bugs possess haemoglobin. Vertebrate haemoglobins have a low affinity for oxygen; i.e. oxygen is obtained from high-oxygen environments and unloaded in an acid (carbonic acid from dissolved carbon dioxide) environment-the Bohr effect.

Where environmental oxygen concentrations are consistently low, as in the virtually anoxic and often acidic sediments of lakes, the Bohr effect would be counterproductive. In contrast to vertebrate haemoglobins, those of chironomids have a high affinity for oxygen.

Chironomid midge larvae can saturate their haemoglobins through undulating their bodies within their silken tubes or substrate burrows to permit the minimally-oxygenated water to flow over the cuticle.

Oxygen is unloaded when the undulations stop, or when recovery from anaerobic respiration is needed. The respiratory pigments allow a much more rapid oxygen release than is available by diffusion alone.

Oxygen Uptake with an Open Spiracular System

For aquatic insects with open spiracular systems, there is a range of possibilities for obtaining oxygen. Many immature stages of Diptera can obtain atmospheric oxygen by suspending themselves from the water meniscus, in the manner of a mosquito larva and pupa.

There are direct connections between the atmosphere and the spiracles in the terminal respiratory siphon of the larva, and in the thoracic respiratory organ of the pupa. Any insect that uses atmospheric oxygen is independent of low dissolved oxygen levels, such as occur in rank or stagnant waters.

This independence from dissolved oxygen is particularly prevalent amongst larvae of flies, such as ephydrids, one species of which can live in oil tar ponds, and certain pollution-tolerant hover flies (Syrphidae), the 'rat-tailed maggots'. Several other larval Diptera and psephenid beetles have cuticular modifications surrounding the spiracular openings, which function as gills, to allow an increase in the extraction rate of dissolved oxygen without spiracular contact with the atmosphere.

An unusual source of oxygen is the vascular system of roots and stems of aquatic macrophytes. Aquatic insects including the immature stages of some mosquitoes, hover flies and *Donacia*, a genus of chrysomelid beetles, can use this source. In *Mansonia* mosquitoes the spiracle-bearing larval respiratory siphon and pupal thoracic respiratory organ both are modified for piercing the plant tissues.

Temporary air stores (*compressible* gills) are common means of

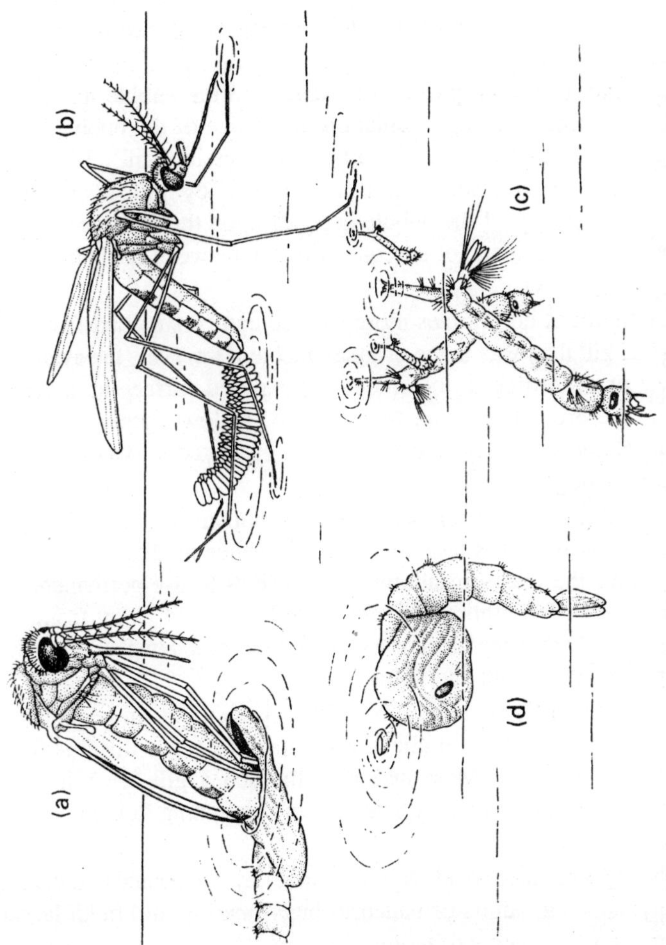

Figure 4.2: The life cycle of the mosquito Culex pipieus (Diptera: Culicidae): (a) adult emerging from its pupal exuviae at the water surface; (b) adult female ovipositing, with her eggs adhering together as a floating raft; (c) larvae obtaining oxygen at the water surface via their siphons; (d) pupa suspended from the water meniscus, with its respiratory horn in contact with the atmosphere.

storing and extracting oxygen. Many adult dytiscid, gyrinid, helodid, hydraenid and hydrophilid beetles, and both nymphs and adults of many belostomatid, corixid, naucorid and pleid hemipterans use this method of enhancing gaseous exchange.

The gill is a bubble of stored air, in contact with the spiracles by various means, including subelytral retention in adephagan water beetles, and fringes of specialized hydrofuge hairs on the body and legs, as in some polyphagan water beetles. When the insect dives from the surface, air is trapped in a bubble in which all gases start at atmospheric equilibrium. As the submerged insect respires, oxygen is used up and the carbon dioxide produced is lost by its high solubility in water.

Within the bubble, as the partial pressure of oxygen drops, more diffuses in from solution in water but not rapidly enough to prevent continued depletion in the bubble.

Meanwhile, as the proportion of nitrogen in the bubble increases, it diffuses outwards, causing diminution in the size of the bubble. This contraction in size gives rise to the term 'compressible gill'. When the bubble has become too small, it is replenished by returning to the surface. The longevity of the bubble depends upon the relative rates of consumption of oxygen and of gaseous diffusion between the bubble and the surrounding water.

A maximum of eight times more oxygen can be supplied from the compressible gill than was in the original bubble. However, the available oxygen varies according to the amount of exposed surface area of the bubble and the prevailing water temperature. At low temperatures the metabolic rate is lower, more gases remain dissolved in water and the gill is long lasting.

Conversely, at higher temperatures metabolism is higher, less gas is dissolved and the gill is less effective. A further modification of the air-bubble gill, the plastron, allows some insects to use permanent air stores, termed an 'incompressible gill'. Water is held away from the body surface by hydrofuge hairs or a cuticular mesh, leaving a permanent gas layer in contact with the spiracles.

Most of the gas is relatively insoluble nitrogen but, in response to metabolic use of oxygen, a gradient is set up and oxygen diffuses from water into the plastron. Most insects with such a gill are relatively sedentary, as the gill is not very effective in responding to high oxygen demand.

Adults of some curculionid, dryopid, elmid, hydraenid and hydrophilid beetles, nymphs and adults of naucorid bugs, and pyralid moth larvae use this mode of oxygen extraction.

Behavioural Ventilation

A consequence of the slow diffusion rate of oxygen through water is the development of an oxygendepleted layer of water that surrounds the gaseous uptake surface, whether it be the cuticle, gill or spiracle. Aquatic insects exhibit a variety of ventilation behaviours that disrupt this oxygen-depleted layer.

Cuticular gaseous diffusers undulate their bodies in tubes (Chironomidae), cases (young caddisfly nymphs) or under shelters (young lepidopteran larvae) to produce fresh currents across the body. This behaviour continues even in later-instar caddisflies and lepidopterans in

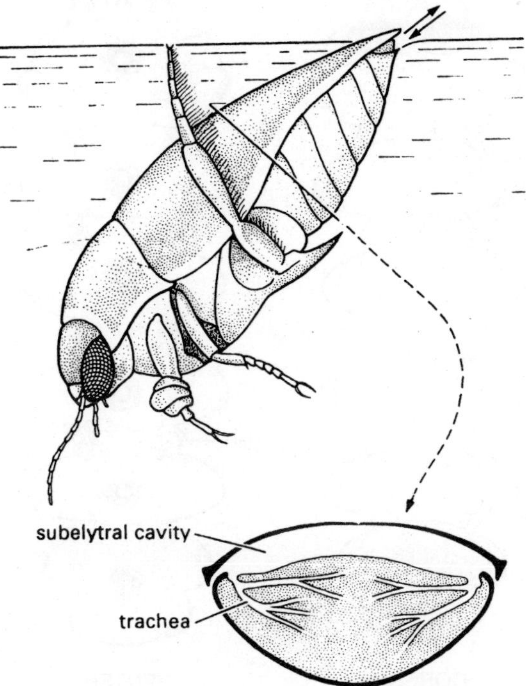

Figure 4.3: A male water beetle of Dytiscus (Coleoptera: Dytiscidae) replenishing its store of air at the water surface. Below is a transverse section of the beetle's abdomen showing the large air store below the elytra and the tracheae opening into this air space. Note: the tarsi of the fore legs are dilated to form adhesive pads that are used to hold the female during copulation.

which gills are developed. Many ungilled aquatic insects select their positions in the water to allow maximum aeration by current flow. Some dipterans, such as blephariceridand deuterophlebiid larvae, are found only in torrents; ungilled simuliids, plecopterans and caseless caddisfly larvae are found commonly in highflow areas.

The very few sedentary aquatic insects with gills, notably black-fly (simuliid) pupae, some adult dryopid beetles and the immature stages of a few lepidopterans, maintain local high oxygenation by positioning themselves in areas of well-oxygenated flow. For mobile insects, swimming actions, such as leg movements, prevent the formation of a low-oxygen boundary layer.

Although most gilled insects use natural water flow to bring oxygenated water to them, they may also undulate their bodies, beat their gills, or pump water in and out of the rectum, as in anisopteran larvae. In lestid zygopteran larvae, ventilation is assisted by 'pull-

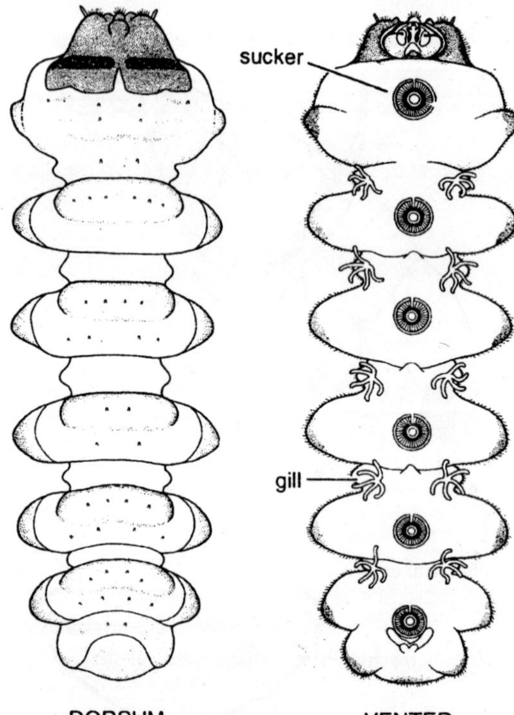

Figure 4.4: Dorsal (left) and ventral (right) views of the larva of Edwardsina palymorpha *(Diptera: Blephariceridae); the venter has suckers which the larva uses to adhere to rock surfaces in fast-flowing water.*

downs' (or 'push-ups') that effectively move oxygen-reduced water away from the gills. When dissolved oxygen is reduced through a rise in temperature, *Siphlonurus* nymphs elevate the frequency and increase the percentage of time spent beating gills.

THE AQUATIC ENVIRONMENT

The two different aquatic physical environments, the lotic (flowing) and lentic (standing), place very different constraints on the organisms living therein. In the following sections, these conditions are highlighted and some of the morphological and behavioural modifications of aquatic insects are discussed.

Lotic Adaptations

In lotic systems, the velocity of flowing water is a major influence on:

- substrate type, with boulders deposited in fastflow and fine sediments in slow-flow areas;

- transport of particles, either as a food source for filter'feeders or, during peak flows, as scouring agents;
- maintenance of high levels of dissolved oxygen.

A stream or river contains heterogeneous microhabitats, with riffles (shallower, stony, fast-flowing sections) interspersed with deeper natural

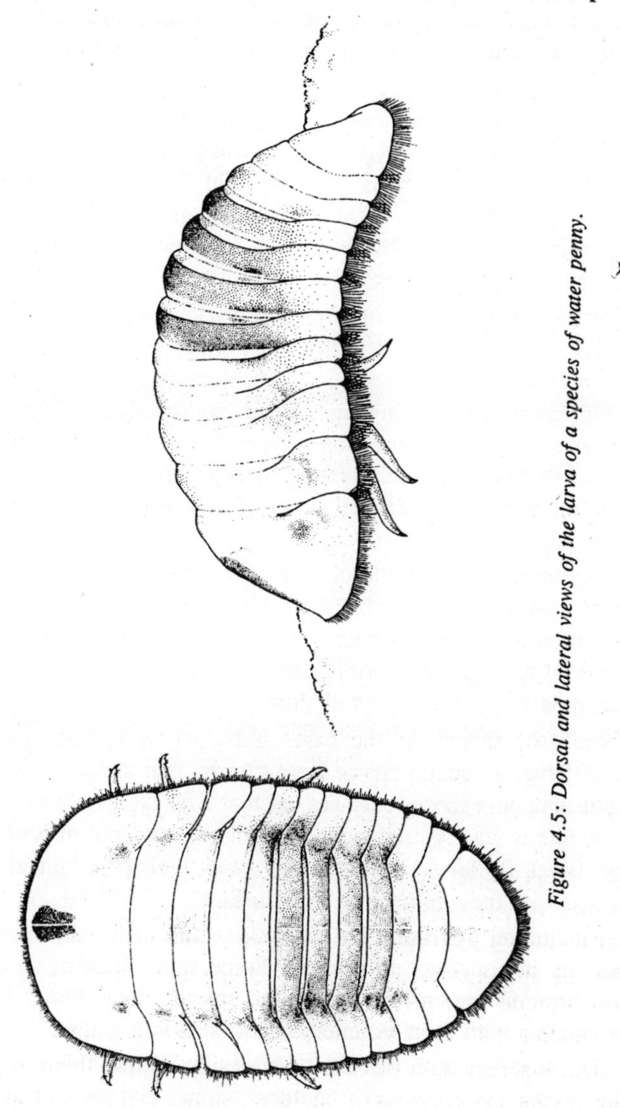

Figure 4.5: Dorsal and lateral views of the larva of a species of water penny.

pools. Areas of erosion of the banks alternate with those where sediments are deposited, and there may be areas of unstable, shifting sandy substrates.

The banks may have trees (a vegetated *riparian* zone) or be unstable, with mobile deposits that change with every flood. Typically, where there is riparian vegetation, there will be local accumulations of drifted *allochthonous* (external to the stream) material such as leaf packs and wood.

In parts of the world where extensive pristine, forested catchments remain, the courses of streams often are periodically blocked by naturally fallen trees. Where the stream is open to light, and nutrient levels allow, *autochthonous* (produced within the stream) growth of plants and macroalgae (macrophytes) will occur, and aquatic flowering plants may be abundant, as in chalk streams.

Characteristic insect faunas inhabit these various substrates, many with particular morphological modifications. Thus those that live in strong currents (*rheophilic* species) tend to be dorsoventrally flattened, sometimes with laterally projecting legs. This is not strictly an adaptation to strong currents, as such modification is found in many aquatic insects, but it permits avoidance or minimization of exposure by allowing the insect to remain within a boundary layer of still water close to the surface of the substrate.

However, the fine-scale hydraulic flow of natural waters is much more complex than was formerly believed, and the relationship between body shape, streamlining and current velocity is not a simple one. The cases constructed by many rheophilic caddisflies assist in streamlining or otherwise modifying the effects of flow.

The variety of shapes of the cases must act as ballast against displacement. Several aquatic larvae have suckers that allow the insect to stick to quite smooth exposed surfaces, such as rock-faces on waterfalls and cascades. Silk is widely produced, allowing maintenance of position in fast flow. Black-fly larvae (Simuliidae) attach their posterior claws to a silken pad that they spin on a rock surface.

Others, including hydropsychid caddisflies and many chironomid midges, use silk in constructing retreats. Some spin silken mesh nets to trap food brought into proximity by the stream flow. Many lotic insects are smaller than their counterparts in standing waters.

Their size, together with flexible body design, allows them to live amongst the cracks and crevices of boulders, stones and pebbles in the bed (*benthos*) of the stream, or even in unstable, sandy substrates.

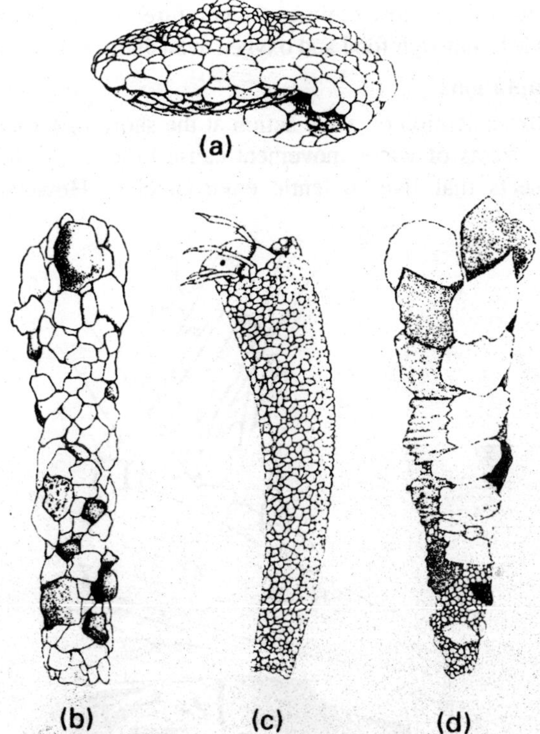

Figure 4.6: Portable larval cases of representative families of caddisflies (Trichoptera): (a) Helicopsychidae; (b) Philorheithridae; (c) and (d) Leptoceridae.

Another means of avoiding the current is to live in accumulations of leaves (leaf packs) or to mine in immersed wood-substrates that are used by many beetles and specialist dipterans, such as cranefly larvae (Diptera: Tipulidae).

Two behavioural strategies are more evident in running waters than elsewhere. The first is the strategic use of the current to allow *drift* from an unsuitable location, with the possibility of finding a more suitable patch. Predatory aquatic insects frequently drift to locate aggregations of prey.

Many other insects, such as stoneflies and mayflies, notably *Baetis* (Ephemeroptera: Baetidae), may show a diurnal periodic pattern of drift. 'Catastrophic' drift is a behavioural response to physical disturbance, such as pollution or severe flow episodes.

An alternative response, of burrowing deep into the substrate (the *hyporheic* zone), is a second particularly lotic behaviour. In the hyporheic zone, the vagaries of flow regime, temperature, and perhaps predation can be avoided, although food and oxygen availability may be diminished.

Lentic Adaptations

With the exception of wave action at the shore of larger bodies of water, the effects of water movement cause little or no difficulty for aquatic insects that live in lentic environments. However, oxygen

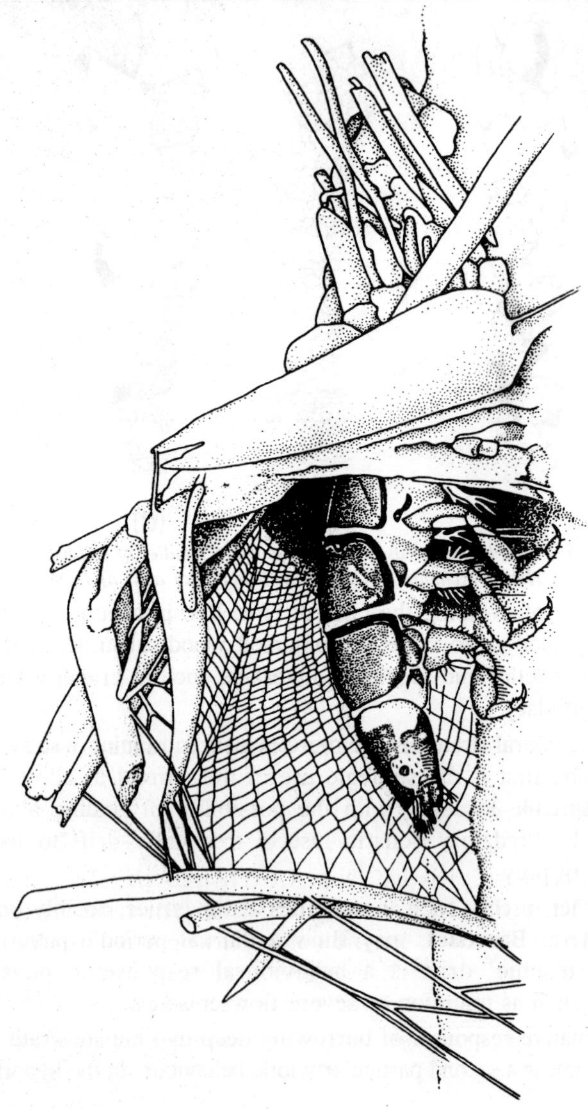

Figure 4.7: A caddisfly larva (Trichoptera: Hydropsychidae) in its retreat; the silk net is used to catch food.

availability is more of a problem and lentic taxa show a greater variety of mechanisms for enhanced oxygen uptake, compared with lotic insects.

The lentic water surface is used by many more species (the neustic community of *semiaquatic* insects) than the lotic surface, because the physical properties of surface tension in standing water that can support an insect are disrupted in turbulent flowing water.

Water-striders (Hemiptera: Gerromorpha: Gerridae, Veliidae) are amongst the most familiar neustic insects that exploit the surface film. They use hydrofuge (water-repellent) hair piles on the legs and venter to avoid breaking the film. Water-striders move with a rowing motion and they locate prey items (and in some species, mates) by detecting vibratory ripples on the water surface.

Certain staphylinid beetles use chemical means to move around the meniscus, by discharging from the anus a detergent-like substance that releases local surface tension and propels the beetle forwards. Some elements of this neustic community can be found in still-water areas of streams and rivers, and related species of Gerromorpha can live in estuarine and even oceanic water surfaces.

Underneath the meniscus of standing water, the larvae of many mosquitoes feed, and hang suspended by their respiratory siphons, as do certain craneflies and stratiomyiids (Diptera). Whirligig beetles (Gyrinidae) also are able to straddle the interface between water and air, with an upper unwettable surface and a lower wettable one.

Uniquely, each eye is divided such that the upper part can observe the aerial environment, and the lower half can see underwater. Between the water surface and the benthos, planktonic organisms live in a zone divisible into an upper *limnetic* zone (i.e. penetrated by light) and a deeper profundal zone. The most abundant planktonic insects belong to *Chaoborus* (Diptera: Chaoboridae); these 'phantom midges' undergo diurnal vertical migration, and their predation on *Daphnia is* discussed elsewhere in this chapter.

Other insects such as diving beetles (Dytiscidae) and many hemipterans, such as Corixidae, dive and swim actively through this zone in search of prey. The profundal zone generally lacks planktonic insects, but may support an abundant benthic community, predominantly of chironomid midge larvae, most of which possess haemoglobin. Even the profundal benthic zone of some deep lakes, such as Lake Baikal in Siberia, supports some midges, although at eclosion the pupa may have to rise more than 1 km to the water surface.

In the *littoral* zone, in which light reaches the benthos and macrophytes can grow, insect diversity is at its maximum. Many differentiated microhabitats are available and physico-chemical factors are less restricting than in the dark, cold and perhaps anoxic conditions of the deeper waters.

ENVIRONMENTAL MONITORING USING AQUATIC INSECTS

Aquatic insects form assemblages that vary with their geographical location, according to historical biogeographic and ecological processes. Within a more restricted area, such as a single lake or river drainage, the community structure derived from within this pool of locally available organisms is constrained largely by physico-chemical factors of the environment.

Amongst the important factors that govern which species live in a particular water body, variations in oxygen availability obviously lead to different insect communities. For example, in low-oxygen conditions, perhaps caused by oxygendemanding sewage pollution, the community is typically species-poor and differs in composition from a comparable well-oxygenated system, as might be found upstream of a pollution site.

Similar changes in community structure can be seen in relation to other physico-chemical factors such as temperature, sediment and substrate type and, of increasing concern, pollutants such as pesticides, acidic materials and heavy metals. All of these factors, which generally are subsumed under the term 'water quality', can be measured physico-chemically.

However, physico-chemical monitoring requires:

- knowledge of which of the hundreds of substances to monitor;
- understanding of the synergistic effects when two or more pollutants interact (which often exacerbates or multiplies the effects of any compound alone);
- continuous monitoring to detect pollutants that may be intermittent, such as nocturnal release of industrial waste products.

The problem is that we often do not know in advance which of the many substances released into waterways are significant biologically; even with such knowledge, continuous monitoring of more than a few is difficult and expensive.

If these impediments could be overcome, the important question remains: what are the biological effects of pollutants? Organisms and communities that are exposed to aquatic pollutants integrate multiple present and immediate-past environmental effects. Increasing insects are used in the description and classification of aquatic ecosystems and in the detection of deleterious effects of human activities.

For the latter purpose, aquatic insect communities (or a subset of the animals that comprise an aquatic community) are used as surrogates for humans: their observed responses give early warning of damaging changes. In this biological *monitoring* of aquatic environments, the advantages of using insects include:

- ability to select amongst the many insect taxa in any aquatic system, according to the resolution required;
- availability of many ubiquitous or widely distributed taxa, allowing elimination of non-ecological reasons why a taxon might be missing from an area;
- functional importance of insects in aquatic ecosystems, ranging from secondary producers to top predators;
- ease and lack of ethical constraints in sampling aquatic insects, giving sufficient numbers of individuals and taxa to be informative, and yet still be able to be handled;
- ability to identify most aquatic insects to a meaningful level;
- predictability and ease of detection of responses of many aquatic insects to disturbances, such as particular types of pollution.

Typical responses observed when aquatic insect communities are disturbed include:

· increased abundance of certain mayflies, such as Caenidae with protected abdominal gills, and caddisflies including filter-feeders such as Hydropsychidae, as particulate material (including sediment) increases;

- increase in numbers of haemoglobin-possessing bloodworms (Chironomidae) as dissolved oxygen is reduced;
- loss of stonefly nymphs (Plecoptera) as water temperature increases;
- substantial reduction in diversity with pesticide run-off;
- increased abundance of a few species but general loss of diversity with elevated nutrient levels (organic enrichment, or *eutrophication*).

More subtle community changes can be observed in response to less overt pollution sources, but it can be difficult to separate environmentally-induced changes from natural variations in community structure.

FUNCTIONAL FEEDING GROUPS

Although aquatic insects are used widely in the context of applied ecology it may not be possible, necessary, or even instructive, to make detailed species-level identifications. Sometimes the taxonomic framework is inadequate to allow identification to this level, or time and effort do not permit resolution. In most aquatic entomological studies there is a necessary trade-off between maximizing ecological information and reducing identification time.

Two solutions to this dilemma involve summary by subsuming taxa into (i) more readily identified higher taxa (e.g. families, genera), or (ii) functional groupings based on feeding mechanisms ('functional feeding groups'). The first strategy assumes that a higher taxonomic category summarizes a consistent ecology or behaviour amongst all member species, and indeed this is evident from some of the broad summary responses noted above.

However, many closely-related taxa diverge in their ecologies, and higher-level aggregates thus contain a diversity of responses. In contrast, functional groupings need make no taxonomic assumptions but use mouthpart morphology as a guide to categorizing feeding modes.

The following categories are generally recognized, with some further subdivisions used by some workers:

- *shredders* feed on living or decomposing plant tissues, including wood, which they chew, mine or gouge;
- collectors feed on fine particulate organic matter by filtering particles from suspension (see the vignette of a filter-feeding black-fly larva of the *Shnulium z'ittntum* complex with body twisted and cephalic feeding fans open) or fine detritus from sediment;
- *scrapers* feed on attached algae and diatoms by grazing solid surfaces;
- *piercers* feed on cell and tissue fluids from vascular plants or larger algae, by piercing and sucking the contents;
- predators feed on living animal tissues by engulfing and eating the whole or parts of animals, or piercing prey and sucking body fluids;
- *parasites* feed on living animal tissue as external or internal parasites of any stage of another organism.

Functional feeding groups traverse taxonomic ones; for example, the grouping 'scrapers' includes some convergent larval mayflies, caddisflies, lepidopterans and dipterans, and within Diptera there are examples of each functional feeding group.

One important ecological observation associated with such functional summary data is the oftenobserved sequential downstream changes in proportions of functional feeding groups. This aspect of the *river continuum concept* relates the sources of energy inputs into the flowing aquatic system to its inhabitants.

Thus in riparian tree-shaded headwaters where light is low, photosynthesis is restricted and energy derives from high inputs of allochthonous materials (leaves, wood, etc.). Here, shredders such as some stoneflies and caddisflies tend to predominate, because they can break up large matter into finer particles.

Further downstream, collectors such as larval black flies (Simuliidae) and hydropsychid caddisflies filter the fine particles generated upstream and themselves add particles (faeces) to the current. Where the waterway becomes broader with increased available light allowing photosynthesis in the midreaches, algae and diatoms (periphyton) develop and serve as food on hard substrates for scrapers, whereas macrophytes provide a resource for piercers.

Predators tend only to track the localized abundance of food resources. There are morphological attributes broadly associated with each of these groups, as grazers in fast-flowing areas tend to be active, flattened and current-resisting, compared with the sessile, clinging filterers; scrapers have characteristic robust, wedge-shaped mandibles.

Changes in functional groups associated with human activities include:

- reduction in shredders with loss of riparian habitat, and consequent reduction in autochthonous inputs;
- increase in scrapers with increased periphyton development resulting from enhanced light and nutrient entry;
- increase in filtering collectors below impoundments, such as dams and reservoirs, associated with increased fine particles in upstream standing waters.

INSECTS OF TEMPORARY WATER BODIES

In a geological timescale, all waterbodies are temporary. Lakes fill with sediment, become marshes and eventually dry out completely. Erosion reduces the catchments of rivers and their courses change. These historical changes are slow compared with the lifespan of insects

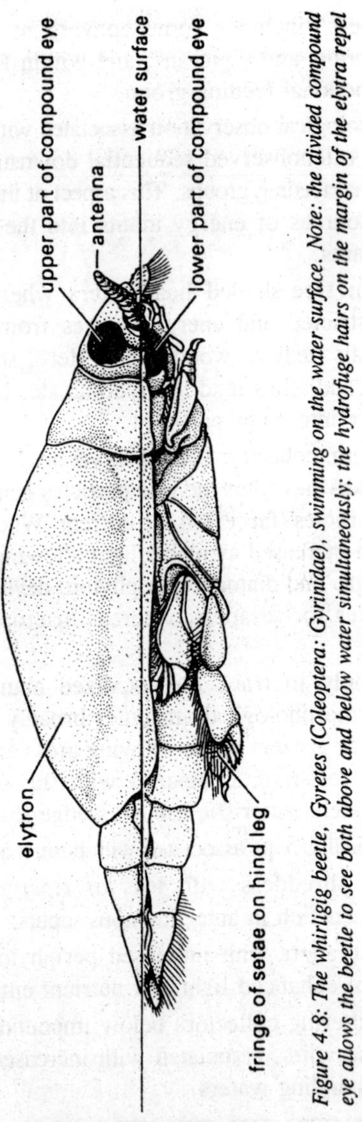

Figure 4.8: The whirligig beetle, Gyretes (Coleoptera: Gyrinidae), swimming on the water surface. Note: the divided compound eye allows the beetle to see both above and below water simultaneously; the hydrofuge hairs on the margin of the elytra repel water.

and have little impact on the aquatic fauna, apart from a gradual alteration in environmental conditions. However, in certain parts of the world, waterbodies may fill and dry on a much shorter timescale. This is particularly evident where rainfall is very seasonal or intermittent, or where high temperatures cause elevated evaporation rates.

Rivers may run during periods of predictable seasonal rainfall, such as the 'winterbournes' on chalk downland in southern England that flow only during, and immediately following, winter rainfall. Others may flow only intermittently after unpredictable heavy rains, such as streams of the arid zone of central Australia and deserts of the western USA.

Temporary bodies of standing waters may last for as little as a few days, as in water-filled footprints of animals, rocky depressions, pools beside a falling river, or in impermeable clay-lined pools filled by flood or snow-melt. Even though temporary, these habitats are very productive and teem with life.

Aquatic organisms appear almost immediately after the formation of such habitats. Amongst the macroinvertebrates, crustaceans are numerous and many insects thrive in ephemeral waterbodies. Some insects lay eggs into a newly-formed aquatic habitat within hours of its filling, and it seems that gravid females of these species are transported to such sites over long distances, associated with the frontal meteorological conditions that bring the rainfall.

An alternative to colonization by the adult is the deposition by the female of desiccation-resistant eggs into the dry site of a future pool. This behaviour is seen in some odonates and many mosquitoes, especially of the genus *Aedes*. Development of the diapausing eggs is induced by environmental factors that include wetting, perhaps requiring several consecutive immersions.

A range of adaptations is shown amongst insects living in ephemeral habitats compared with their relatives in permanent waters. First, development to the adult often is more rapid, perhaps because of increased food quality and lowered interspecific competition.

Second, development may be staggered or asynchronous, with some individuals reaching maturity very rapidly, thereby increasing the possibility of at least some adult emergence from a short-lived habitat. Associated with this is a greater variation in size of adult insects from ephemeral habitats-with metamorphosis hastened as a habitat diminishes. Certain larval midges (Diptera: Chironomidae and Ceratopogonidae) can survive drying of an ephemeral habitat by resting in silk- or mucuslined cocoons amongst the debris at the bottom of a pool, or by complete dehydration.

In a cocoon, desiccation of the body can be tolerated and development continues when the next rains fill the pool. In the dehydrated condition temperature extremes can be withstood. Persistent temporary pools develop a fauna of predators, including immature beetles, bugs and odonates, which are the offspring of aerial colonists. These colonization events are important in the genesis of faunas of newly-flowing intermittent rivers and streams. In addition, immature stages present in remnant water beneath the stream bed may move into the main channel, or colonists maybe derived from permanent waters with which the temporary water connects.

It is a frequent observation that novel flowing waters are colonized initially by a single species, often otherwise rare, that rapidly attains high population densities and then declines rapidly with the development of a more complex community, including predators. Temporary waters are often saline, because evaporation concentrates salts, and this type of pool develops communities of specialist saline-tolerant organisms.

However, few if any species of insect living in saline inland waters also occur in the marine zone-nearly all of the former have freshwater relatives.

INSECTS OF THE MARINE, INTERTIDAL AND LITTORAL ZONES

The estuarine and subtropical and tropical mangrove zones are transitions between fresh and marine waters. Here, the extremes of the truly marine environment, such as wave and tidal actions, and some osmotic effects, are ameliorated. Mangroves and 'saltmarsh' communities (such as *Spnrtincr*, *Sarcocornin*, *Halosarein* and *Sporobolus*) support a complex phytophagous insect fauna on the emergent vegetation. In intertidal substrates and tidal pools, biting flies (mosquitoes and biting midges) are abundant and may be diverse.

At the littoral margin, species of any of four families of hemipterans stride on the surface, some venturing onto the open water. A few other insects, including some *Bledius* staphylinid beetles, cixid fulgoroid bugs and root-feeding *Pemphigus* aphids, occupy the zone of prolonged inundation by salt water.

This fauna is restricted compared with freshwater and terrestrial ecosystems. Splash-zone pools on rocky shores have salinities that vary as a result of rainwater dilution and solar concentration. They can be occupied by many species of corixid bugs and several larval mosquitoes and craneflies.

Flies and beetles are diverse on sandy and muddy marine shores, with some larvae and adults feeding along the strandline, often aggregated on and under stranded seaweeds. Within the intertidal zone, which lies between high and low neap-tide marks, the period of tidal inundation varies with the location within the zone.

The insect fauna of the upper level is indistinguishable from the strandline fauna. At the lower end of the zone, in conditions that are virtually fully marine, craneflies, chironomid midges and species of several families of beetles can be fairly abundant. The female of a remarkable Australasian marine trichopteran (Chathamiidae: *Philanisus plebeius*) *lays* its eggs in a starfish coelom.

The early-instar caddisflies feed on starfish tissues, but later free-living instars construct cases of algal fragments. Three lineages of chironomid midges are amongst the few insects that have diversified in the marine zone. *Tehnatogeton* is common in mats of green algae, such as *Ulva*, and occurs worldwide, including many isolated oceanic islands. In Hawaii the genus has re-invaded freshwater.

The ecologically convergent *Clunio* also is found worldwide. In some species adult emergence from marine rockpools is synchronized by the lunar cycle to coincide with the lowest tides. A third lineage, *Pontomyia*, ranges from intertidal to oceanic, with larvae found at depths of up to 30 m on coral reefs.

The only insects on open oceans are pelagic waterstriders (*Halobates*), which have been sighted hundreds of kilometres from shore in the Pacific Ocean. The distribution of these insects coincides with midoceanic accumulations of flotsam, where food of terrestrial origin supplements a diet of chironomids.

Physiology is unlikely to be a factor restraining diversification in the marine environment because so many different taxa are able to live in inland saline waters and in various marine zones. When living in highly saline waters, submerged insects can alter their osmoregulation to reduce chloride uptake and increase the concentration of their excretion through Malpighian tubules and rectal glands.

In the pelagic water-striders, which live on the surface film, contact with saline waters must be limited. As physiological adaptation appears to be a surmountable problem, explanations for the failure of insects to diversify in the sea must be sought elsewhere.

The most likely explanation is that the insects originated well after other invertebrates, such as the Crustacea and Mollusca, had already dominated the sea.

The advantages to terrestrial (including freshwater) insects of internal fertilization and flight are superfluous in the marine environment, where gametes can be shed directly into the sea and the tide and oceanic currents aid dispersal. Notably, of the few successful marine insects, many have modified wings or have lost them altogether.

5

Saprophytic Insects

A profile of a typical soil shows an upper layer of recently derived vegetational material, termed *litter*, overlying more decayed material intergrading with humus-enriched organic soils. These organic materials lie above the mineralized soil layers, which vary with local geology and climate, such as rainfall and temperature.

For subterranean organisms, particle size and soil moisture are important in influencing their microdistributions. An integral part of the soil system is the decompositional habitat, comprising decaying wood, leaf litter, carrion and dung. The processes of decay of vegetation and animal matter and return of nutrients to the soil involve many organisms, notably fungi; their hyphae and fruiting bodies provide a medium exploited by many insects.

All decompositional substrates have associated faunas that include insects and other hexapods. This chapter considers the taxonomic range and ecology of soil and decompositional faunas in relation to the differing macrohabitats of soil and decaying vegetation and humus, dead and decaying wood, dung and carrion.

The importance of insect-fungal interactions is stressed, and two intimate associations are examined. There is a description of a specialized subterranean habitat (caves), followed by a discussion of some uses of terrestrial hexapods in environmental monitoring.

The chapter concludes with seven taxonomic boxes that deal with: non-insect hexapods (Collembola, Protura and Diplura); primitively wingless bristletails and silverfish (Archaeognatha and Thysanura); three small hemimetabolous orders, the Grylloblattodea, Embiidina and Zoraptera; earwigs (Dermaptera); and cockroaches (Blattodea).

INSECTS OF LITTER AND SOIL

Litter is fallen vegetative debris, comprising materials such as leaves, twigs, wood, fruit and flowers in various states of decay. The processes that lead to the incorporation of recently fallen vegetation into the humus layer of the soil involve degradation by microorganisms, such as bacteria, protists and fungi.

The actions of nematodes, earthworms and terrestrial arthropods, including crustaceans, mites and a range of hexapods, mechanically break down large particles and deposit finer particles as faeces. Acari (mites), termites (Isoptera), ants (Formicidae) and many beetles (Coleoptera) are important arthropods of litter and humus-rich soils.

The immature stages of many insects, including beetles, flies (Diptera) and moths (Lepidoptera), may be abundant in litter and soils. For example, in Australian forests and woodlands, the eucalypt leaf litter is consumed by the larvae of many oecophorid moths and some chrysomelid leaf beetles.

The soil fauna also includes many of the non-insect hexapods (Collembola, Protura and Diplura) and the primitively wingless insects, the Archaeognatha and Thysanura. Many Blattodea, Orthoptera and Dermaptera occur only in terrestrial litter-a habitat to which several of the minor orders of insects, the Zoraptera, Embiidina and Grylloblattodea are restricted.

Soils that are permanently or regularly waterlogged, such as marshes and riparian (stream marginal) habitats, intergrade into the fully aquatic habitats described elsewhere in this chpater and have many faunal similarities. In a profile of soil the transition from the upper, recently-fallen litter to the lower well-decomposed litter to the humus-rich soil below may be gradual.

Certain arthropods may be confined to a particular layer or depth and show a distinct behaviour and morphology appropriate to the depth in the soil. For example, amongst the Collembola, *Onychurus* lives in deep soil layers and has reduced appendages, is blind and white, and lacks a furcula, the characteristic collembolan springing organ.

At intermediate soil depths, *Hypogastrura* has simple eyes, and short appendages with the furcula shorter than half the body length. In contrast, Collembola such as *Orchesella* that live amongst the superficial leaf litter have larger eyes, longer appendages, and an elongate furcula, more than half as long as the body.

A suite of morphological variations can be seen in soil insects.

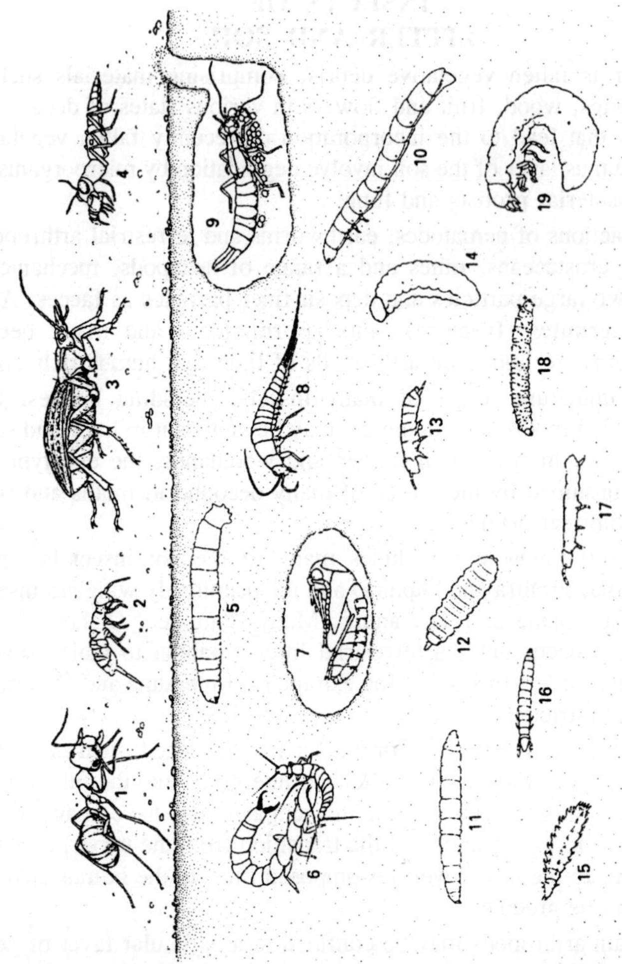

Figure 5.1: Diagrammatic view of a soil profile showing some typical litter and soil insects and other hexapods. The organisms depicted are: (1) worker of a wood ant (Hymenoptera: Formicidae); (2) springtail (Collembola: Isotomidae); (3) ground beetle (Coleoptera: Carabidae); (4) rove beetle (Coleoptera: Staphylinidae) eating a springtail; (5) larva of a cranefly (Diptera: Tipulidae); (6) japygid d ipluran (Diplura: Japygidae) attacking a smaller campodeid dipluran; (7) pupa of a ground beetle (Coleoptera: Carabidae); (8) bristletail (Archaeognatha: Machilidae); (9) female earwig (Dermaptera: Labiduridae) tending her eggs; (10) wireworm, larva of a tenebrionid beetle (Coleoptera: Tenebrionidae); (11) larva of a robber fly *(Diptera: Asilidae); (12) larva of a soldier fly (Diptera: Stratiomyidae); (13) springtail (Collembola: Isotomidae); (14) larva of a weevil (Coleoptera: Curculionidae); (15) larva of a muscid* fly *(Diptera: Muscidae); (16) proturan (Protura: Sinentomidae); (17) springtail (Collembola: Isotomidae); (18) larva of a march fly (Diptera: Bibionidae); (19) larva of a scarab beetle (Coleoptera: Scarabaeidae).*

Larvae often have well-developed legs to permit active movement through the soil, and pupae frequently have spinose transverse bands that assist the movement to the soil surface for eclosion.

Many adult soil-dwelling insects have reduced eyes and their wings are protected by hardened fore wings, or are reduced (brachypterous), or lost altogether (apterous) or, as in the reproductives of ants and termites, shed after the dispersal flight (deciduous, or caducous).

Flightlessness (either primary or secondary) in ground-dwelling organisms may be countered by development of jumping as a means of evading predation: the collembolan furcula is a spring mechanism and the alticine Coleoptera ('*fleabeetles*') and terrestrial Orthoptera can jump to safety.

However, jumping is of little value in subterranean organisms. In these insects, the fore legs may be developed as fossorial limbs, modified for digging, as seen in some groups that construct tunnels, such as mole crickets (as depicted in the vignette of this chapter), immature cicadas and many beetles.

The distribution of subterranean insects shows seasonal changes. The constant temperatures at greater soil depths are attractive in winter as a means of avoiding low temperatures above ground. The level of water in the soil is important in governing both vertical and horizontal distributions.

Frequently, larvae of subterranean insects that live in moist soils will seek drier sites for pupation, perhaps to reduce the risks of fungal disease during the immobile pupa] stage. The subterranean nests of ants usually are located in drier areas, or the nest entrance is elevated above the soil surface to prevent flooding during rain, or the whole nest may be elevated to avoid excess ground moisture.

Location and design of the nests of ants and termites is very important to the regulation of both humidity and temperature because, unlike social wasps and bees, they cannot ventilate their nests by fanning, although they can migrate within nests or, in some species, between them.

The passive regulation of the internal nest environment is exemplified by termites of *A. nitermes* and *Macrotermes*, which maintain an internal environment suitable for the growth of particular fungi that serve as food. Many soil-dwelling hexapods derive their nutrition from ingesting large volumes of soil containing dead and decaying vegetable and animal debris and associated microorganisms. These bulk-feeders, known as saprophages or *detritivores*, include hexapods such as some Collembola,

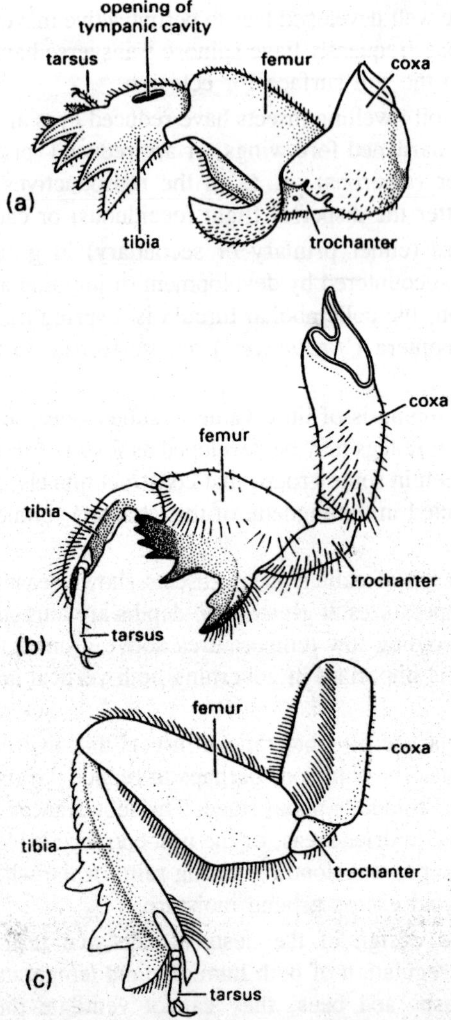

Figure 5.2: Fossorial fore legs of: (a) a mole cricket of Gryllotalha (Orthoptera: Gryllotalpidae); (b) a nymphal periodical cicada of Magicicada (Hemiptera: Cicadidae); and (c) a scarab beetle of Canthon (Coleoptera: Scarabaeidae).

beetle larvae and certain termites (Isoptera: Termitinae, including *Termes* and relatives) that have not been demonstrated to possess symbiotic gut protists yet appear able to digest cellulose from the humus layers of the soil. Copious excreta is produced, and these organisms clearly play a significant role in structuring soils of the tropics and subtropics.

For arthropods that consume humic soils, the subsoil parts of plants

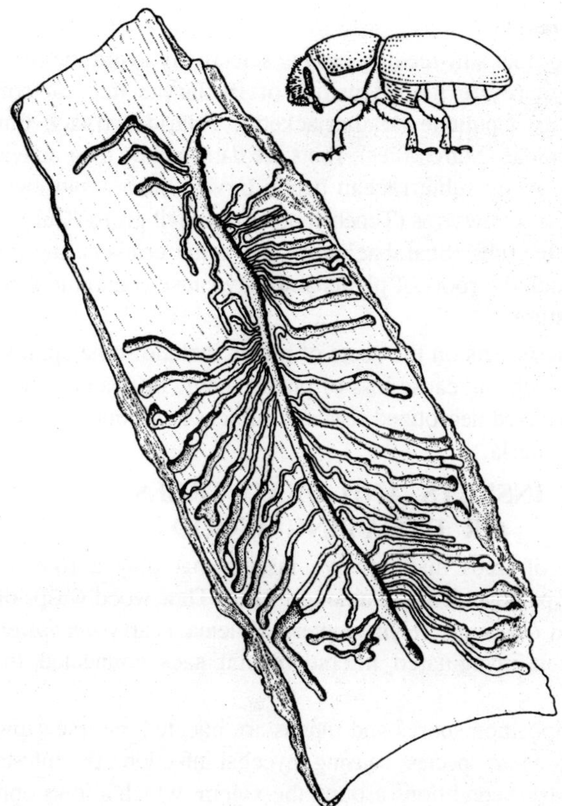

Figure 5.3: A plume-shaped tunnel excavated by the bark beetle Scolytus unispinosus (Coleoptera: Scolytidae) showing eggs at the ends of a number of galleries; enlargement shows an adult beetle.

(the roots) will be encountered frequently. The fine parts of roots often have particular associations with fungal mycorrhizae and rhizobacteria, forming a zone called the *rhizosphere*. Bacterial and fungal densities are an order of magnitude higher in soil close to the rhizosphere compared with soil distant from roots, and microarthropod densities are correspondingly higher close to the rhizosphere.

The selective grazing of Collembola, for example, can curtail growth of fungi that are pathogenic to plants, and their movements aid in transport of beneficial fungi and bacteria to the rhizosphere.

Furthermore, interactions between microarthropods and fungi in the rhizosphere and elsewhere may aid in mineralization of nitrogen and phosphates, making these elements available to plants, but further experimental evidence is required to quantify these beneficial roles.

Root-Feeding Insects

It is unlikely that soil-feeding insects selectively avoid the roots of plants. Where there are high densities of fly larvae that eat soil in pastures, such as Tipulidae (leatherjackets), Sciaridae (black fungus gnats) and Bibionidae (March flies), roots are damaged by their activities. Within the soil, many subterranean beetle larvae, such as wireworms (Elateridae), false wireworms (Tenebrionidae), weevil grubs (Curculionidae) and scarab grubs (Scarabaeidae), and some crickets and a few moth larvae attack the roots of plants and may cause economic damage in managed pastures.

Sap-sucking insects on the roots of plants include some aphids and scale insects, which can cause loss of plant vigour, or death, especially when insect-damaged necrotized tissue is subject to secondary invasion by fungi and bacteria.

INSECTS AND DEAD TREES OR DECAYING WOOD

The death of trees may involve insects that play a role in the transmission of pathogenic fungi amongst trees. Thus wood wasps of the genera *Sirex* and *Urocercus* (Hymenoptera: Siricidae) carry *Amylostereum* fungal spores in invaginated intersegmental sacs connected to the ovipositor.

During oviposition spores and mucus are injected into the sapwood of trees, notably *Pinus* species, causing mycelial infection. The infestation causes locally drier conditions around the xylem, which allows optimal development of larval *Sirex*.

In Australia and New Zealand the fungal disease can cause death of fire-damaged trees or those stressed by drought conditions. The role of *Scolytus* beetles (Coleoptera: Scolytidae) in the spread of Dutch elm disease is discussed elsewhere in this chapter, and there are several other insect-borne fungal diseases that are transmitted to live trees and may result in tree mortality.

The continued decay of these trees, and those that die of natural causes, often involves further interactions between insects and fungi. The ambrosia beetles (Platypodidae and some Scolytidae) are involved in a notable association between beetles, fungus and dead wood. Adult beetles excavate tunnels, predominantly in dead wood though some attack live wood.

Mines are made in the phloem, wood, twigs or woody fruits, which the beetles infect with wood-inhabiting ectosymbiotic 'ambrosia' fungi.

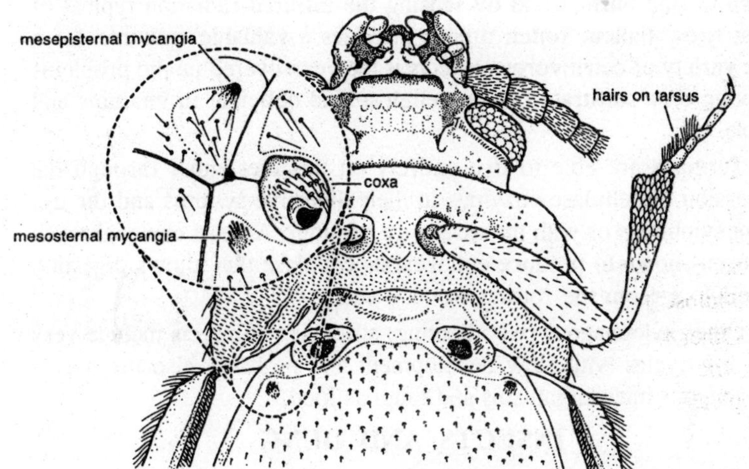

Figure 5.4: Underside of the thorax of the beetle Henoticus scrratus *(Coleoptera: Cryptophagidae) showing the depressions, called mycangia, which the beetle uses to transport fungal material that inoculates new substrate on recentlyburnt wood.*

The fungi, which come from a wide taxonomic range, break down wood, making it more nutritious for the beetles. Both larvae and adults feed on the conditioned wood and directly on the extremely nutritious fungi.

The cultivation of fungi on nutrient-poor, cellulose-rich woody substrates is particularly well developed in leafcutter ants and certain termites. Some mycophagous insects, such as beetles of the families Lathridiidae and Cryptophagidae, are strongly attracted to recently-burned forest. These insects can carry fungi in special cuticular pockets called mycangia, which probably store the fungi during the insects' aestivation or dispersal.

The cryptophagid beetle *Henoticus serratus*, which is an early colonizer of burned forest in some areas of Europe, has deep depressions on the underside of its pterothorax, from which glandular secretions and material of the ascomycete fungus *Trichoderma* have been isolated.

The beetle probably uses its legs to fill its mycangia with fungal material, which it transports to newly-burnt habitats as an inoculum. Ascomycte fungi are important food sources for many pyrophilous insects, i.e. species strongly attracted to burning or newly-burned areas or that occur mainly in burned forest for a few years postfire.

Some predatory and wood-feeding insects are also pyrophilous. A number of pyrophilous heteropterans (Aradidae), flies (Empididae and Platypezidae) and beetles (Carabidae and Buprestidae) have been shown to be attracted to the heat or smoke of fires, and often from a great distance. A species of jewel beetle (Buprestidae: *Melanophila*) has been shown to find burnt wood by sensing the infrared radiation typical of forest fires. Fallen, rotten timber provides a valuable resource for a wide variety of detritivorous insects if they can overcome the problems of living on a substrate rich in cellulose and deficient in vitamins and sterols.

Termites are able to live entirely on this diet either through the possession of cellulase enzymes in their digestive systems and the use of gut symbionts or with the assistance of fungi. At least one cockroach has been shown to produce endogenous cellulase that allows digestion of cellulose from the rotting wood it eats.

Other xylophagous (wood-eating) strategies of insects include very long life cycles with slow development and probably also the use of xylophagous microorganisms and fungi as food.

INSECTS AND DUNG

The excreta or dung produced by vertebrates may be a rich source of nutrients. In the grasslands and rangelands of North America and Africa, large ungulates produce substantial volumes of fibrous and nitrogen-rich dung that contains many bacteria and protists.

Insect *coprophages* (dung-feeding organisms) utilize this resource in a number of ways. Certain higher flies-such as the Scathophagidae, Muscidae (notably the worldwide housefly, *Musca domestica*, the Australian *M. vetustissirna*, and the widespread tropical buffalo *fly*, *Haematohia irritans*), Faniidae and Calliphoridae-oviposit or larviposit into freshly laid dung.

Development can be completed before the medium becomes too desiccated. Within the dung medium, predatory fly larvae (notably other species of Muscidae) can seriously limit survival of coprophages. However, in the absence of predators or disturbance of the dung, nuisance-level populations of flies can be generated from larvae developing in dung in pastures.

The insects primarily responsible for disturbing dung, and thereby limiting fly breeding in the medium, are scarab dung beetles, belonging to the family Scarabaeidae. Not all larvae of scarabs use dung: some ingest general soil organic matter, whereas some others are herbivorous on plant roots.

However, many are coprophages. In Africa, where there are many large herbivores that produce large volumes of dung, several thousand species of scarabs are coprophagous, showing a wide variety of strategies

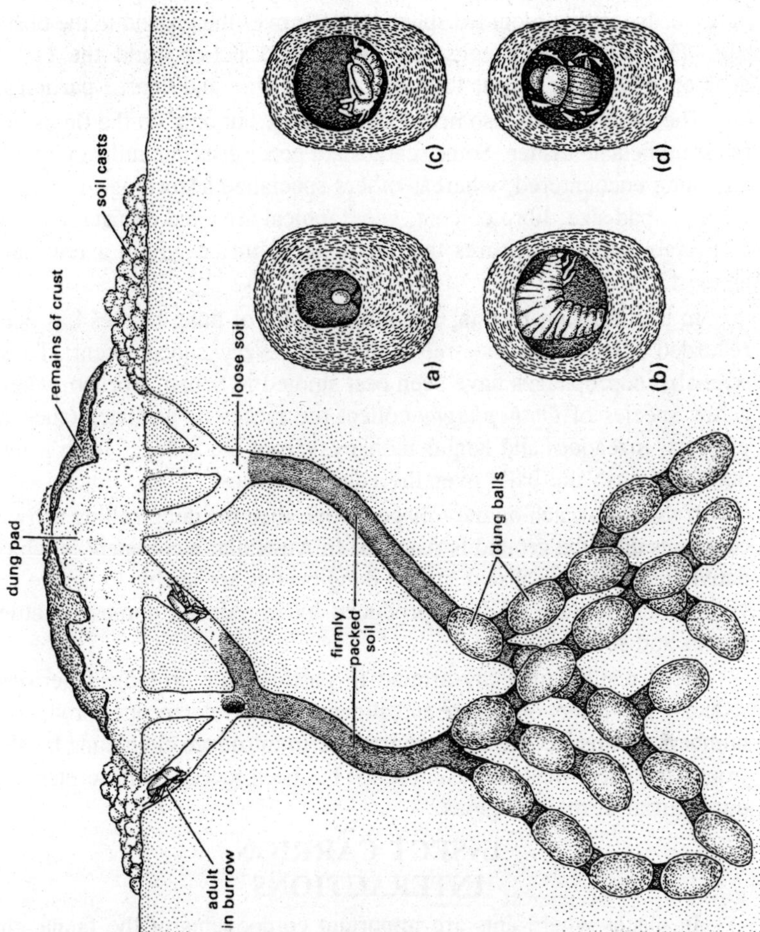

Figure 5.5: A pair of dung beetles of OnHwphe ;us gn-eila (Coleoptera: Scarabaeidae) filling in the tunnels that they have excavated below a dung pad. The inset shows an individual dung ball within which beetle development takes place: (a) egg; (b) larva, which feeds on the dung; (c) pupa; and (d) adult just prior to emergence.

to obtain the resource. Many are able to detect dung as it is produced by the herbivore, and from the time it falls to the ground invasion is *very* rapid and many individuals may arrive, for example up to many thousands for a fresh elephant dropping.

Most dung beetles excavate networks of tunnels immediately beneath or beside the pad (also called a pat), and pull down pellets of dung. Other beetles excise a chunk of dung and move it some distance to a dug-out chamber, also often within a network of tunnels. This movement from pad to nest chamber either may occur by head-butting an unformed lump, or by rolling moulded spherical balls over the ground to the burial site. The female lays eggs into the buried pellets, and the larvae develop within the faecal food ball, eating fine and coarse particles.

The adult scarabs also may feed on dung, but only on the fluids and finest particulate matter. Some scarabs are generalists and utilize virtually any dung encountered, whereas others specialize according to texture, wetness, pad size, fibre content, geographical area and climate; a range of scarab activities ensures that all dung is buried within a few days at most.

In tropical rain forests, an unusual guild of dung beetles has been recorded foraging in the tree canopy on every subcontinent. These specialist coprophages have been best studied in Sabah, Borneo, where a few species of *Onthophagus* collect the faeces of primates (such as gibbons, macaques and langur monkeys) from the foliage, form it into balls and push the balls over the edge of leaves.

If the balls catch on the foliage below, then the dung-rolling activity continues until the ground is reached. In Australia, a continent in which native ungulates are absent, native dung beetles are unable to handle the volume and texture of dung produced by introduced domestic cattle, horses and sheep.

As a result, dung lay around in pastures for prolonged periods, reducing the quality of pasture and allowing the development of prodigious numbers of nuisance flies. A programme to introduce alien dung beetles from Africa and Mediterranean Europe has been successful in accelerating dung burial in many regions.

INSECT-CARRION INTERACTIONS

In places where ants are important components of the fauna, the corpses of invertebrates are discovered and removed rapidly by ants, which scavenge widely and efficiently. In contrast, vertebrate corpses (carrion) support a wide diversity of organisms, many of which are insects.

These form a succession -a non-seasonal, directional and continuous sequential pattern of populations of species colonizing and being eliminated as carrion decay progresses. The nature and timing of the succession depends upon the size of the corpse, and seasonal and ambient climatic conditions, and the surrounding non-biological (edaphic) environment, such as soil type. The organisms involved in the succession vary according to whether they are upon or within the carrion, in the substrate immediately below the corpse or in the soil at an intermediate distance below or away from the corpse.

Furthermore, each succession will comprise different species in different geographical areas, even in places with similar climates. This is because few species are very widespread in distribution, and each biogeographic area will have its own specialist carrion faunas. However, the broad taxonomic categories of cadaver specialists are similar worldwide.

The first stage in carrion decomposition, initial decay, involves only microorganisms already present in the body, but within a few days the second stage, called *putrefaction*, begins. About two weeks later, amidst strong odours of decay, the third black *putrefaction* stage begins, followed by a fourth, *butyric fermentation* stage, in which the cheesy odour of butyric acid is present.

This terminates in an almost dry carcass and the fifth stage, slow dry decay, completes the process, leaving only bones. The typical sequence of corpse *necrophages*, saprophages and their parasites is often referred to as following 'waves' of colonization. The first wave involves certain blowflies (Diptera: Calliphoridae) and houseflies (Muscidae) that arrive within hours or a few days at most.

The second wave is of sarcophagids (Diptera) and additional muscids and calliphorids that follow shortly thereafter, as the corpse develops an odour. All these flies either lay eggs or larviposit on the corpse. The principal predators on the insects of the corpse fauna are staphylinid, silphid and histerid beetles, and hymenopteran parasitoids may be entomophagous on all the above hosts.

At this stage blowfly activity ceases as their larvae leave the corpse and pupate in the ground. When the fat of the corpse turns rancid, a third wave of species enter this modified substrate, notably more dipterans, such as certain Phoridae, Drosophilidae and *Eristalis* rat-tailed maggots (Syrphidae) in the liquid parts.

As the corpse becomes butyric, a fourth wave of cheese-skippers (Diptera: Piophilidae) and related flies use the body A fifth wave occurs as the ammonia-smelling carrion dries out, and adult and larval Dermestidae and Cleridae (Coleoptera) become abundant, feeding on keratin. In the final stages of dry decay, some tineid larvae ('clothes moths') feed on any remnant hair.

Immediately beneath the corpse, larvae and adults of the beetle families Staphylinidae, Histeridae and Dermestidae are abundant during the putrefaction stage. However, the normal, soil-inhabiting groups are absent during the carrion phase, and only slowly return as the corpse enters late decay.

The rather predictable sequence of colonization and extinction of carrion insects allows forensic entomologists to estimate the age of a corpse, which can have medicolegal implications in homicide investigations.

INSECT-FUNGAL INTERACTIONS

Fungivorous Insects

Fungi and, to a lesser extent, slime moulds are eaten by many insects, termed fungivores or mycophages, which belong to a range of orders. Amongst insects that use fungal resources, Collembola and larval and adult Coleoptera and Diptera are numerous. Two feeding strategies can be identified: *microphages* gather small particles such as spores and hyphal fragments or use more liquid media, whereas macrophages use the fungal material of fruiting bodies, which must be torn apart with strong mandibles.

The relationship between fungivores and the specificity of their fungus feeding varies. Insects that develop as larvae in the fruiting bodies of large fungi are often obligate fungivores, and may even be restricted to a narrow range of fungi, whereas insects that enter such fungi late in development or during actual decomposition of the fungus are more likely to be saprophagous or generalists than specialist mycophages.

Longer-lasting macrofungi such as the pored mushrooms, Polyporaceae, have a higher proportion of mono- or oligophagous associates than ephemeral and patchily distributed mushrooms such as the gilled mushrooms (Agaricales). Smaller and more cryptic fungal food resources also are used by insects but the associations tend to be less well studied. Yeasts are naturally abundant on live and fallen fruits and leaves, and *fructivores* (fruit-eaters) such as larvae of certain nitidulid beetles and drosophilid fruitflies are known to seek and eat yeasts.

Apparently fungivorous drosophilids that live in decomposing fruiting bodies of fungi also use yeasts, and specialization on particular fungi may reflect variations in preferences for particular yeasts. The fungal component of lichens is probably used by grazing larval lepidopterans and adult plecopterans.

Amongst the Diptera that utilize fungal fruiting bodies, the Mycetophilidae (fungus-gnats) are diverse and speciose, and many appear to have oligophagous relationships with fungi from amongst a wide range used by the family. The use by insects of subterranean fungal bodies in the form of mycorrhizae and hyphae within the soil is poorly known.

The phylogenetic relationships of the Sciaridae (Diptera) to the mycetophilid 'fungus-gnats' and evidence from commercial mushroom farms all suggest that sciarid larvae normally eat fungal mycelia. Other dipteran larvae, such as certain phorids and cecidomyiids, feed on commercial mushroom mycelia and associated microorganisms, and may also use this resource in nature.

Fungus Farming by Leaf-Cutter Ants

The subterranean ant nests of the genus *Atta* and the rather smaller colonies of *Acromyrmex* are amongst the major earthen constructions in neotropical rain forest. Calculations suggest that the largest nests of *Atta* species involve excavation of some 40tonnes of soil.

Both these genera are members of a tribe of myrmecine ants, the Attini, in which the larvae have an obligate dependence on symbiotic fungi for food. Other genera of Attini have monomorphic workers (of a single morphology) and cultivate fungi on dead vegetable matter, insect faeces (including their own and, e.g. caterpillar 'frass'), flowers and fruit.

In contrast, *Atta* and *Acromyrmex*, the more derived genera of Attini, have polymorphic workers of several different kinds or castes that exhibit an elaborate range of behaviours including cutting living plant tissues, hence the name 'leaf-cutter ants'. In *Atta*, the largest worker ants excise sections of live vegetation with their mandibles and transport the pieces to the nest.

During these processes the working ant has its mandibles full, and may be the target of attack by a particular parasitic phorid fly. The smallest worker is recruited as a defender, and is carried on the leaf fragment. When the material reaches the nest, other individuals lick any waxy cuticle from the leaves and macerate the plant tissue with their mandibles.

The mash is then inoculated with a faecal cocktail of enzymes from the hind gut. This initiates digestion of the fresh plant material, which acts as an incubation medium for fungus, known only from these 'fungus gardens' of leaf-cutter ants.

Another specialized group of workers tends the gardens by inoculating new substrate with fungal hyphae and removing other species of undesirable fungus in order to maintain a monoculture. Control of alien fungus

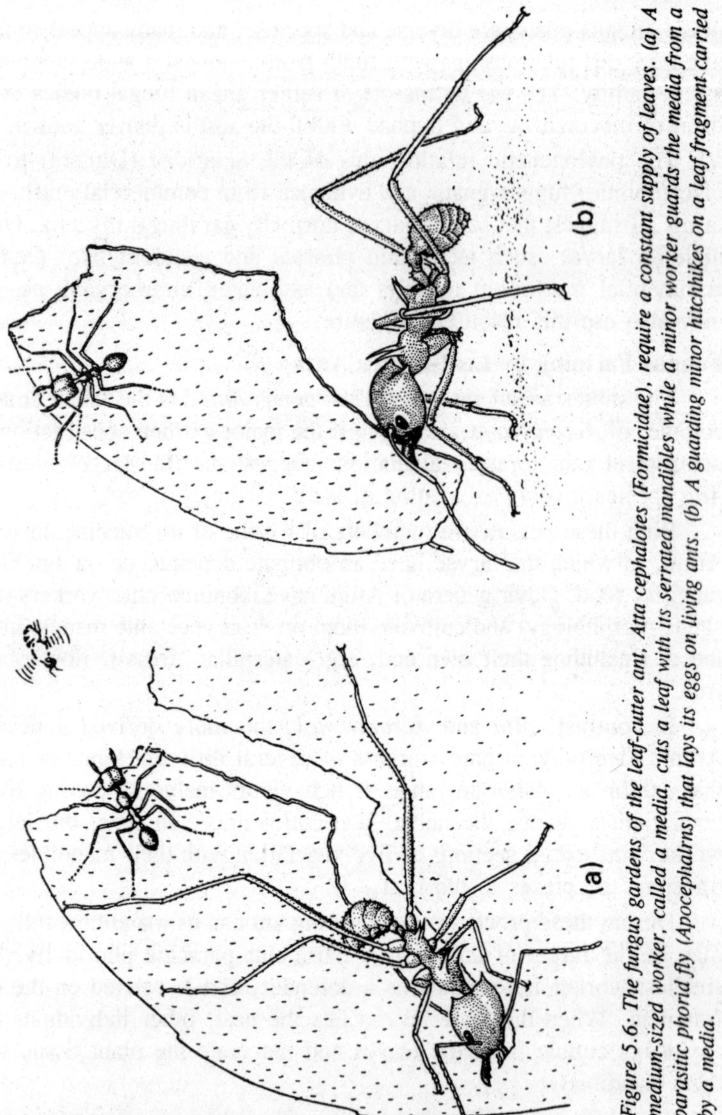

Figure 5.6: The fungus gardens of the leaf-cutter ant, Atta cephalotes (Formicidae), require a constant supply of leaves. (a) A medium-sized worker, called a media, cuts a leaf with its serrated mandibles while a minor worker guards the media from a parasitic phorid fly (Apocephalrns) that lays its eggs on living ants. (b) A guarding minor hitchhikes on a leaf fragment carried by a media.

and bacteria is facilitated by pH regulation (4.5-5.0) and by antibiotics, including those produced by mutualistic *Streptomyces* bacteria associated with ant cuticle. In darkness, and at optimal humidity and a temperature close to 25°C, the cultivated fungal mycelia produce nutritive hyphal bodies called gongylidia. These are not sporophores, and appear to have no function other than to provide food for ants in a mutualistic relationship in which the fungus gains access to the controlled environment. Gongylidia are easily manipulated by the ants, providing food for adults, and are the exclusive food eaten by larval attine ants.

Digestion of fungi requires specialized enzymes, which include chitinases produced by ants from their labial glands. Although one might expect a single origin of fungus domestication, molecular phylogenetic studies of the fungi shows domestication from freeliving stocks has taken place on a minimum of five occasions.

All but one of these domesticates are basidiomycetes of the tribe Leucocoprini in the family Lepiotaceae, propagated as a mycelium or occasionally as a unicellular yeast. Although each attine nest has a single species of fungus, amongst different nests of a single species a range of fungus species are tended. Obviously some ant species can change their fungus when a new nest is constructed. For example, lateral transfer was observed in the case of a central American species introduced to Florida that rapidly adopted the local attine-tended fungus for its gardens.

Leaf-cutter ants dominate the ecosystems in which they occur; some grassland *Atta* species consume as much vegetation per hectare as domestic cattle, and certain rain-forest species are estimated to cause up to 80% of all leaf damage and to consume up to 17% of all leaf production.

The system is an effective converter of plant cellulose to usable carbohydrate, with at least 45% of the original cellulose of fresh leaves converted by the time the spent substrate is ejected as refuse from the fungus garden. However, fungal gongylidia contribute only a modest fraction of the metabolic energy of the ants, because about 95% of the respiratory requirements of the colony is provided by adult feeding on plant sap. Leaf-cutter ants may be termed highly polyphagous, as studies have shown them to utilize between 50 and 70% of all neotropical rainforest plant species.

However, as the adults feed on the sap of fewer species, and the larvae are monophagous on fungus, the term polyphagy strictly may be incorrect. The key to the relationship is the ability of the worker ants to harvest from a wide variety of sources, and the cultivated fungus to grow on a wide range of hosts.

Coarse texture and latex production by leaves can discourage attines, and chemical defences may play a role in deterrence. However, leaf-cutter ants have adopted a strategy to evade plant defensive chemicals that act on the digestive system; they use the fungus to digest the plant tissue. The ants and fungus co-operate to break down plant defences, with the ants removing protective leaf waxes that deter fungi, and the fungi in turn producing carbohydrates from cellulose indigestible to the ants.

Fungus Cultivation by Termites

The terrestrial microfauna of tropical savannas (grasslands and open woodlands) and some forests of the Afrotropical and Oriental (Indomalayan) zoogeographic regions can be dominated by a single subfamily of Termitidae, the Macrotermitinae. These termites may form conspicuous above-ground mounds up to 9m high, but more often their nests consist of huge underground structures.

Abundance, density and production of macrotermitines may be very high and, with estimates of a live biomass of 10 gm-2, termites consume over 25% of all terrestrial litter (wood, grass and leaf) produced annually in some west African savannas. The litter-derived food resources are ingested, but not digested by the termites: the food is passed rapidly though the gut and, upon defecation, the undigested faeces are added to comb-like structures within the nest.

The combs may be located within many small subterranean chambers or one large central hive or brood chamber. Upon these combs of faeces, a *Termitomyces* fungus develops. The fungi are restricted to Macrotermitinae nests, or occur within the bodies of termites. The combs are constantly replenished and older parts eaten, on a cycle of 5-8 weeks.

Fungus action on the termite faecal substrate raises the nitrogen content of the substrate from about 0.3%% until in the asexual stages of *Termitomyces* it may reach 8%. These asexual spores (mycotetes) are eaten by the termites, as well as the nutrientenriched older comb.

Although some species of *Termitomyces* have no sexual stage, others develop above-ground basidiocarps (fruiting bodies, or 'mushrooms') at a time that coincides with colonyfounding forays of termites from the nest. A new termite colony is inoculated with fungus by means of asexual or sexual spores transferred in the gut of the founder termite(s).

Termitomyces lives as a monoculture on termiteattended combs, but if the termites are removed experimentally or a termite colony dies out, or if the comb is extracted from the nest, many other fungi invade the comb and *Termitomyces* dies. Termite saliva has some antibiotic properties but there is little evidence for *Termitomyces* being able to reduce local competition from other fungi.

It seems that *Termitomyces* is favoured in the fungal comb by the remarkably constant microclimate at the comb, with a temperature of 30°C and scarcely varying humidity together with an acid pH of 4.1-4.6. The heat generated by fungal metabolism is regulated appropriately via a complex circulation of air through the passageways of the nest, as illustrated for the aboveground nest of the African *Macrotermes natalensis* in Figure elsewhere in this chapter.

The origin of the mutualistic relationship between termite and fungus seems not to derive from joint attack on plant defences, in contrast to the antfungus interaction seen in section 8.5.2 above. Termites are closely associated with fungi, and fungusinfested rotting wood is likely to have been a primitive food preference.

Termites can digest complex substances such as pectins and chitins, and there is good evidence that they have endogenous cellulases, which break down dietary cellulose. However, the Macrotermitinae have shifted some of their digestion to *Tennitomyces* outside of the gut.

The fungus facilitates conversion of plant compounds to more nutritious products and probably allows a wider range of cellulose-containing foods to be consumed by the termites. Thus the macrotermitines successfully utilize the abundant resource of dead vegetation.

CAVERNICOLOUS INSECTS

Caves are often perceived as extensions of the subterranean environment, resembling deep soil habitats in the lack of light and the uniform temperature, but differing in the scarcity of food. Food sources in shallow caves include roots of terrestrial plants, but in deeper caves there is no plant material other than that originating from any stream-derived debris.

In many caves nutrient supplies come from fungi and the faeces (guano) of bats and certain cave-dwelling birds, such as swiftlets in the Orient. *Cavernicolous* (cave-dwelling) insects include those that seek refuge from adverse external environmental conditions-such as moths and adult flies, including mosquitoes, that hibernate to avoid winter cold, or aestivate to avoid summer heat and desiccation.

Troglobiont or *troglobite* insects are restricted to caves, and often are phylogenetically related to soil-dwelling ones. The troglobite assemblage may be dominated by Collembola (especially the family Entomobryidae), and other important groups include the Diplura (especially the family Campodeidae), orthopteroids (including cave crickets, Raphidophoridae) and beetles (chiefly carabids but including fungivorous silphids). In Hawaii, past and present volcanic activity produces a spectacular range of 'lava tubes' of different isolation in space and time from other volcanic caves.

Here studies of the wide range of troglobitic insects and spiders living in lava tubes have helped us to gain an understanding of the possible rapidity of morphological divergence rates under these unusual conditions. Even caves formed by very recent lava flows such as on Kilauea have endemic or incipient species of *Caconemobius* cave crickets. Dermaptera and Blattodea may be abundant in tropical caves, where they are active in guano deposits.

In southeast Asian caves one troglobite earwig is ectoparasitic on roosting bats. Associated with cavernicolous vertebrates there are many more conventional ectoparasites, such as hippoboscid, nycteribid and streblid flies, fleas and lice.

ENVIRONMENTAL MONITORING USING GROUND-DWELLING HEXAPODS

Human activities such as agriculture, forestry and pastoralism have resulted in the simplification of many terrestrial ecosystems. Attempts to quantify the effects of such practices -for the purposes of conservation assessment, classification of land-types and monitoring of impacts-have tended to be phytosociological, emphasizing the use of vegetational mapping data.

More recently, data on vertebrate distributions and communities have been incorporated into surveys for conservation purposes. Although arthropod diversity is estimated to be very great, it is rare for data derived from this group to be available routinely in conservation and monitoring.

There are several reasons for this neglect. Firstly, when 'flagship' species elicit public reaction to a conservation issue, such as loss of a particular habitat, these organisms are predominantly furry mammals, such as pandas and koalas, or birds; rarely are they insects.

Excepting perhaps some butterflies, insects often lack the necessary charisma in the public perception. Secondly, insects generally are difficult to sample in a comparable manner within and between sites. Abundance and diversity fluctuate on a relatively short timescale, in response to factors that may be little understood.

In contrast, vegetation often shows less temporal variation; and with knowledge of mammal seasonality and of the migration habits of birds, the seasonal variations of vertebrate populations can be taken into account.

Thirdly, arthropods often are more difficult to identify accurately, as a result of the numbers of taxa and some deficiencies in taxonomic knowledge. Whereas competent mammalogists, ornithologists or field botanists might expect to identify to species level, respectively, all mammals, birds and plants of a geographically restricted area (outside the tropical rain forests), no entomologist could aspire to do so.

Nonetheless, aquatic biologists routinely sample and identify all macroinvertebrates (mostly insects) in regularly surveyed aquatic ecosystems, for purposes including monitoring of deleterious change in environmental quality.

Comparable studies of terrestrial systems, with objectives such as establishment of rationales for conservation and the detection of pollution-induced changes, are undertaken in some countries. The problems outlined above have been addressed in the following ways.

Some charismatic insect species have been highlighted, usually under 'endangered-species' legislation designed with vertebrate conservation in mind. These species predominantly have been lepidopterans and much has been learnt of the biology of selected species.

However, from the perspective of site classification for conservation purposes, the structure of selected soil and litter communities has greater realized and potential value than any singlespecies study. Sampling problems are alleviated by using a single collection method, often that of pit-fall trapping, but including the extraction of arthropods from litter samples by a variety of means.

Pit-fall traps collect mobile terrestrial arthropods by capturing them in containers filled with preserving fluid and sunken level with the substrate. Traps can be aligned along a transect, or dispersed according to a standard quadrat-based sampling regime.

According to the sample size required, they can be left *in situ* for several days or up to a few weeks. Depending on the sites surveyed, arthropod collections may be dominated by Collembola, Formicidae, and Coleoptera, particularly ground beetles (Carabidae), Tenebrionidae, Scarabaeidae and Staphylinidae, with some terrestrial representatives of many other orders.

Taxonomic difficulties often are alleviated by selecting (from amongst the organisms collected) one or more higher taxonomic groups for specieslevel identification. The carabids are often selected for study because of the diversity of species sampled, the pre-existing ecological knowledge and availability of taxonomic keys to species level, although these are largely restricted to temperate northern hemisphere taxa. Studies to date are ambivalent concerning correlates between species diversity (including taxon richness) established from vegetational survey and those from terrestrial insect trapping.

Evidence from the well-documented British biota suggests that vegetational diversity does not predict insect diversity. However, a study in more natural, less humanaffected environments in southern Norway showed congruence between carabid faunal indices and those obtained by vegetational and bird survey.

Further studies are required into the relationships (if any) between terrestrial insect richness and diversity and data obtained by conventional biological survey of selected plants and vertebrates.

6

Parasitic Insects

In other chapter we saw that many insects are phytophagous, feeding directly on primary producers, the algae and higher plants. These phytophages comprise a substantial food resource, which is fed upon by a range of other organisms. Individuals within this broad carnivorous group may be categorized as follows.

A *predator* kills and consumes a number of prey animals during its life. *Predation* involves the interactions in space and time between predator foraging and prey availability, although often it is treated in a one-sided manner as if predation is what the predator does. Animals that live at the expense of another animal (a *host*) that eventually dies as a result are called parasitoids, which may live externally (ectoparasitoids) or internally (endoparasitoids).

Those that live at the expense of another animal (also a host) that they do not kill, are parasites, which likewise can be internal (*endoparasites*) or external (*ectoparasites*). A host attacked by a parasitoid or parasite is *parasitized*, and parasitization is the condition of being parasitized. *Parasitism* describes the relationship between parasitoid or parasite and the host.

Predators, parasitoids and parasites, although defined above as if distinct, may not be so clear-cut, as parasitoids may be viewed as specialized predators. By some estimates, about 25% of insect species are predatory or parasitic in feeding habit in some lifehistory stage. Representatives from amongst nearly every order of insects are predatory, with adults and immature stages of the Mantodea, the neuropteroid orders (Neuroptera, Megaloptera and Raphidioptera) and the Mecoptera being almost exclusively predatory.

The latter orders are considered elsewhere in this chapter that complete this chapter, and the vignette for this chapter depicts a female mecopteran, *Panorpa coaumuuis* (Panorpidae), feeding on a dead pupa of a small tortoiseshell butterfly, *Ag/cats urticae*. The speciose Hymenoptera have a preponderance of parasitoid taxa almost exclusively using invertebrate hosts, and the uncommon Strepsiptera are unusual in being endoparasites in other insects.

Other parasites that are of medical or veterinary importance, such as lice, adult fleas and many Diptera, are dealt elsewhere in this book. Insects are amenable to field and laboratory studies of predator-prey interactions as they are unresponsive to human attention, easy to manipulate, may have several generations a year and show a range of predatory and defensive strategies and life histories.

Furthermore, studies of predator-prey and parasitoid-host interactions are fundamental to understanding and effecting biocontrol strategies for pest insects. Attempts to model predator-prey interactions mathematically often emphasize parasitoids, as some simplifications can be made.

These include the ability to simplify search strategies, as only the adult female parasitoid seeks hosts, and the number of offspring per unit host remains relatively constant from generation to generation. In this chapter we show how predators, parasitoids and parasites forage, i.e. locate and select their prey or hosts.

We look at morphological modifications of predators for handling prey, and how some of the prey defences covered in other chapter of this book are overcome. The means by which parasitoids overcome host defences and develop within their hosts is examined, and different strategies of host use by parasitoids are explained.

The host use and specificity of ectoparasites is discussed from a phylogenetic perspective. Finally, we conclude with a consideration of the relationships between predator/parasitoid/ parasite and prey/host abundances and evolutionary histories. In the taxonomic boxes at the end of the chapter, the Mantodea, neuropteroid orders, Mecoptera and Strepsiptera are described.

PREY/HOST LOCATION

The foraging behaviours of insects, like all other behaviours, comprise a stereotyped sequence of components. These lead a predatory or host-seeking insect towards the resource, and on contact, to recognize and use it. Various stimuli along the route elicit an appropriate ensuing response, involving either action or inhibition. The foraging strategies of predators, parasitoids and parasites involve tradeoffs between profits or benefits (the quality and quantity of resource obtained) and cost, in the form of time expenditure, exposure to suboptimal or adverse environments and the risks of being eaten.

Recognition of the time component is important, as all time spent in activities other than reproduction can be viewed, in an evolutionary sense, as time wasted. In an optimal foraging strategy, the difference between costs and benefits is maximized, either through increasing nutrient gain from prey capture, or reducing effort expended to catch prey, or both. Choices available are:

- where and how to search;
- how much time to expend in fruitless search in one area before moving;
- how much (if any) energy to expend in capture of suboptimal food, once located.

A primary requirement is that the insect be in the appropriate habitat for the resource sought. For many insects this may seem trivial, especially if development takes place in the area which contained the resources used by the parental generation.

However, circumstances such as seasonality, climatic vagaries, ephemerality or major resource depletion, may necessitate local dispersal or perhaps major movement (migration) in order to reach an appropriate location. Even in a suitable habitat, resources rarely are evenly distributed but occur in more or less discrete microhabitat clumps, termed patches. Insects show a gradient of responses to these patches.

At one extreme, the insect waits in a suitable patch for prey or host organisms to appear. The insect may be camouflaged or apparent, and a trap may be constructed. At the other extreme, the prey or host is actively sought within a patch. As seen in Figure elsewhere in this chapter, the waiting strategy is economically effective, but time consuming; the active strategy is energy intensive but time-efficient, and trapping lies intermediate between these two. Patch selection is vital to successful foraging.

Sitting-and-Waiting

Sit-and-wait predators find a suitable patch and wait for mobile prey to come within striking range. As the vision of many insects limits them to recognition of movement rather than precise shape, a sit-andwait predator may need only remain motionless in order to be unobserved by its prey.

Nonetheless, amongst those that wait, many have some form of camouflage (crypsis). This may be defensive, directed against highly visual predators such as birds, rather than evolved to mislead invertebrate prey.

Cryptic predators modelled on a feature that is of no interest to the prey (such as tree bark, lichen, a twig or even a stone) can be separated from those that model on a feature of some significance to prey, such as a flower that acts as an insect attractant. In an example of the latter case, the Malaysian mantid *Hymenopus bicornis* closely resembles the red flowers of the orchid *Melastoma palyanthum* amongst which it rests.

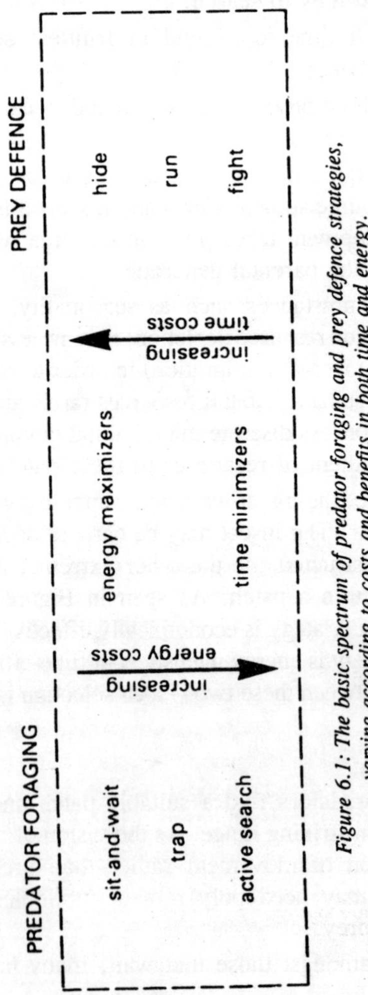

Figure 6.1: The basic spectrum of predator foraging and prey defence strategies, varying according to costs and benefits in both time and energy.

Flies are encouraged to land, assisted by the presence of marks resembling flies on the body of the mantid: larger flies that land are eaten by the mantid. In another related example of *aggressive foraging mimicry*, the African flower-mimicking mantid *Idolum* does not rest hidden in a flower, but actually resembles one due to petal-shaped, coloured outgrowths of the prothorax and the coxae of the anterior legs.

Butterflies and flies that are attracted to this hanging 'flower' are snatched and eaten. Ambushers include cryptic, sedentary insects such as mantids, which prey fail to distinguish from the inert, non-floral plant background. Although these predators rely on the general traffic of invertebrates associated with vegetation, often they locate close to flowers, to take advantage of the increased visiting rate of flower feeders and pollinators.

Odonate larvae, which are major predators in many aquatic systems, are classic ambushers, which rest concealed in submerged vegetation or in the substrate awaiting prey to pass. These predators may show dual strategies: if waiting fails to provide food, the hungry insect may change to a more active searching mode, after a fixed period.

This energy expenditure may bring the predator into an area of higher prey density. In running waters, a disproportionately high number of organisms found drifting passively with the current are predators: this drift constitutes a low-energy means for sit-and-wait predators to relocate, induced by local prey shortage.

Sitting-and-waiting strategies are not restricted to cryptic and slow-moving predators. Fast-flying, diurnal, visual, rapacious predators such as many robber flies (Diptera: Asilidae) and adult odonates spend much time perched prominently on vegetation. From these conspicuous locations their excellent sight allows them to detect passing flying insects.

With rapid and accurately controlled flight, the predator makes only a short foray to capture appropriately-sized prey. This strategy combines energy saving, through not needing to fly incessantly in search of prey, with time efficiency, as prey is taken from outside the immediate area of reach of the predator.

Another sit-and-wait technique involving greater energy expenditure is the use of traps to ambush prey. Although spiders are the prime exponents of this method, in the warmer parts of the world the pits of certain larval antlions (Neuroptera: Myrmeleontidae) are familiar. The larvae either dig pits directly or form them by spiralling backwards into soft soil or sand.

Trapping effectiveness depends upon the steepness of the sides, the

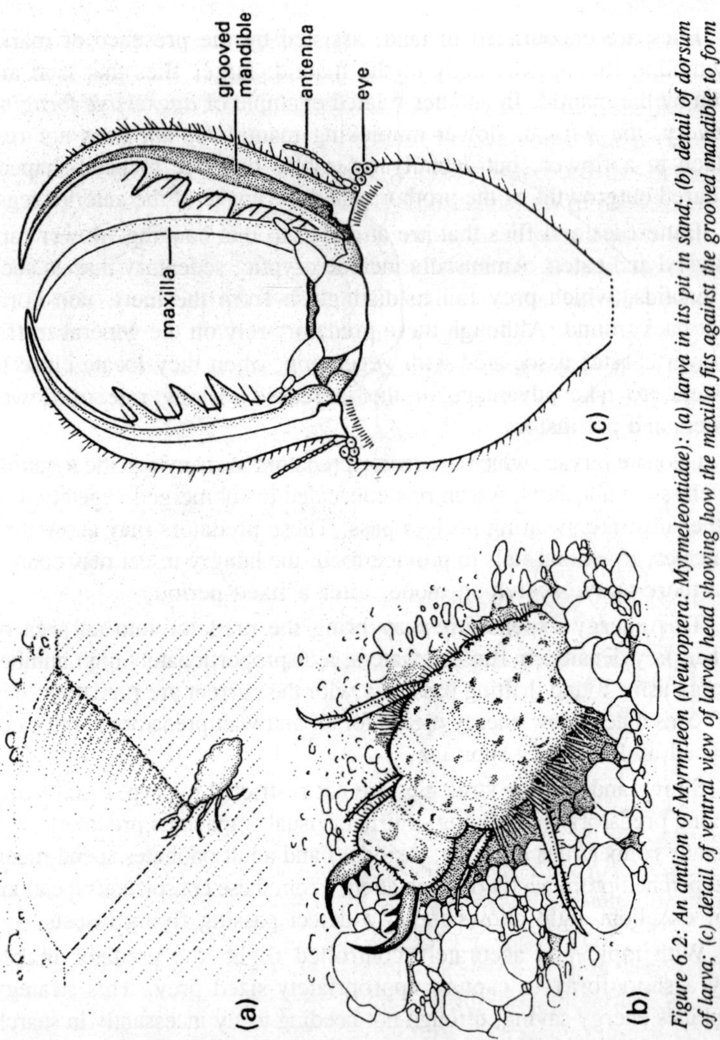

Figure 6.2: An antlion of Myrmleon (Neuroptera: Myrmeleontidae): (a) larva in its pit in sand; (b) detail of dorsum of larva; (c) detail of ventral view of larval head showing how the maxilla fits against the grooved mandible to form a sucking tube.

diameter and the depth of the pit, which vary with species and instar. The larva waits, buried at the base of the conical pit, for passing prey to fall in. Escape is prevented physically by the slipperiness of the slope, and the larva may also flick sand at prey before dragging it underground to restrict its defensive movements.

The location, construction and maintenance of the pit are vitally important to capture efficiency but construction and repair is energetically very expensive. Experimentally it has been shown that even starved

Japanese antlions (*Mi nncleon bore*) would not relocate their pits to an area where prey was provided artificially. Instead larvae of this species of antlion reduce their metabolic rate to tolerate famine, even if death by starvation is the result.

In holometabolous ectoparasites, such as fleas and parasitic flies, immature development takes place away from their vertebrate hosts. Following pupation, the adult must locate the appropriate host. Since in many the eyes are reduced or absent, vision cannot be used. Furthermore, as many ectoparasites are flightless, mobility is restricted.

In fleas and some Diptera, in which larval development often takes place in the nest of a host vertebrate, the adult insect waits quiescent in the pupal cocoon until the presence of a host is detected. The duration of this quiescent period may be a year or longer, as in the cat flea (*Ctenocephali(Ies felis*)-*a* familiar phenomenon to humans that enter an empty dwelling that previously housed flea-infested cats.

The stimuli to cease dormancy include some or all of: vibration, rise in temperature, increased carbon dioxide or another stimulus generated by the host. In contrast, the hemimetabolan lice spend their lives entirely on a host, with all developmental stages ectoparasitic. Any transfer between hosts is either through phoresy (see below) or when host individuals make direct contact, as from mother to young within a nest.

Active Foraging

More energetic foraging involves active searching for suitable patches, and once there, for prey or for hosts. Movements associated with foraging and with other locomotory activities, such as seeking a mate, are so similar that the 'motivation' may be recognized only in retrospect, by resultant prey capture or host finding.

The locomotory search patterns used to locate prey or hosts are those described for general orientation elsewhere in this chapter, and comprise nondirectional (random) and directional (non-random) locomotion.

Random, or Non-directional Foraging

The foraging of aphidophagous larval coccinellid beetles and syrphid flies amongst their clumped prey illustrates several features of random food searching. The larvae advance, stop periodically and 'cast' about by swinging their raised anterior bodies from side to side. Subsequent behaviour depends upon whether or not an aphid is encountered. If no prey is encountered, motion continues, interspersed with casting and turning at a fundamental frequency.

However, if contact is made and feeding has taken place or if the prey is encountered and lost, searching intensifies with an enhanced frequency of casting, and, if the larva is in motion, increased turning or direction-changing. Actual feeding is unnecessary to stimulate this more concentrated search: an unsuccessful encounter is adequate.

For early-instar larvae that are very active but have limited ability to handle prey, this stimulus to search intensively near a lost feeding opportunity is important to survival. Most laboratory-based experimental evidence, and models of foraging based thereon, are derived from single species of walking predators, frequently assumed to encounter a single species of prey randomly distributed within selected patches.

Such premises may be justified in modelling grossly simplified ecosystems, such as an agricultural monoculture with a single pest controlled by one predator. Despite the limitations of such laboratory-based models, certain findings appear to have general biological relevance. An important consideration is that the time allocated to different patches by a foraging predator depends upon the criteria for leaving a patch.

Four mechanisms have been recognized to trigger departure from a patch:

- a certain number of food items have been encountered (fixed number);
- a certain time has elapsed (fixed time);
- a certain searching time has elapsed (fixed searching time);
- the prey capture rate falls below a certain threshold (fixed rate).

The fixed rate mechanism has been favoured by modellers of optimal foraging, but even this is likely to be a simplification if the forager's responsiveness to prey is non-linear (e.g. declines with exposure time) and/or derives from more than simple prey encounter rate, or prey density.

Differences between predator-prey interactions in simplified laboratory conditions and the actuality of the field cause many problems, including failure to recognize variation in prey behaviour that results from exposure to predation (perhaps multiple predators).

Furthermore, there are difficulties in interpreting the actions of polyphagous predators, including the causes of predator/ parasitoid / parasite behavioural switching between different prey animals or hosts.

Non-random, or Directional Foraging

Several more specific directional means of host finding can be recognized, including the use of chemicals, sound, and light. Experimentally these are rather difficult to establish, and to separate, and it may be that the use of these cues is very widespread, if little understood.

Of the variety of cues available, many insects probably use more than one, depending upon distance or proximity to the resource sought. Thus the European crabronid wasp *Philnnthins*, which eats only bees, relies initially on vision to locate moving insects of appropriate size.

Only bees, or other insects to which bee odours have been applied experimentally, are captured, indicating a role for odour when near the prey. However, the sting is applied only to actual bees, and not to beesmelling alternatives, demonstrating a final tactile recognition.

Not only may a step-wise sequence of stimuli be necessary, as seen above, but also appropriate stimuli may have to be present simultaneously in order to elicit appropriate behaviour. Thus *Telenomits heliothidis* (Hymenoptera: Scelionidae), an egg parasitoid of *Heliothis z'irescens* (Lepidoptera: Noctuidae), will investigate and probe at appropriate-sized round glass beads that emulate *Heliothis* eggs, if they are coated with female moth proteins.

However, the scelionid makes no response to glass beads alone, or to female moth proteins applied to improperly shaped beads.

Chemicals

The world of insect communication is dominated by chemicals, or pheromones. Ability to detect the chemical odours and messages produced by prey or hosts (kairomones) allows specialist predators and parasitoids to locate these resources.

Certain parasitic tachinid flies and braconid wasps can locate their respective stink bug or coccoid host by tuning to their hosts' long-distance sex attractant pheromones. Several unrelated parasitoid hymenopterans use the aggregation pheromones of their bark and timber beetle hosts.

Chemicals emitted by stressed plants, such as terpenes produced by pines when attacked by an insect, act as *synomones* (communication chemicals that benefit both producer and receiver); for example, certain pteromalid (Hymenoptera) parasitoids locate their hosts, the damage-causing scolytid timber beetles, in this way.

Some species of tiny wasps (Trichogrammatidae) that are egg endoparasitoids are able to locate the eggs laid by their preferred host moth by the sex attractant pheromones released by the moth. Furthermore, there are several examples of parasitoids that locate their specific insect larval hosts by 'frass' odours-the smells of their faeces. Chemical location is particularly valuable when hosts are concealed from visual inspection, for example, when encased in plant or other tissues.

Chemical detection need not be restricted to tracking volatile compounds produced by the prospective host. Thus many parasitoids searching for phytophagous insect hosts are attracted initially, and at a distance, to host-plant chemicals, in the same manner that the phytophage located the resource.

At close range, chemicals produced by the feeding damage and/or frass of phytophages may allow precise targeting of the host. Once located, the acceptance of a host as suitable is likely to involve similar or other chemicals, judging by the increased use of rapidly vibrating antennae in sensing the prospective host. Blood-feeding adult insects locate their hosts using cues that include chemicals emitted by the host.

Many female biting flies can detect increased carbon dioxide levels associated with animal respiration and fly upwind towards the source. Highly host-specific biters probably also are able to detect subtle odours: thus, human-biting black flies (Diptera: Simuliidae) respond to components of human exocrine sweat glands. Both sexes of tsetse flies (Diptera: Glossinidae) track the odour of exhaled breath, notably carbon dioxide, octanols, acetone, and ketones emitted by their preferred cattle hosts.

Sonnd

The sound signals produced by animals, including those made by insects to attract mates, have been utilized by some parasites to locate their preferred hosts acoustically. Thus the blood-sucking females of *Corethrella* (Diptera: Corethrellidae) locate their favoured host, hylid treefrogs, by following the frogs' calls.

The details of the host-finding behaviour of ormiine tachinid flies are considered in detail elsewhere in this chapter. Flies of two other dipteran species are known to be attracted by the songs of their hosts: females of the larviparous tachinid *Euphasiopteryx ochracea* locate the male crickets of *Gryllus integer*, and the sarcophagid *Colcondamyia auditrix* finds its male cicada host, *Okanagana rimosa*, in this manner.

This allows precise deposition of the parasitic immature stages in, or close to, the hosts in which they are to develop. Predatory biting midges (Ceratopogonidae) that prey upon swarm-forming flies, such as midges (Chironomidae), appear to use cues similar to those used by their prey to locate the swarm; cues may include the sounds produced by wing-beat frequency of the members of the swarm.

Vibrations produced by their hosts can be detected by ectoparasites, notably amongst the fleas. There is also evidence that certain parasitoids can detect at close range the substrate vibration produced by the feeding activity of their hosts. Thus *Biosteres longicaudatus*, a braconid hymenopteran endoparasitoid of a larval tephritid fruit fly (Diptera: *Anastrepha suspensa*), detects vibrations made by the larvae moving and feeding within fruit. These sounds act as a behavioural releaser, stimulating host-finding behaviour as well as acting as a directional cue for their concealed hosts.

Light

The larvae of the Australian cave-dwelling mycetophilid fly *Arachnocampa* and its New Zealand counterpart, *Bolitophila lurninosa*, use bioluminescent lures to catch small flies in sticky threads that they suspend from the cave ceiling. Luminescence, as with all communication systems, provides scope for abuse; in this case, the luminescent courtship signalling between beetles is misappropriated.

Carnivorous female lampyrids of some *Photurus* species, in an example of aggressive foraging mimicry, imitate the flashing signals of females of up to five other firefly species. The males of these different species flash their responses and are deluded into landing close by the mimetic female, whereupon she devours them.

The mimicking *Photurits* female will eat the males of her own species, but cannibalism is avoided or reduced as the *Photurus* female is most piratic only after mating, at which time she becomes relatively unresponsive to the signals of males of her own species.

Phoresy

Phoresy is a phenomenon in which an individual of one species is transported by an individual of another species. This relationship benefits the carried and does not directly affect the carrier, although in some cases its progeny may be disadvantaged (as we shall see below). Phoresy provides a means of finding a new host or food source.

An often-observed example involves ischnoceran lice (Phthiraptera) transported by the winged adults of *Ornithomyia* (Diptera: Hippoboscidae). Hippoboscidae are bloodsucking ectoparasitic flies and *Ornithomyia* occurs on many avian hosts.

When a host bird dies, lice can reach a new host by attaching themselves by their mandibles to a hippoboscid, which may fly to a new host. However, lice are highly host-specific but hippoboscids are much less so, and the chances of any hitchhiking louse arriving at the appropriate host may not be great.

In some other associations, such as a biting midge (*Forcipoinyia*) found on the thorax of various adult dragonflies in Borneo, it is difficult to determine whether the hitchhiker is merely phoretic or actually parasitic.

Amongst the egg-parasitizing hymenopterans (notably the Scelionidae, Trichogrammatidae and Torymidae), some attach themselves to adult females of the host species, thereby gaining immediate access to the eggs at oviposition. *Matibaria manticida* (Scelionidae), an egg parasitoid of the European praying mantid (*Mantis religiosa*), *is* phoretic, predominantly on female hosts.

The adult wasp sheds its wings and may feed on the mantid, and therefore can be an ectoparasite. It moves to the wing bases and amputates the female mantid's wings and then oviposits into the mantid's egg mass whilst it is frothy, before the ootheca hardens. Individuals of *M. manticida* that are phoretic on male mantids may transfer to the female during mating.

Certain chalcid hymenopterans (including species of Eucharitidae) have active planidium larvae that actively seek worker ants, on which they attach, thereby gaining transport to the ant nest. Here the remainder of the immature life cycle comprises typical sedentary grubs that develop within ant larvae or pupae.

An extreme example of phoresy involves the human bot fly, *Dermatobia hominis* (Diptera: Cuterebridae) of the Neotropical region (Central and South America), which causes myiasis of humans and cattle. The female fly does not seek out the vertebrate host herself, but uses the services of blood-sucking flies, particularly mosquitoes and muscoid flies.

The female bot fly, which produces up to 1000 eggs in her lifetime, captures a phoretic intermediary and glues around 30 eggs to its body in such a way that flight is not impaired. When the intermediary finds a vertebrate host on which it feeds, an elevation of temperature induces the eggs to hatch rapidly and the larvae transfer to the host, where they penetrate the skin via hair follicles and develop within the resultant pus-filled boil.

PREY/HOST ACCEPTANCE AND MANIPULATION

During foraging, there are some similarities in location of prey by a predator and of the host by a parasitoid or parasite. When contact is made with the potential prey or host, its acceptability must be established, by checking the identity, size and age of the prey/host. For example, many parasitoids reject old larvae, which are close to pupation. Chemical and tactile stimuli are involved in specific identification, and in subsequent behaviours including biting, ingestion and continuance of feeding.

Chemoreceptors on the antennae and ovipositor of parasitoids are vital in chemically detecting host suitability and exact location. Different manipulations follow acceptance: the predator attempts to eat suitable prey, whereas parasitoids and parasites exhibit a range of behaviours regarding their hosts.

A parasitoid either oviposits (or larviposits) directly or subdues and may carry the host elsewhere, for instance to a nest, prior to the offspring developing within or on it. An ectoparasite needs to gain a hold and obtain a meal. The different behavioural and morphological modifications associated with prey and host manipulation are covered in separate sections below, from the perspectives of predator, parasitoid and parasite.

Prey Manipulation by Predators

When a predator detects and locates suitable prey, it must be captured and restrained before feeding. As predation has arisen many times, and in nearly every order, the morphological modifications associated with this lifestyle are highly convergent. Nevertheless, in most predatory insects the principal organs used in capture and manipulation of prey are the legs and mouthparts.

Typically, *raptorial* legs of adult insects are elongate and bear spines on the inner surface of at least one of the segments. Prey is captured by closing the spinose segment against another segment, which may itself be spinose, i.e. the femur against the tibia, or tibia against the tarsus.

As well as spines, there may be elongate spurs on the apex of the tibia, and the apical claws may be strongly developed on the raptorial legs in predators with leg modifications, usually it is the anterior legs that are raptorial, but some hemipterans also employ the mid-legs, and scorpionflies grasp prey with their hind legs.

Mouthpart modifications associated with predation arc of two principal kinds: (i) incorporation of a variable number of elements into a tubular rostrum to allow piercing and sucking of fluids; or (ii) development of strengthened and elongate mandibles. Mouthparts modified as a rostrum are seen in bugs (Hemiptera) and function in sucking fluids from plants or from dead arthropods (as in many gerrid bugs) or in predation on living prey, as in many other aquatic insects, including

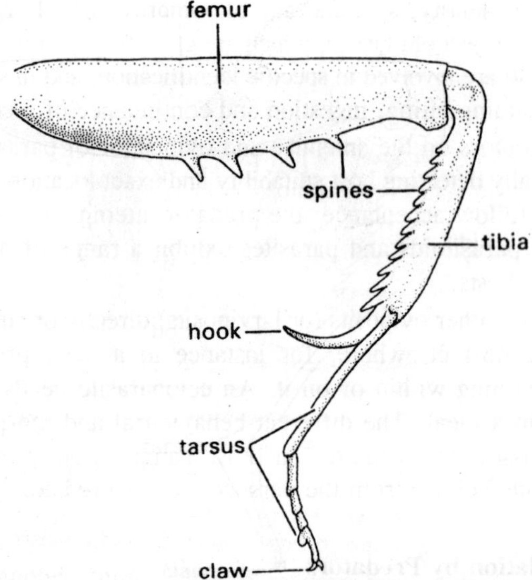

Figure 6.3: Distal part of the leg of a mantid showing the opposing rows of spines that interlock when the tibia is drawn upwards against the femur.

species of Nepidae, Belostomatidae and Notonectidae. Amongst the terrestrial bugs, assassin bugs (Reduviidae), which use raptorial fore legs to capture other terrestrial arthropods, are major predators.

They inject toxins and proteolytic saliva into captured prey, and suck the body fluids through the rostrum. Similar hemipteran mouthparts are used in bloodsucking, as demonstrated by *Rhodnius*, *a* reduviid that has attained fame for its role in experimental insect physiology, and the family Cimicidae, including the bed bug, *Citnex lectularius*.

In the Diptera, mandibles are vital for wound production by the blood-sucking Nematocera (mosquitoes, midges and black flies) but have been lost in the higher flies, some of which have regained the bloodsucking habit. Thus in the stable flies (*Stomoxys*) and tsetse flies (*Glossina*), for example, alternative mouthpart structures have evolved; some specialized mouthparts of blood-sucking Diptera are described and illustrated elsewhere in this chapter.

Many predatory larvae and some adults have hardened, elongate and apically pointed mandibles capable of piercing durable cuticle. Larval neuropterans (lacewings and antlions) have the slender maxilla and sharply pointed and grooved mandible, which are pressed together to form a composite sucking tube.

The composite structure may be straight, as in active pursuers of

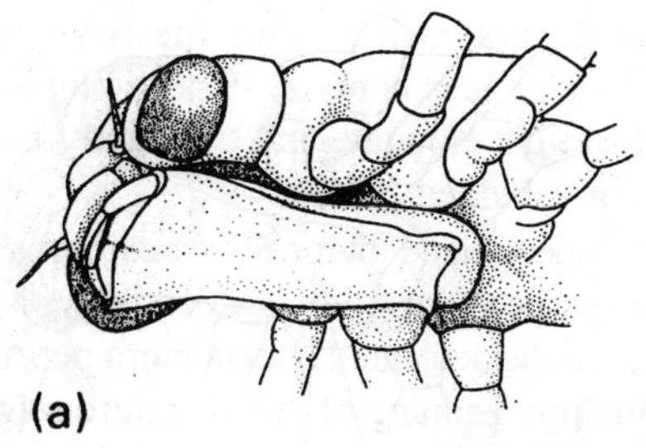

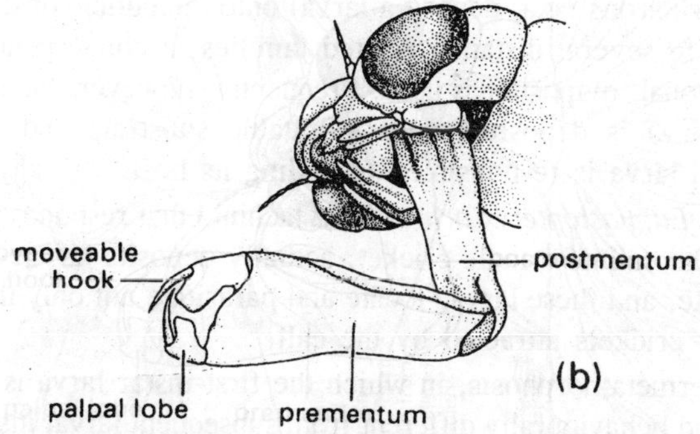

Figure 6.4: Ventrolateral view of the head of a dragonfly larva (Odonata: Aeshnidae Aeshna) showing the labial 'mask': (a) in folded position, and (b) extended during prey capture with opposing hooks of the palpal lobes forming claw-like pincers.

prey, or curved, as in the sit-and-wait ambushers such as antlions. Liquid may be sucked (or pumped) from the prey, using a range of mandibular modifications after enzymatic predigestion has liquefied the contents (*extraoral digestion*).

There are some unusual morphological modifications for predation, such as in the larvae of Chaoboridae (Diptera) that use modified antennae to grasp their planktonic cladoceran prey. Odonate larvae capture passing prey by striking with a highly modified labium, which is projected rapidly outwards by release of hydrostatic pressure, rather than by muscular means.

Host Acceptance and Manipulation by Parasitoids

The two orders with greatest numbers and diversity of larval parasitoids are the Diptera and Hymenoptera. Two basic approaches are displayed once a potential host is located, though there are exceptions. Firstly, as seen in many hymenopterans, it is the adult that seeks out the actual larval development site.

In contrast, in many Diptera it is often the first-instar planidium larva that makes the close-up host contact. Parasitic hymenopterans use sensory information from the elongate and constantly mobile antennae to precisely locate even a hidden host.

The antennae and specialized ovipositor bear sensilla that allow host acceptance and accurate oviposition, respectively. Modification of the ovipositor as a sting in the aculeate Hymenoptera permits behavioural modifications, including provisioning of the immature stages with a food source captured by the adult and maintained alive in a paralysed state.

Endoparasitoid dipterans, including the Tachinidae, may oviposit (or in larviparous taxa, deposit a larva) onto the cuticle or directly into the host. In several distantly related families, a convergently evolved 'substitutional' ovipositor is used. Frequently, however, the parasitoid's egg or larva is deposited onto a suitable substrate and the mobile planidium larva is responsible for finding its host.

Thus *Euphasiopteryx ochracea, a* tachinid that responds phonotactically to the call of a male cricket, actually deposits larvae around the calling site, and these larvae locate and parasitize not only the vocalist, but other crickets attracted by the call.

Hypermetamorphosis, in which the first-instar larva is morphologically and behaviourally different from subsequent larval instars (which are sedentary parasitic maggots), is common amongst parasitoids. Certain parasitic and parasitoid dipterans and some hymenopterans use their aerial flying skills to gain access to a potential host. Some are able to intercept their hosts in flight, others can make rapid lunges at an alert and defended target.

Some of the inquilines of social insects are able to gain access to the nest via an egg laid upon a worker whilst it is active outside the nest. For example, certain phorid flies, lured by ant odours, may be seen darting at ants in an attempt to oviposit on them. A West Indian leafcutter ant (*Atta* sp.) cannot defend itself from such attacks whilst bearing leaf fragments in its mandibles.

This problem frequently is addressed (but is unlikely to be completely overcome) by stationing a guard on the leaf during transport; the guard is a small (minima) worker that uses its jaws to threaten any approaching phorid fly. The success of attacks of such insects against active and well-defended hosts demonstrates great rapidity in host acceptance, probing and oviposition.

This may contrast with the sometimes leisurely manner of many parasitoids of sessile hosts, such as scale insects, pupae, or immature stages that are restrained within confined spaces, such as plant tissue and unguarded eggs.

Overcoming Host Immune Responses

Insects that develop within the body of other insects must cope with the active immune responses of the host. An adapted or compatible parasitoid is not eliminated by the cellular immune defences of the host. These defences protect the host by acting against incompatible parasitoids, pathogens and abiotic matter that may invade the host's body cavity.

Host immune responses entail mechanisms for (i) recognizing introduced material as non-self, and (ii) inactivating, suppressing or removing the foreign material. The usual host reaction to an incompatible parasitoid is encapsulation, i.e. surrounding the invading egg or larva by an aggregation of haemocytes.

The haemocytes become flattened onto the surface of the parasitoid and phagocytosis commences as the haemocytes build up, eventually forming a capsule that encloses and kills the intruder.

This type of reaction rarely occurs when parasitoids infect their normal hosts, presumably because the parasitoid or some factor(s) associated with it alters the host's ability to recognize the parasitoid as foreign and/or to respond to it. Parasitoids that cope successfully with the host immune system do so in one or more of the following ways:

- Avoidance-for example, ectoparasitoids feed externally on the host (in the manner of predators), egg parasitoids lay into host eggs that are incapable of immune response, and many other parasitoids at least temporarily occupy host organs (such as the brain, a ganglion, a salivary gland or the gut) and thus escape the immune reaction of the host haemolymph.
- Evasion-this includes molecular mimicry (the parasitoid is coated with a substance similar to host proteins and is not recognized as non-self by the host), cloaking (e.g. the parasitoid may insulate itself in a membrane or capsule, derived from either embryonic membranes or host tissues; see also 'subversion' below) and/or by rapid development in the host.
- Destruction-the host immune system may be blocked by attrition of the host such as by gross feeding that weakens host defence reactions, and/or by destruction of responding cells (the host haemocytes).
- Suppression-host cellular immune responses may be suppressed by viruses associated with the parasitoids; often suppression

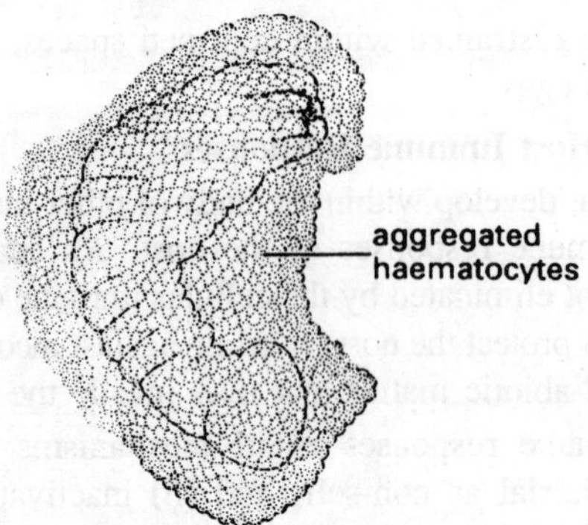

Figure 6.5: Encapsulation of a living larva of Apontelcs (Hymenoptera: Braconidae) by the haemocytes of a cater pillar of Ephestia (Lepidoptera: Pyralidae).

is accompanied by reduction in host haemocyte counts and other changes in host physiology.

- Subversion-in many cases parasitoid development occurs despite host response; for example, physical resistance to encapsulation is known for wasp parasitoids, and in dipteran parasitoids the host's haemocytic capsule is subverted for use as a sheath that the fly larva keeps open at one end by vigorous feeding. In many parasitic Hymenoptera, the serosa or trophamnion associated with the parasitoid egg fragments into individual cells that float free in the host haemolymph and grow to form giant cells, or teratocytes, that may assist in overwhelming the host defences.

Obviously the various ways of coping with host immune reactions are not discrete and most adapted parasitoids probably use a combination of methods to allow development within their respective hosts. Parasitoid-host interactions at the level of cellular and humoral immunity are complex and vary greatly among different taxa.

Our understanding of these systems is still relatively limited but this field of research is producing exciting findings concerning parasitoid genomes and coevolved associations between insects and viruses.

PREY/HOST SELECTION AND SPECIFICITY

As we have seen in other chapters of this book, insects vary in the breadth of food sources they use. Thus some predatory insects are monophagous, utilizing a single species of prey, others are oligophagous, using few species, and many are polyphagous, feeding on a variety of prey species. As a broad generalization, predators are mostly polyphagous, as a single prey species rarely will provide adequate resources. However, sit-and-wait (ambush) predators, by virtue of their chosen location, may have a restricted diet-for example, antlions may predominantly trap small ants in their pits.

Furthermore, some predators select gregarious prey, such as certain eusocial insects, because the predictable behaviour and abundance of this prey allows monophagy. Although these prey insects may be aggregated, often they are aposematic and chemically defended. Nonetheless, if the defences can be countered, these predictable and often abundant food sources permit predator specialization.

Predator-prey interactions are not discussed further: the remainder of this section concerns the more complicated host relations of parasitoids and parasites. In referring to parasitoids and their range of hosts, the terminology of monophagous, oligophagous and polyphagous is applied, as for phytophages and predators.

However, a different, parallel terminology exists for parasites: *monoxenous* parasites are restricted to a single host, *oligoxenous* to few, and polyxenous ones avail themselves of many hosts. In the following sections, we discuss first the variety of strategies for host selection by parasitoids, followed by the ways in which a parasitized host may be manipulated by the developing parasitoid.

In the final section, patterns of host use by parasites are discussed, with particular reference to coevolution.

Host Use by Parasitoids

Parasitoids require only a single individual in which to complete development, always kill their immature host, and rarely are parasitic in the adult stage. Insect-eating (*entomophagous*) parasitoids show a range of strategies for development on their selected insect hosts. The larva may be ectoparasitic, developing externally, or endoparasitic, developing within the host.

Eggs (or larvae) of ectoparasitoids are laid close to or upon the body of the host, as are sometimes those of endoparasitoids; however, in the latter group, more often the eggs are laid within the body of the host, using a piercing ovipositor (in hymenopterans) or a substitutional ovipositor (in parasitoid dipterans).

Certain parasitoids that feed within host pupal cases or under the covers and protective cases of scale insects and the like, actually are ectophages (external feeding), living internal to the protection but external to the insect host body. These different feeding modes give different exposures to the host immune system, with endoparasitoids encountering and ectoparasitoids avoiding the host defences. Ectoparasitoids are often less host specific compared with endoparasitoids, as they have less intimate association with the host compared with the endoparasitoid, which must counter the species-specific variations of the host immune system.

Parasitoids may be solitary on or in their host or gregarious. The number of parasitoids that can develop on a host relates to the size of the host, its postinfected longevity, and the size (and biomass) of the parasitoid.

Development of several parasitoids in one individual host arises commonly through the female ovipositing several eggs on a single host, or, less often, by polyembryony, in which a single egg laid by the mother divides and can give rise to numerous offspring. Gregarious parasitoids appear able to regulate the clutch size in relation to the quality and size of the host.

Most parasitoids *host* discriminate; i.e. they can recognize, and generally reject, hosts that are parasitized already, either by themselves, their conspecifics or another species. Distinguishing unparasitized from parasitized hosts generally involves a marking pheromone placed inside or externally on the host at the time of oviposition.

However, not all parasitoids avoid alreadyparasitized hosts. In *superparasitism*, a host receives multiple eggs either from a single individual or several individuals of the same parasitoid species, although the host cannot sustain the total parasitoid burden to maturity.

The outcome of multiple oviposition is discussed elsewhere in this chapter. Theoretical models, some of which have been substantiated experimentally, imply that superparasitism will increase:

- as unparasitized hosts are depleted;
- as parasitoid numbers searching any patch increase;
- in species with high fecundity and small eggs.

Although historically all such instances were deemed to have been 'mistakes', there is some evidence of adaptive benefits deriving from the strategy. Superparasitism is adaptive for individual parasitoids when there is competition for scarce hosts, but avoidance is adaptive when hosts are abundant.

Very direct benefits accrue in the case of a solitary parasitoid that uses a host that is able to encapsulate a parasitoid egg. Here, a first-laid egg may use all the host haemocytes, and a subsequent egg may thereby escape encapsulation. In *multiparasitism*, a host receives eggs of more than one species of parasitoid. Multiparasitism occurs more often than superparasitism, perhaps because parasitoid species are less able to recognize the marking pheromones placed by species other than their own.

Closely-related parasitoids may recognize each others' marks, whereas more distantlyrelated species may be unable to do so. However, secondary parasitoids, called *hyperparasitoids*, appear able to detect the odours left by a primary parasitoid, allowing accurate location of the site for the development of the hyperparasite.

Hyperparasitic development involves a secondary parasitoid developing at the expense of the primary parasitoid. Some insects are obligate hyper parasitoids, developing only within primary parasitoids, whereas others are facultative and may develop also as primary parasitoids.

Development may be external or internal to the primary parasitoid host, with oviposition into the primary host in the former, or into the primary parasitoid in the latter. External feeding is frequent, and predominantly restricted to the host larval stage: hyperparasitoids of eggs of adult hosts are very rare.

Hyperparasitoids belong to two families of Diptera (certain Bombyliidae and Conopidae), two families of Coleoptera (a few Rhipiphoridae and Cleridae) and notably the Hymenoptera, principally amongst 11 of the 17 families of the superfamily Chalcidoidea and in four subfamilies of ichneumonidae.

However, many parasitoid insects are not attacked by hyperparasitoids, notably the Tachinidae (Diptera) and, amongst the Hymenoptera, the aphidiine Braconidae and the egg parasitoids, Trichogrammatidae, Scelionidae and Mymaridae. Within the Hymenoptera, hyperparasitism has evolved several times, each originating in some manner from primary

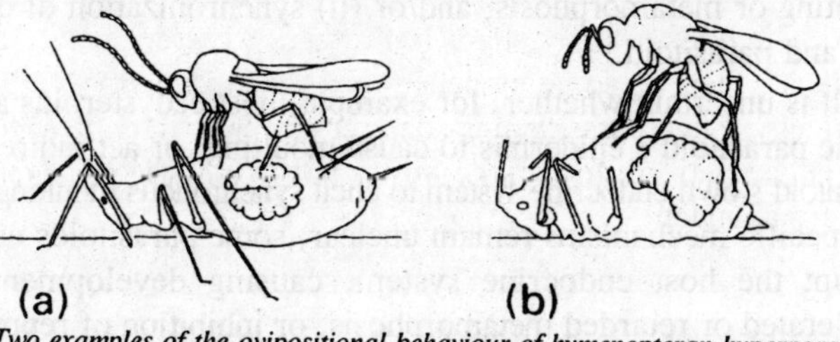

Figure 6.6: Two examples of the ovipositional behaviour of hymenopteran hyperparasitoids of aphids: (a) endophagous Alluxlista victrix (Hymenoptera: Cynipidae) ovipositing into a primary parasitoid inside a live aphid; (b) ectophagous Asaphcs hams (Hymenoptera: Ptcromalidae) ovipositing onto a primary parasitoid in a mummified aphid.

parasitism, with facultative hyperparasitism demonstrating the ease of the transition.

Hymenopteran hyperparasitoids attack a wide range of hymenopteran-parasitized insects, predominantly amongst the homopterans (especially Sternorrhyncha) and Lepidoptera. Hyperparasitoids often have a broader host range than the frequently oligophagous or monophagous primary parasitoids.

However, as with primary parasitoids, edophagous hyperparasitoids seem to be more host specific than those that feed externally, relating to the greater physiological problems experienced when developing within another living organism.

Additionally, foraging and assessment of host suitability of a complexity comparable with that of primary parasitoids is known, at least for cynipid hyperparasitoids of aphidophagous parasitoids. As explained elsewhere in this book, hyperparasitism and the degree of host specificity is fundamental information in biological control programmes.

Host Manipulation and Development of Parasitoids

Parasitization may kill or paralyse the host, and the developing parasitoid, called an *idiobiont*, develops rapidly, in a situation that differs only slightly from predation. Of greater interest and much more complexity is the *konobiont* parasitoid that lays its egg(s) in a young host, which continues to grow, thereby providing an increasing food resource.

Parasitoid development can be delayed until the host has attained a sufficient size to sustain it. *Host regulation* is a feature of konobionts, with certain parasitoids able to manipulate host physiology, including suppression of its pupation to produce a 'super host'. Many konobionts respond to hormones of the host, as demonstrated by (i) the frequent moulting or emergence of parasitoids in synchrony with the host's moulting or metamorphosis, and/or (ii) synchronization of diapause of host and parasitoid.

It is uncertain whether, for example, host ecdysteroids act directly on the parasitoid's epidermis to cause moulting, or act indirectly on the parasitoid's own endocrine system to elicit synchronous moulting. Although the specific mechanisms remain unclear, some parasitoids undoubtedly disrupt the host endocrine system, causing developmental arrest, accelerated or retarded metamorphosis, or inhibition of reproduction in an adult host.

This may arise through production of hormones (including mimetic ones) by the parasitoid, or through regulation of the host's endocrine

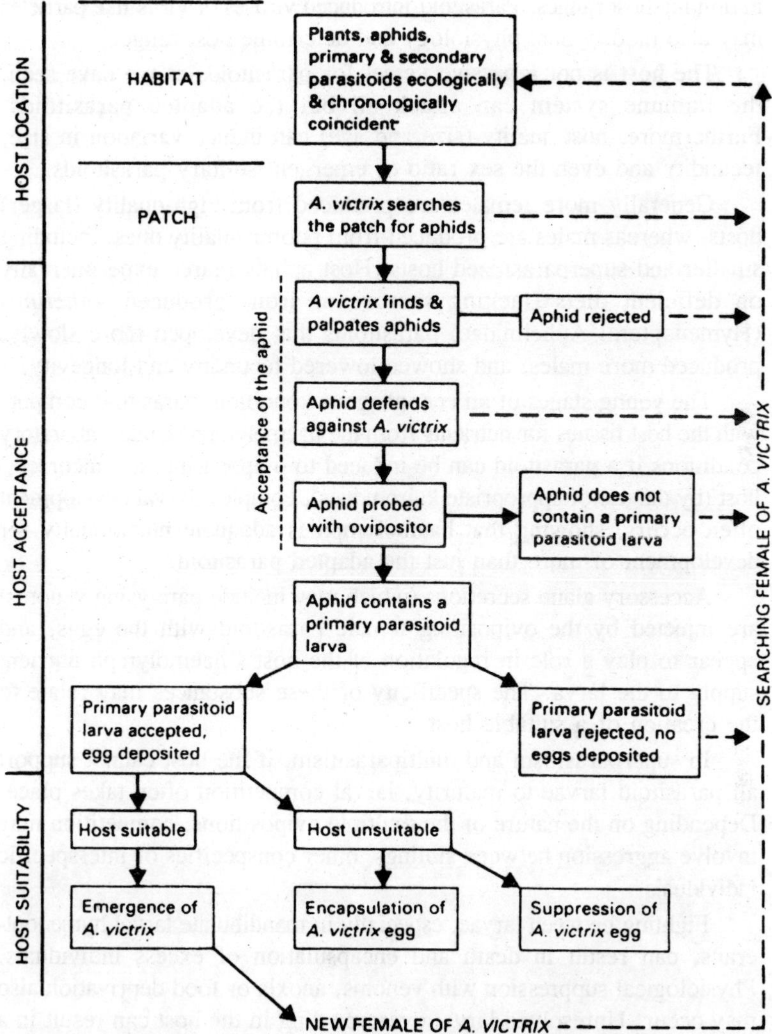

Figure 6.7: Steps in host selection by the hyperparasitoid Alloxysta victrix.

system, or both. In cases of delayed parasitism, such as is seen in certain platygastrine and braconid hymenopterans, development of an egg laid in the host egg is delayed for up to a year, until the host is a late-stage larva.

Host hormonal changes approaching metamorphosis are implicated in the stimulation of parasitoid development. Specific interactions between the endocrine systems of endoparasitoids and their hosts will play a role in limiting host ranges. Parasitoid-introduced viruses or virus-like particles may also modify host physiology and determine host range.

The host is not a passive vessel for parasitoids-as we have seen, the immune system can attack all but the adapted parasitoids. Furthermore, host quality (size and age) can induce variation in size, fecundity and even the sex ratio of emergent solitary parasitoids.

Generally more females are produced from high-quality (larger) hosts, whereas males are produced from poorer quality ones, including smaller and superparasitized hosts. Host aphids reared experimentally on deficient diets (lacking sucrose or iron) produced *Aphelinus* (Hymenoptera: Aphelinidae) parasitoids that developed more slowly, produced more males, and showed lowered fecundity and longevity.

The young stages of an endophagous konobiont parasitoid compete with the host tissues for nutrients from the haemolymph. Under laboratory conditions if a parasitoid can be induced to oviposit into an 'incorrect' host (by the use of appropriate kairomones), complete larval development often occurs, showing that haemolymph is adequate nutritionally for development of more than just the adapted parasitoid.

Accessory gland secretions (which may include paralysing venoms) are injected by the ovipositing female parasitoid with the eggs, and appear to play a role in regulation of the host's haemolymph nutrient supply to the larva. The specificity of these substances may relate to the creation of a suitable host.

In superparasitism and multiparasitism, if the host cannot support all parasitoid larvae to maturity, larval competition often takes place. Depending on the nature of the multiple ovipositions, competition may involve aggression between siblings, other conspecifics or interspecific individuals.

Fighting between larvae, especially in mandibulate larval hymenopterans, can result in death and encapsulation of excess individuals. Physiological suppression with venoms, anoxia or food deprivation also may occur. Unresolved larval overcrowding in the host can result in a few weak and small individuals emerging, or no parasitoids at all if the host dies prematurely, or resources are depleted before pupation.

Gregariousness may have evolved from solitary parasitism in circumstances in which multiple larval development is permitted by greater host size. Evolution of gregariousness may be facilitated when the potential competitors for resources within a single host are relatives. This is particularly so in polyembryony, which produces clonal, genetically identical larvae.

Patterns of Host Use and Specificity in Parasites

The wide array of insects that are ectoparasitic upon vertebrate hosts are of such significance to the health of humans and their domestic animals that we devote a complete chapter to them and medical issues will not be considered further here.

In contrast to the radiation of ectoparasitic insects using vertebrate hosts and the immense numbers of species of insect parasitoids seen above, there are remarkably few insect parasites of other insects, or indeed, of other arthropods. The largest group of endoparasitic insects using other insects as hosts belongs to the Strepsiptera, an order comprising a few hundred exclusively parasitic species.

The characteristically aberrant bodies of their predominantly hemipteran and hymenopteran hosts are termed 'stylopized', socalled for a common strepsipteran genus, *Stylops*. Within the host's body cavity, growth of larvae and pupae of both sexes, and the adult female strepsipteran causes malformations including displacement of the internal organs.

The host's sexual organs degenerate, or fail to develop appropriately. Although larval Dryinidae (Hymenoptera) develop parasitically part-externally, part-internally in hemipterans, virtually all other insect-insect parasitic interactions involve ectoparasitism. The Braulidae is a family of Diptera comprising some aberrant, mite-like flies belonging to a single genus, *Braula*, intimately associated with *Apis* (honey bees).

Larval braulids scavenge on pollen and wax in the hive, and the adults usurp nectar and saliva from the proboscis of the bee. This association certainly involves phoresy, with adult braulids always found on their hosts' bodies, but whether the relationship is ectoparasitic is open to debate.

Likewise, the relationship of several genera of aquatic chironomid larvae with nymphal hosts, such as mayflies, stoneflies and dragonflies, ranges from phoresy to suggested ectoparasitism. Generally there is little evidence that any of these ecto- and endoparasites using insects show a high degree of specificity at the species level. However, this is not necessarily the case for insect parasites with vertebrate hosts.

The patterns of host specificity and preferences of parasites raise some of the most fascinating questions in parasitology. For example, most orders of mammals bear lice (Phthiraptera), many of which are monoxenic or found amongst a limited range of hosts.

Even some marine mammals, namely certain seals, have lice, although whales do not. None of the Chiroptera (bats) harbour lice, despite their apparent suitability, although they are host to many other ectoparasitic insects, including the Strebilidae and Nycteribiidae-two families of ectoparasitic Diptera restricted to bats.

Some terrestrial hosts are free of all ectoparasites, others have very specific associations with one or a few guests, and in Panama the opossum *Didelphis marsupialis* has been found to harbour 41 species of ectoparasitic insects and mites. Although four or five of these are commonly present, none are restricted to the opossum and the remainder are found on a variety of hosts ranging from distantly-related mammals to reptiles, birds and bats.

We can examine some principles concerning the different patterns of distribution of parasites and their hosts, by looking in some detail at cases where close associations of parasites and hosts are expected. The findings can then be related to ectoparasite-host relations in general.

The Phthiraptera are obligate permanent ectoparasites, spending all their lives on their hosts, and lacking any free-living stage. Extensive surveys, such as one concerning the lice of Neotropical birds that showed an average of 1.1 lice species per bird species across 127 species and 26 families of birds, indicate that lice are highly monoxenous (restricted to one host species).

A high level of coevolution between louse and host might be expected, and in general, related animals have related lice. The widely quoted Fahrenholz's rule formally states that the phylogenies of hosts and parasites are identical, with every speciation event affecting hosts being matched by a synchronous speciation of the parasites, as shown in Figure elsewhere in this chpater.

It follows that:

- phylogenetic trees of hosts can be derived from the trees of their ectoparasites;
- ectoparasite phylogenetic trees are derivable from the trees of their hosts (the potential for circularity of reasoning is evident);
- the number of parasite species in the group under consideration is identical to the number of host species considered;
- no species of host has more than one species of parasite in the taxon under consideration;
- no species of parasite parasitizes more than one species of host.

Fahrenholz's rule has been tested for mammal lice selected from amongst the family Trichodectidae, for which robust phylogenetic trees, derived independently of any host mammal phylogeny, are available. Amongst a sample of these trichodectids, 337 lice species parasitize 244 host species, with 34% of host species parasitized by more than one trichodectid.

Several possible explanations exist for these mismatches. Firstly, speciation may have occurred independently amongst certain lice on a single host. This is substantiated, with at least 7% of all speciation events in the sampled Trichodectidae showing this pattern of independent speciation.

A second explanation involves secondary transfer of lice species to phylogenetically unrelated host taxa. Amongst extant species, when cases arising from human-induced unnatural host proximity are excluded (accounting for 6% of cases), unmistakable and presumed natural transfers (i.e. between marsupial and eutherian mammal, or bird and mammal) occur in about 2% of speciation events.

However, hidden within the phylogenies of host and parasite are speciation events that involve lateral transfer between rather more closely-related host taxa, but these transfers fail to match precisely the phylogeny.

Examination of the detailed phylogeny of the sampled Trichodectidae shows that a minimum of 20% of all speciation events are associated with distant and lateral secondary transfer, including historical transfers (lying deeper in the phylogenetic trees).

In detailed examinations of relationships between a smaller subset of trichodectids and eight of their pocket gopher (Rodentia: Geomyidae) hosts, substantial concordance was claimed between trees derived from biochemical data for hosts and parasites, and some evidence of cospeciation was found.

However, many of the hosts were shown to have two lice species, and unconsidered data show most species of gopher to have a substantial suite of associated lice. Furthermore, a minimum of three instances of lateral transfer (host switching) appeared to have occurred, in all cases between hosts with geographically contiguous ranges.

Although many speciation events in these lice 'track' speciation in the host and some estimates even indicate similar ages of host and parasite species, it is evident from the Trichodectidae that strict cospeciation of host and parasite is not the sole explanation of the associations observed.

The reasons why apparently monoxenic lice sometimes do deviate

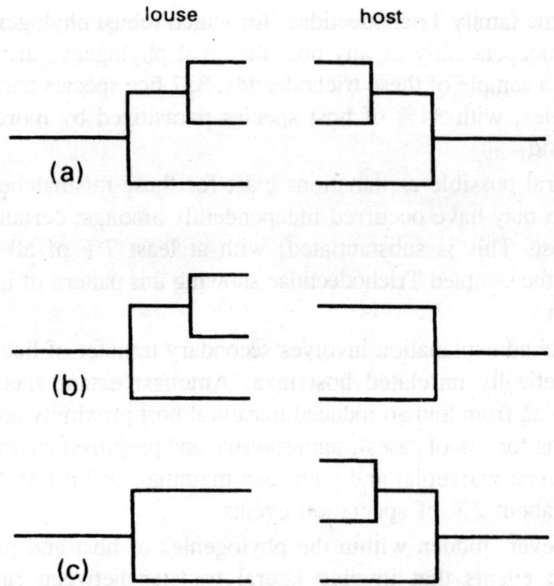

Figure 6.8: Comparisons of louse and host phylogenetic trees: (a) adherence to Fahrenholz's rule; (b) independent speciation of the lice; (c) independent speciation of the hosts.

from strict coevolution and cospeciation apply equally to other ectoparasites, many of which show similar variation in complexity of host relationships. Deviations from strict cospeciation arise if host speciation occurs without commensurate parasite speciation.

This resulting pattern of relationships is identical to that seen if one of two parasite sister taxa generated by co-speciation in concert with the host, subsequently became extinct. Frequently a parasite is not present throughout the complete range of its host, resulting perhaps from the parasite being restricted in range by environmental factors independent of those controlling the range of the host.

Hemimetabolous ectoparasites, such as lice, which spend their entire lives on the host, might be expected to closely follow the ranges of their hosts, but there are exceptions in which the ectoparasite distribution is restricted by external environmental factors. For holometabolous ectoparasites, which spend some of their lives away from their hosts, such external factors will be even more influential in governing parasite range.

For example, a homeothermic vertebrate may tolerate environmental conditions that cannot be sustained by the free-living stage of a poikilothermic ectoparasite, such as a larval flea. As speciation may occur in any part of the distribution of a host, host speciation may be expected to occur without necessarily involving the parasite. Furthermore, a parasite may show geographical variation within all or part of the host range that is incongruent with the variation of the host.

If either or both variations leads to eventual species formation, there will be incongruence between parasite and host phylogeny. Furthermore, poor knowledge of host and parasite interactions may result in misleading conclusions.

A true host may be defined as one that provides the conditions for parasite reproduction to continue indefinitely. When there is more than one true host, there may be a principal (preferred) or exceptional host, depending on the proportional frequencies of ectoparasite occurrence.

An intermediate category may be recognized-the sporadic or secondary host-on which parasite development cannot normally take place, but an association arises frequently, perhaps through predator-prey interactions or environmental encounters (such as a shared nest).

Small sample sizes and limited biological information can allow an accidental or secondary host to be mistaken for a true host, giving rise to a possible erroneous 'refutation' of cospeciation. Extinctions of certain parasites and true hosts (leaving the parasite extant on a secondary host) will refute Fahrenholz's rule.

Even assuming perfect recognition of true host specificity and knowledge of the historical existence of all parasites and hosts, it is evident that successful parasite transfers between hosts have taken place throughout the history of host-parasite interactions.

Cospeciation is fundamental to host-parasite relations, but the factors encouraging deviations must be considered. Predominantly these concern (i) geographical and social proximity of different hosts, allowing opportunities for parasite colonization of the new host, together with (ii) ecological similarity of different hosts, allowing establishment, survival and reproduction of the ectoparasite on the novel host.

The results of these factors have been termed *resource* tracking, to contrast with the phyletic tracking implied by Fahrenholz's rule. As with all matters biological, most situations lie somewhere along a continuum between these two extremes, and rather than forcing patterns into one category or the other, interesting questions arise from recognizing and interpreting the different patterns observed.

If all host-parasite relationships are examined, some of the factors that govern host specificity can be identified:

- the stronger the life-history integration with that of the host, the greater the likelihood of monoxeny;

- the greater the vagility (mobility) of the parasite, the more likely it is to be polyxenous;
- the number of accidental and secondary parasite species increases with decreasing ecological specialization and with increase in geographical range of the host, as we saw for the widespread and unspecialized opossum earlier in this section.

If a single host shares a number of ectoparasites, there may be some ecological or temporal segregation on the host. For example, in haematophagous (blood-sucking) black flies (Simuliidae) that attack cattle, the belly is more attractive to certain species, whereas others feed only on the ears.

Pediculus capitis and *P. humanus* (Phthiraptera), human head and body lice, are ecologically separated examples of sibling species in which proven reproductive isolation is reflected by only slight morphological differences.

MODELS OF ABUNDANCES OF PREDATOR/PARASITOIDS AND PREY/HOSTS

There is a substantial body of experimental and theoretical evidence that predators (taken to include parasitoids in this discussion) impose a structure on the ecological communities in which they operate.

Experiments show that removal of the most important ('top') predator can give a major shift in community structure, demonstrating that predators control the abundance of subdominant predators and certain prey species. Ecologists have attempted to model the complex relationship between predators and prey, frequently motivated by a desire to understand interactions of biological control agents and target pest species.

Mathematical models may commence from simple interactions between a single monophagous predator and its prey. Experiments and simulations concerning the long-term trend in numbers of each show a regular cycling of numbers of predators and prey: when prey are abundant, predator survival is high; as more predators become available, prey abundance is reduced; predator numbers decrease as do those of prey; reduction in predation allows the prey to escape and rebuild numbers. The sinusoidal, timelagged cycles of predator and prey abundances may occur in some simple natural systems, such as the aquatic planktonic predator *Chaoborus* (Diptera: Chaoboridae) and its cladoceran prey *Daphnia*.

Examination of shorter-term feeding responses using laboratory studies of simple systems shows that predators vary in their responses to prey density, with an early assumption of a linear relationship (increased prey density leading to increased predator feeding) being superseded. A common pattern of functional response of a predator to prey density involves a gradual slowing of the rate of predation relative to increased prey density, until an asymptote is reached.

This upper limit beyond which no increased rate of prey capture occurs is due to the time constraints of foraging and handling prey in which there is a finite limit to the time spent in feeding activities, including a recovery period.

The rate of prey capture does not depend upon prey abundance alone: individuals of different instars have different feeding rate profiles, and in poikilothermic insects there is an important effect of ambient temperature on activity rates. The assumptions of predator monophagy usually are biologically unrealistic, and more complex models include multiple prey items.

Predator behaviour is based upon optimal foraging strategies involving simulated prey selection varying with changes in proportional availability of different prey items. However, predators may not switch between prey items based upon simple relative numerical abundance; other factors include differences in prey profitability (nutritional content, ease of handling, etc.), the hunger-level of the predator, and perhaps predator learning and development of a searchimage for particular prey,

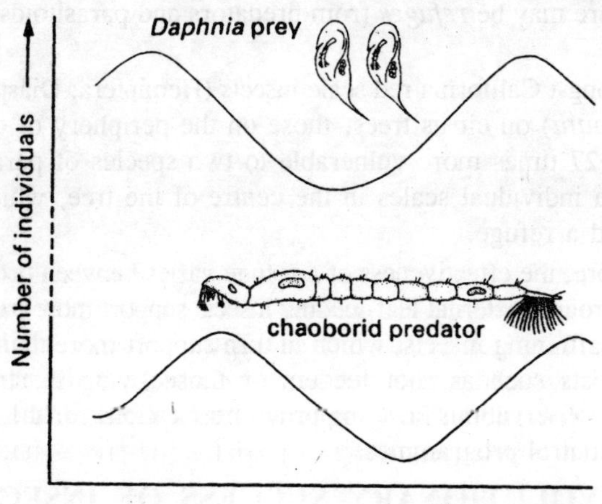

Figure 6.9: An example of the regular cycling of numbers of predators and their prey: the aquatic planktonic predator Chaoborus (Diptera: Chaoboridae) and its cladoceran prey Daphnia (Crustacea).

irrespective of abundance.

Models of prey foraging and handling by predators, in which a more realistic choice between profitable and less profitable prey items is available, indicate that:

- prey specialization ought to occur when the most profitable prey is abundant;
- predators should switch rapidly from complete dependence on one prey to the other, with partial preference (mixed feeding) being rare;
- the actual abundance of a less-abundant prey should be irrelevant to the decision of a predator to specialize on the most abundant prey.

Further problems are associated with the unrealistic assumptions that parasitoid searching behaviour resembles that of a random-searching predator, in being independent of host abundance, the proportion of hosts already parasitized and the distribution of the hosts. As we have seen above, parasitoids often are able to identify and respond behaviourally to already-parasitized hosts.

Furthermore, prey (and hosts) are not distributed at random, but occur in patches, and within patches the density is likely to vary. As predators and parasitoids aggregate in areas of high resource density, interactions between predators/parasitoids (*interference*) become significant, perhaps making a profitable area unprofitable. For a number of reasons, there may be *refuges* from predators and parasitoids within a patch.

Thus, amongst California red scale insects (Hemiptera: Diaspididae: *Aoiidiella auraittii*) on citrus trees, those on the periphery of the tree may be up to 27 times more vulnerable to two species of parasitoids compared with individual scales in the centre of the tree, which thus may be termed a refuge.

Furthermore, the effectiveness of a refuge varies between taxonomic or ecological groups: external leaf-feeding insects support more parasitoid species than leafmining insects, which in turn support more than highly concealed insects such as root feeders or those living in structural refuges. These observations have important implications for the success of biological control programmes.

THE EVOLUTIONARY SUCCESS OF INSECT PREDATION AND PARASITISM

In Chapter elsewhere in this book we saw how the development of angiosperms and their colonization by specific planteating insects could be seen as an explanation for a substantial diversification of phytophagous insects relative to their non-phytophagous sister taxa. Applying similar reasoning to the Hymenoptera, comparison of the phytophagous suborder

Symphyta with its primarily parasitic sister group, the suborder Apocrita, implies that, in this case, adoption of a parasitic lifestyle is associated with a major evolutionary radiation. An explanation may lie in the degree of host restriction: if each species of phytophagous insect were host to a more or less monophagous parasitoid, then we would expect to see a diversification (radiation) of insect parasitoids that corresponded to that of phytophagous insects.

Two assumptions need examination in this context -the degree of host specificity and the number of parasitoids harboured by each host. The question of the degree of monophagy amongst parasites and parasitoids is not answered conclusively. For example, many parasitic hymenopterans are extremely small, and the basic taxonomy and host associations are yet to be fully worked out.

However, there is no doubt that the parasitic hymenopterans are extremely speciose, and show a varying pattern of host specificity from strict monophagy to oligophagy. Amongst parasitoids within the Diptera, the species-rich Tachinidae are relatively general feeders, specializing only in hosts belonging to families or even ordinal groups. Amongst the ectoparasites, lice are predominantly monoxenic, as are many fleas and flies.

However, even if several species of ectoparasitic insects were borne by each host species, as the vertebrates are not numerous, ectoparasites contribute relatively little with biological diversification in comparison with the parasitoids of insect (and other diverse arthropod) hosts.

Concerning the numbers of parasitoid species on each potential host, there is substantial evidence, much of it acquired by the diligence of amateur entomologists, that many hosts support multiple parasitoids. This phenomenon is well known to lepidopterists that endeavour to rear adult butterflies or moths from wild-caught larvae-the frequency and diversity of parasitization is very high.

Suites of parasitoid and hyperparasitoid species may attack the same species of host at different seasons, in different locations and in different life-history stages. There are many records of more than 10 parasitoid species throughout the range of some widespread lepidopterans, and although this is true also for certain well-studied coleopterans, the situation is less clear for other orders of insects.

Finally, some evolutionary interactions between parasites and parasitoids and their hosts may be considered. Firstly, patchiness of potential host abundance throughout the host range seems to provide opportunity for increased specialization, perhaps leading to species formation within the guild of parasites/parasitoids.

This can be seen as a form of niche differentiation, where the total range of a host provides a niche that is ecologically partitioned. Hosts may escape from parasitization within refuges within the range, or by modification of the life cycle, with the introduction of a phase that the parasitoid cannot track.

Host diapause may be a mechanism for evading a parasite that is restricted to continuous generations, with an extreme example of escape perhaps seen in the periodic cicada. These species of *Mac icicada* grow concealed for many years as nymphs beneath the ground, with the very visible adults appearing only every 13 or 17 years.

This cycle of a prime number of years may allow avoidance of predators or parasitoids that are able only to adapt to a predictable cyclical life history. Life-cycle shifts in attempts to evade predators may be important in species formation.

Strategies of prey/hosts and predators/parasitoids have been envisaged as evolutionary arms races, with a step-wise sequence of prey/host escape by evolution of successful defences, followed by radiation before the predator/parasitoid 'catchesup', in a form of prey/host tracking.

An alternative evolutionary model envisages both prey/host and predator/ parasitoid evolving defences and circumventing them in virtual synchrony, in an evolutionarily stable strategy termed the 'Red Queen' hypothesis (after the description in *Alice in Wonderland of* Alice and the Red Queen running faster and faster to stand still).

Tests of each can be devised and models for either can be justified, and it is unlikely that conclusive evidence will be found in the short term. What is clear is that parasitoids and predators do exert great selective pressure on their hosts or prey, and remarkable defences have arisen, as we shall see elsewhere in this book.

7

PATHOGENIC INSECTS

Aside from their impact on agricultural and horticultural crops, insects impinge on us mainly through the diseases they can transmit to humans and their domestic animals. The number of insect species involved is not large, but the insects that transmit disease (vectors), cause wounds, inject venom or create nuisance have serious social and economic consequences.

Thus the study of the veterinary and medical impact of insects is a major scientific discipline. Medical and veterinary entomology differs from, and is often much broader in scope than, other areas of entomological pursuit. Firstly, the frequent motivation (and funding) for study is rarely the insect itself, but the insect-borne human or animal disease(s).

Secondly, the scientist studying medical and veterinary aspects of entomology must have a wide understanding not only of the insect vector of disease, but of the biology of host and parasite. Thirdly, most practitioners do not restrict themselves to insects, but have to consider other arthropods, notably ticks, mites and perhaps spiders and scorpions. For brevity in this chapter, we refer to medical entomologists as those who study all arthropodborne diseases, including diseases of livestock.

The insect, though a vital cog in the chain of disease, need not be the central focus of medical research. Medical entomologists rarely work in isolation but usually function in multidisciplinary teams that may include medical practitioners and researchers, epidemiologists, virologists and immunologists, and ought to include those with skills in insect control. In this chapter, we deal with entomophobia, followed by allergic reactions, venoms and urtication caused by insects.

This is followed by details of transmission of a specific disease, namely malaria, an exemplar of insect-borne disease. This is followed by a review of additional diseases in which insects play an important role, finishing with a section on forensic entomology.

The chapter is concluded with taxonomic boxes dealing with the Phthiraptera (lice), Siphonaptera (fleas) and Diptera (flies), especially medically-significant ones.

INSECT NUISANCE AND PHOBIA

Our perceptions of nuisance may be little related to the role of insects in disease transmission. Insect nuisance is often perceived as a product of high densities of a particular species, such as bush flies (Musca *o'tustissima*) in rural Australia, or ants and silverfish around the house.

Most people have a more justifiable avoidance of filth-frequenting insects such as blowflies and cockroaches, biters such as some ants, and venomous stingers such as bees and wasps. Many serious disease vectors are rather uncommon and have inconspicuous behaviours, aside from their biting habits, such that the lay public may not perceive them as particular nuisances.

Harmless insects and arachnids sometimes arouse reactions such as unwarranted phobic responses (arachnophobia or *entomophobia* or *delusory parasitosis*). These cases may cause time-consuming and fruitless inquiry by medical entomologists, when the more appropriate investigations ought to be psychological.

Nonetheless there certainly are cases in which sufferers of persistent 'insect bites' and persistent skin rashes, in which no physical cause can be established, actually suffer from undiagnosed local or widespread infestation with microscopic mites.

In these circumstances, diagnosis of delusory parasitosis, through medical failure to identify the true cause, and referral to psychological counselling is unhelpful to say the least. There are, however, some insects that transmit no disease, but feed on blood and whose attentions almost universally cause distress-bed bugs.

Our vignette for this chapter shows *Cimex lectularius* (Hemiptera: Cimicidae), the cosmopolitan common bed bug, whose presence between the sheets indicates poor hygiene conditions.

VENOMS AND ALLERGENS

Insect Venoms

Some people's earliest experiences with insects are memorable for their pain. Although the sting of the females of many social hymenopterans (bees, wasps and ants) can seem unprovoked, it is an aggressive defence of the nest. The delivery of venom is through the sting, a modified female ovipositor.

The honey-bee sting has backwardly directed barbs that allows only one use, as the bee is fatally damaged when it leaves the sting and accompanying venom sac in the wound as it struggles to retract the sting. In contrast, wasp and ant stings are unbarbed, can be retracted and are capable of repeated use.

In some ants, the ovipositor sting is greatly reduced and venom is either sprayed around liberally, or it can be directed with great accuracy into a wound made by the jaws. The venoms of social insects are discussed in more detail elsewhere in this book.

Blister and Urtica (itch)-Inducing Insects

Some toxins produced by insects can cause injury to humans, even though they are not inoculated through a sting. Blister beetles (Meloidae) contain toxic chemicals, cantharidins, that are released if the beetle is crushed or handled. Cantharidins cause blistering of the skin and, if taken orally, inflammation of the urinary and genital tracts, which gave rise to its notoriety (as 'Spanish fly') as a supposed aphrodisiac.

Staphylinid beetles of the genus *Paederus* produce potent contact poisons including paederin, that cause delayed onset of severe blistering and long-lasting ulceration. Lepidopteran caterpillars, notably moths, are a frequent cause of skin irritation, or urtication (a description derived from a similarity to the reaction to nettles, genus *Urtica*).

Some species have hollow spines containing the products of a subcutaneous venom gland, which are released when the spine is broken. Other species have setae (bristles and hairs) containing toxins, which cause intense irritation when the setae contact human skin.

Urticating caterpillars include the processionary caterpillars (Notodontidae) and some cup moths (Limacodidae). Processionary caterpillars combine frass (dry insect faeces), cast larval skins and shed hairs into bags suspended in trees and bushes, in which pupation occurs.

If the bag is damaged by contact or by high wind, urticating hairs are widely dispersed. The pain caused by hymenopteran stings may last a few hours, urtication may last a few days, and the most ulcerated beetle-induced blisters may last some weeks. However, increased medical significance of these injurious insects comes when repeated exposure leads to allergic disease in some humans.

Insect Allergenicity

Insects and other arthropods are often implicated in allergic disease, which occurs when exposure to some arthropod allergen (a moderate-sized molecular weight chemical component, usually a protein) triggers excessive immunological reaction in some exposed people or animals.

Those who handle insects in their occupations, such as in entomological rearing facilities, tropical fish food production or research laboratories, frequently develop allergic reactions to one or more of a range of insects. Mealworms (beetle larvae of *Tcnebrio spp.*), bloodworms (larvae of *Chironomus spp.*), locusts and blowflies have all been implicated.

Stored products infested with astigmatic mites give rise to allergic diseases such as baker's and grocer's itch. The most significant arthropod-mediated allergy arises through the faecal material of house-dust mites (*Dermatophagoides pteronyssinus*), which are ubiquitous and abundant in houses throughout the temperate regions of the world.

Exposure to naturally occurring allergenic arthropods and their products maybe underestimated, although the role of house-dust mites in allergy is now well recognized. The venomous and urticating insects discussed above can cause greater danger when some *sensitized* (previously exposed and allergy-susceptible) individuals are bitten again, as anaphylactic shock is possible, with death occurring if untreated.

Individuals showing indications of allergic reaction to hymenopteran stings must take appropriate precautions, including allergen avoidance and carrying adrenaline.

INSECTS AS CAUSES AND VECTORS OF DISEASE

In tropical and subtropical regions, scientific, if not public, attention is drawn to the role of insects in transmitting protists, viruses and nematodes. Such pathogens are the causative agents of many important and widespread human diseases, including malaria, dengue, yellow fever, onchocerciasis (river blindness), leishmaniasis (oriental sore, kala-azar), filariasis (elephantiasis) and trypanosomiasis (sleeping sickness).

The causative agent of diseases may be the insect itself, such as the human body or head louse (*Pediculns human us* and *P. capitis*, respectively), which cause pediculosis, or the mite *Sarcoptes scabiei*, whose skinburrowing activities cause scabies.

In myiasis (from *myia*, the Greek for fly) the maggots or larvae of blowflies, houseflies and their relatives (Diptera: Calliphoridae, Sarcophagidae and Muscidae) can develop in living flesh, either as primary agents or subsequently following wounding or damage by other insects, such as ticks and biting flies.

If untreated, the animal victim may die. As death approaches and the flesh putrefies through bacterial activity, there may be third wave of specialist fly larvae, and these colonizers are present at death. One particular form of myiasis affecting livestock is known as 'strike' and is caused in the Old World by *Chnisamya hezziana* and in the Americas by the New World screw-worm *fly*, *Cochliomyia hominivorax*.

The name 'screw-worm' derives from the distinct rings of setae on the maggot resembling a screw. Virtually all myiases, including screw-worm, can affect humans, particularly under conditions of poor hygiene. Further groups of 'higher' Diptera develop in mammals as endoparasitic larvae in the dermis, intestine or, as in the sheep nostril fly, *Oestrus ovis*, in the nasal and head sinuses.

In many parts of the world, losses caused by fly-induced damage to hides and meat, and death as a result of myiases may amount to many millions of dollars. Even more frequent than direct injury by insects is their action as vectors, transmitting disease-inducing pathogens from one animal or human *host* to another.

This transfer may be by mechanical or biological means. *Mechanical transfer* occurs, for example, when a mosquito transfers myxomatosis from rabbit to rabbit in the blood on its proboscis. Likewise, when a cockroach or housefly acquires bacteria when feeding on faeces it may physically transfer some bacteria from its mouthparts, legs or body to human food, thereby transferring enteric diseases.

The causative agent of the disease is passively transported from host to host, and does not increase in the vector. Usually in mechanical transfer, the arthropod is only one of several means of pathogen transfer, with poor public and personal hygiene often providing additional pathways.

In contrast, biological transfer is a much more specific association between insect vector, pathogen and host, and transfer never occurs naturally without all three components. The disease agent replicates (increases) within the vector insect, and there is often close specificity between vector and disease agent.

The insect is thus a vital link in biological transfer, and efforts to curb disease nearly always involve attempts to reduce vector numbers. In addition, biologically transferred disease may be controlled by seeking to interrupt contact between vector and host, and by direct attack on the pathogen, usually whilst in the host.

Disease control comprises a combination of these approaches, each of which requires detailed knowledge of the biology of all three components-vector, pathogen and host.

GENERALIZED DISEASE CYCLES

In all biologically transferred diseases, a biting (blood-feeding or sucking) adult arthropod, often an insect, particularly a true fly (Diptera), transmits a parasite from human to human, or from animal to human, or, more rarely, from human to animal. Some human pathogens (causative agents of human disease such as malaria parasites) can complete their parasitic life cycles solely within the insect vector and the human host.

Human malaria is an example of a disease with a *single cycle* involving *Anopheles* mosquitoes, malaria parasites and humans. Although related malaria parasites occur in animals, notably other primates and birds, these hosts and parasites are not involved in the human malarial cycle.

Only a few human insect-borne diseases have single cycles, as in malaria, because these diseases require coevolution of pathogen and vector and *Homo sapiens*. As *H. sapiens* is of relatively recent origin in evolutionary terms, there has been only a short time for the development of unique insectborne diseases that require specifically a human rather than any alternative vertebrates for completion of the disease-causing organism's life cycle.

In contrast to single-cycle diseases, many other insect-borne diseases that affect humans include a (non-human) vertebrate host, as for instance in yellow fever in monkeys, plague in rats and leishmaniasis in desert rodents. In these cases it is clear that the non-human cycle is primary and the sporadic inclusion of humans in a *secondary* cycle is not essential to maintain the disease.

However, when outbreaks do occur, these diseases can spread in human populations and may involve many cases. Outbreaks in humans often stem from human actions, such as the spread of people into the natural ranges of the vector and animal hosts, which act as disease *reservoirs*. For example, yellow fever in native forested Uganda (central Africa) has a 'sylvan' (woodland) cycle, remaining within canopy-dwelling primates with the exclusively primate-feeding mosquito *Aedes africanus* as the vector.

It is only when monkeys and humans coincide at banana plantations close to or within the forest, that *Aedes siuipsoni*, a second mosquito vector that feeds on both humans and monkeys, can transfer yellow fever to humans. In a second example, *Phlebotomus* sand flies (Psychodidae) depend upon Arabian arid-zone burrowing rodents and, in feeding, transmit *Leishmania* parasites between rodent hosts.

Leishmaniasis, a disfiguring ailment showing a dramatic increase in the Neotropics, is transmitted to humans when suburban expansion places humans within this rodent reservoir, but unlike yellow fever, there appears to be no change in vector when humans enter the cycle.

In epidemiological terms, the natural cycle is maintained in animal reservoirs: sylvan primates for yellow fever and desert rodents for leishmania. Disease control clearly is complicated by the presence of these reservoirs in addition to a human cycle.

PATHOGENS

The disease-causing organisms transferred by the insect may be viruses (termed 'arboviruses', an abbreviation of arthropod-borne *viruses*), rickettsias, bacteria, protists or filarial nematode worms. Replication of these parasites in both vectors and hosts is required and some complex life cycles have developed, notably amongst the protists and filarial nematodes.

The presence of a parasite in the vector insect (which can be determined by dissection and microscopy and/or biochemical means) generally appears not to harm the host insect. When the parasite is at an appropriate developmental stage, and following multiplication or replication (amplification and/or concentration in the vector), transmission can occur.

Transfer of parasites from vector to host or vice versa takes place when the bloodfeeding insect takes a meal from a vertebrate host. The transfer from host to previously uninfected vector is through parasite-infected blood. Transmission to a host by an infected insect usually is by injection along with anticoagulant salivary gland products that keep the wound open during feeding.

However, transmission may also be through deposition of infected faeces close to the wound site. In the following survey of major arthropod-borne disease, malaria will be dealt with in some detail. Malaria is the most devastating and debilitating disease in the world, and it illustrates a number of general points concerning medical entomology.

This is followed by briefer sections reviewing the range of pathogenic diseases involving insects, arranged by phylogenetic sequence of parasite, from virus to filarial worm.

Malaria

The Disease

Malaria affects more people, more persistently, throughout more of the world than any other insectborne disease. Some 120 million new cases arise each year. The World Health Organization calculated that malaria control during the period 1950-72 reduced the proportion of the world's (excluding China's) population exposed to malaria from 64% to 38%.

Since then, however, exposure rates to malaria in many countries have risen towards the rates of half a century ago, as a result of concern over the unwanted side-effects of DDT, resistance of insects to modern pesticides and of malaria parasites to antimalarial drugs, and civil unrest and poverty in a number of countries.

Even in countries such as Australia, in which there is no transmission of malaria, the disease is on the increase among travellers, as demonstrated by the number of cases having risen from 199 in 1970, to 629 in 1980 and 700-800 in the early 1990s with 1-5 deaths per annum.

The parasitic protists that cause malaria are sporozoans, belonging to the genus *Plasmodium.* Four species are responsible for the human malarias, with others described from, but not necessarily causing diseases in, primates, some other mammals, birds and lizards.

There is developing molecular evidence that at least some of these species of *Plasmodium* are not restricted to humans, but are shared (under different names) with other primates. The vectors of mammalian malaria are always *Anopheles* mosquitoes, with other genera involved in bird plasmodia) transmission.

The disease follows a course of a prepatent period between infective bite and *patenty*, the first appearance of parasites (sporozoites, see below) in the erythrocytes (red blood cells). The first clinical symptoms define the end of n *incubation period*, some 9 (*P. falciparum*) to 21 (*P malariae*) days after infection.

Periods of fever followed by severe sweating recur cyclically and follow several hours after synchronous rupture of infected erythrocytes. The spleen is characteristically enlarged. The four malaria parasites each provoke rather different symptoms:

- *Plasmodium falciparum*, or malignant tertian malaria, kills many untreated sufferers through, for example, cerebral malaria or renal failure. Fever recurrence is at 48 h intervals (tertian is Latin for third day, the name for the fever being derived from fever on day one, normal on day two, with fever recurrent on the third day). *P. falciparum* is limited by a minimum 20°C isotherm and is thus most common in the warmest areas of the world.

- *Plasmodium vivax*, or benign tertian malaria, is a less serious disease that rarely kills. However, it is more widespread than *P. falciparum*, and has a wider temperature tolerance, extending as far as the 16°C summer isotherm. Recurrence of fever is every 48h, and the disease may persist for up to 8 years with relapses some months apart.
- *Plasmodium malariae* is known as quartan malaria, and is a widespread, but rarer parasite than P. *falciparum* or *P. vivax*. If allowed to persist for an extended period death occurs through chronic renal failure. Recurrence of fever is at 72 h, hence quartan (fever on day one, recurrence on the fourth day). It is persistent, with relapses up to half a century after the initial attack.
- *Plasmodium ovate* is a rare tertian malaria with limited pathogenicity and a very long incubation period, with relapse at three-monthly intervals.

Life cycle of Plasmodium

The malarial cycle commences with an infected female *Anopheles* mosquito taking a blood meal from a human host. As it feeds, it injects saliva contaminated with the *sporozoite* stage of the *Plasinodium*. The sporozoite circulates in the blood until reaching the liver, where a *pre-* (or *exo-*) *erythrocytic schizogonous* cycle takes place in the parenchyma cells of the liver.

This leads to the formation of a large schizont, containing from 2000-40000 *merozoites*, according to *Plasmodium* species. The prepatent period of infection, which started with an infective bite, ends when the merozoites are released (Figure elsewhere in this chapter to either infect more liver cells or enter the bloodstream and invade the erythrocytes.

Invasion occurs by the erythrocyte invaginating to engulf the merozoite, which subsequently feeds as a *trophozoite* within a vacuole. The first and several subsequent *erythrocyte schizogonous* cycles produce a trophozoite that becomes a schizont, which releases from 6 to 16 merozoites, which commence the repetition of the erythrocytic cycle.

This synchronous release of merozoites from the erythrocytes liberates parasite products that stimulate the host's cells to release cytokines (a class of immunological mediators) and these provoke the fever and illness of a malaria attack. Thus the duration of the erythrocyte schizogonous cycle is the duration of the interval between attacks (i.e. 48h for tertian, 72h for quartan).

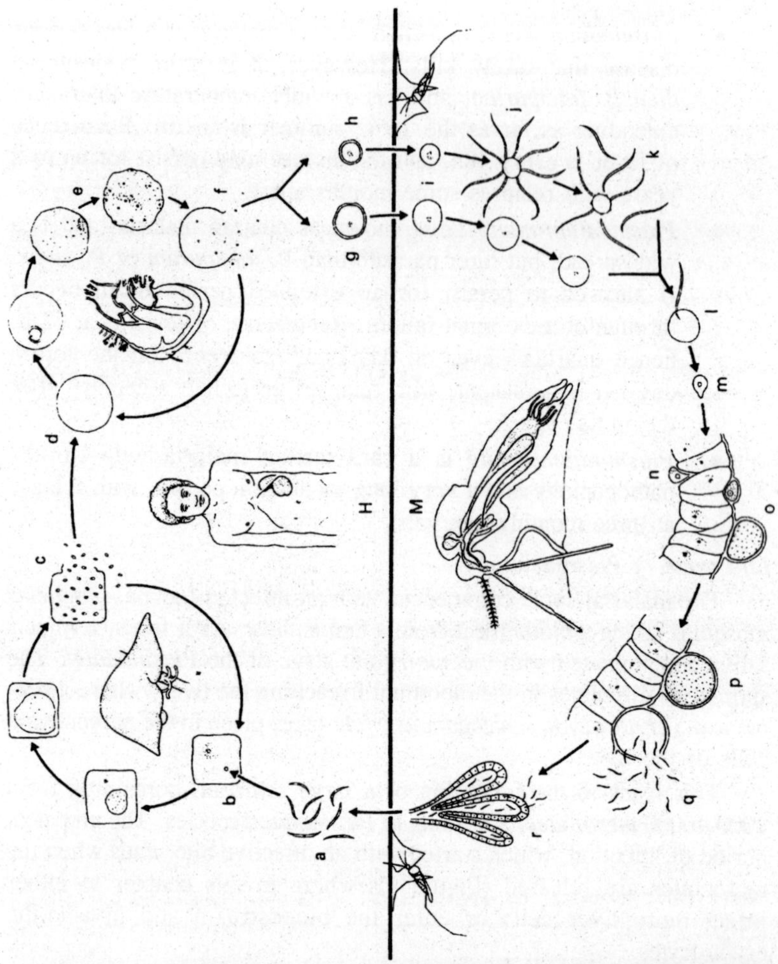

Figure 7.1: The life cycle of a Plasmodium, the malaria pathogen, in human (H) and mosquito (M): (a) injection of sporozoites into human host by feeding mosquito; (b) sporozoite enters liver parenchyma cell; (c) rupture of schizont to release merozoites; (d) merozoites enter erythrocyte; (e) trophozoite becoming schizont; (f) schizont releasing merozoites; (g) female macrogamete formation; (h) male gametocyte formation; (i) gametes lacking erythrocyte coat; (j) flagellate microgametes; (k) exflagellation; (1) zygote formation; (m) ookinete; (n) oocyst forming on mosquito inner midgut wall; (o,p) oocyst maturation and sporogeny; (q) release of sporozoites; (r) sporozoites entering salivary gland.

After several erythrocyte cycles, some trophozoites do not undergo division but mature to gametocytes, a process that takes 8 days for *P. falciparum* but only 4 days for *P. vivax*. If a female *Anopheles* feeds on an infected human host at this stage in the cycle, she ingests blood containing erythrocytes, some of which contain two types of gametocytes.

Within a susceptible mosquito the erythrocyte is disposed of and the two types of gametocytes develop further: half are female gametocytes, which remain large and are termed *macrogametes*; the other half are males, which divide into eight flagellate *microgametes*, which rapidly deflagellate, and seek and fuse with a macrogamete to form a *zygote*.

All this sexual activity has taken place in a matter of 15 min or so while the blood meal passes towards the midgut of the female mosquito. In the midgut, the initially inactive zygote becomes an active *ookinete*, which burrows into the epithelial lining of the midgut to form an oocyst.

Asexual reproduction (*sporogony*) now takes place within the expanding oocyst. In a temperature-dependent process numerous nuclear divisions give rise to sporozoites. Sporogony does not occur below 16°C or above 33°C, thus explaining the temperature limitations for *Plasmodium* development noted above.

The mature oocyst may contain 10000 sporozoites, which are shed into the haemocoel, from whence they migrate into the mosquito's salivary glands. This sporogonic cycle takes a minimum of 8-9 days and produces sporozoites that are active for up to 12 weeks, which is several times the complete life expectancy of the mosquito.

At each subsequent feeding, the infective female *Anopheles* injects sporozoites into the next host along with the saliva containing an anticoagulant, and the cycle recommences.

Malaria Epidemiology

Malaria exists in many parts of the world but the incidence varies from place to place. As with other diseases, malaria is said to be *endemic* in an area when it occurs at a relatively constant incidence by natural transmission over successive years. Categories of endemicity have been recognized based on the incidence and severity of symptoms (spleen enlargement) in both adults and children.

An *epidemic* occurs when the incidence in an endemic area rises or a number of cases of the disease occur in a new area. Malaria is said to be in a stable state when there is little seasonal or annual variation in the disease incidence, predominantly transmitted by a strongly *anthropophilic* (human-loving) *Anopheles* vector species.

Stable malaria is found in the warmer areas of the world where conditions encourage rapid sporogeny and usually are associated with the *P. falciparum* pathogen. In contrast, unstable malaria is associated with sporadic epidemics, often with a short-lived and more *zoophilic* (preferring other animals to humans) vector that may occur in massive numbers.

Often ambient temperatures are lower than for areas with stable malaria, sporogeny is slower and the pathogen is more often *P. vivax*. Disease transmission can be understood only in relation to the potential of each vector to transmit the particular disease. This involves the variously complex relationship between:

- vector distribution;
- vector abundance;
- life expectancy (survivorship) of the vector;
- predilection of the vector to feed on humans (anthropophily);
- feeding rate of the vector;
- vector competence.

With reference to *Anopheles* and malaria, these factors can be detailed as follows.

Vector Distribution

Anopheles mosquitoes occur almost worldwide, with the exception of cold temperate areas, and there are over 400 known species. However, the four species of human pathogenic *Plasinodium* are transmitted significantly in nature only by some 30 species of *Anopheles*.

Some species have very local significance, others can be infected experimentally but have no natural role, and perhaps 75% of *Anopheles* are rather refractory (intolerant) to malaria. Of the vectorial species, a handful are important in stable malaria, whereas others only become involved in epidemic spread of unstable malaria.

Vectorial status can vary across the range of a taxon, an observation that may be due to the hidden presence of sibling species that lack morphological differentiation, but differ slightly in biology and have substantially different epidemiological significance, as in the *Anc gambiae* complex.

Vector abundance

Anopheles development is temperature dependent, as in *Aedes aegypti*, with one or two generations per year in areas where winter temperatures force hibernation of adult females, but with generation times of perhaps six weeks at 16°C and as short as 10 days in tropical conditions. Under optimal conditions, with batches of over 100 eggs laid every two to three days, and a development time of 10 days, hundred-fold increases in adult *Anopheles* can take place within 14 days.

As *Anopheles* larvae develop in water, rainfall significantly governs numbers. The dominant African malaria vector, *An. gambiae* (in the restricted sense), breeds in short-lived pools that require replenishment; increased rainfall obviously increases the number of *Anopheles* breeding sites.

On the other hand, rivers where other *Anopheles* species develop in lateral pools or stream-bed pools during a low- or no-flow period will be scoured out by excessive wet season rainfall. Adult survivorship is clearly related to elevated humidity and, for the female, availability of blood meals and a source of carbohydrate.

Vector survival rate

The duration of the adult life of the female infective *Anopheles* mosquito is of great significance in its effectiveness as a disease transmitter. As seen above, there is a minimum period between feeding on an infected host and the sporozoites becoming available for transmission.

If a mosquito survives less than eight or nine days after an initial infected blood meal, it does not live long enough to transmit malaria. The age of a mosquito can be calculated by finding the physiological age based on the ovarian 'relicts' left by each ovarian cycle. With knowledge of this physiological age and the duration of the sporogonic cycle, the proportion of each *Anopheles* vector population of sufficient age to be infective can be calculated.

In African *An. gamhiae*, three ovarian cycles are completed before infectivity is detected. Maximum transmission of P. *falciparum* to humans occurs in *An. gamhiae* that has completed four to six ovarian cycles. Despite these old individuals forming only 16% of the population, they constitute 73% of infective individuals.

Clearly adult longevity is important in epidemiological calculations. Raised humidity prolongs adult life and the most important cause of mortality is desiccation.

Anthropophily of the vector

To act as a vector, a female *Anopheles* mosquito must feed at least twice, once to gain the pathogenic *Plasmodium* and a second time to transmit the disease. *Host preference* is the term for the propensity of a vector mosquito to feed on a particular host species. In malaria, the host preference for humans (anthropophily) rather than alternative hosts (zoophily) is crucial to human malaria epidemiology.

As seen above, stable malaria is associated with vectors that are so strongly anthropophilic that they may never feed on other hosts. In these circumstances the probability of two consecutive meals being taken from a human is very high, and disease transmission can take place even when mosquito densities are low.

In contrast, if the vector has a low rate of anthropophily (a low probability of human feeding) the probability of consecutive blood meals being taken from humans is slight and human malarial transmission by this particular vector is correspondingly low. Transmission takes place only if the vector is present in very high numbers, as occurs in epidemics of unstable malaria.

Feeding interval

The frequency of feeding of the female *Anopheles* vector is important in disease transmission. This frequency can be estimated from mark-release-recapture data or from survey of the ovarian-age classes of indoor resting mosquitoes. It is commonly assumed that one blood meal is needed to mature each batch of eggs.

However, some mosquitoes may mature a first egg batch without a meal, whereas some anophelines require two meals. Already-infected vectors may experience difficulty in feeding to satiation at one meal, because of blockage of the feeding apparatus by parasites, and may probe many times. This, as well as disturbance during feeding by an irritated host, may lead to feeding on more than one host.

Vector competence

Even if an uninfected *Anopheles* feeds on an infectious host, either the mosquito may not acquire a viable infection, or the *Plasmodium* parasite may fail to replicate within the vector. Furthermore, the mosquito may not transmit the infection onwards at a subsequent meal.

Thus, there is scope for substantial variation, both within and between species, in the competence to act as a disease vector. Allowance must also be made for the density, infective condition and age profiles of the human population, as human immunity to malaria increases with age.

Vectorial capacity

The *vectorial capacity* of a given *Anopheles* vector to transmit malaria in a circumscribed human population can be modelled. This involves a relationship between the:

- number of female mosquitoes per person;
- daily biting rate on humans;
- daily mosquito survival rate;

- time between mosquito infection and sporozoite production in the salivary glands;
- vectoral competence;
- some factor expressing the human recovery rate from infection.

This vectorial capacity must be related to some estimate concerning the biology and prevalence of the parasite when modelling disease transmission, and in monitoring disease control programmes. In malarial studies, the infantile conversion *rate* (ICR), the rate at which young children develop antibodies to malaria, may be used.

In Nigeria (West Africa), the Garki Malaria Project found that over 60% of the variation in the ICR derived from the human-biting rate of the two dominant *Anopheles* species. Only 2.2% of the remaining variation is explained by all other components of vectorial capacity, casting some doubt on the value of any measurements other than human-biting rate.

This was particularly reinforced by the difficulties and biases involved in obtaining reasonably accurate estimates of many of the vectorial factors listed above.

Arboviruses

Viruses which multiply in an invertebrate vector and a vertebrate host are termed arboviruses. This definition excludes the mechanically transmitted viruses, such as the myxoma virus that causes myxomatosis in rabbits. There is no viral amplification in myxomatosis vectors such as the rabbit flea, *Spilopsyllus eunieuli*, and, in Australia, *Anopheles* and *Aedes* mosquitoes. Arboviruses are united by their ecologies, notably their ability to replicate in an arthropod.

It is an unnatural grouping rather than one based upon virus phylogeny, as arboviruses belong to several virus families. These include some Bunyaviridae, Reoviridae and Rhabdoviridae, and notably many Flaviviridae and Togaviridae.

Alphavirus (Togaviridae) includes exclusively mosquito-transmitted viruses, notably the agents of equine encephalitides. Members of *Flavivirus* (Flaviviridae), which includes yellow fever, dengue, Japanese encephalitis and other encephalitis viruses, are borne by mosquitoes or ticks.

Yellow fever exemplifies a flavivirus life cycle. We have seen something of the African sylvan (forest) cycle elsewhere in this chapter, and a similar cycle involving a primate host occurs in Central and South America (though with different mosquito vectors from Africa).

Although sylvan transmission to humans takes place, as we have seen in the Ugandan banana plantations, the disease makes its greatest fatal impact in urban epidemics. The urban and peridomestic insect vector on both continents is the female of the yellow fever mosquito, *Aedes (Stegomyia) aegypti.*

This mosquito acquires the virus by feeding on a human yellow fever sufferer in the early stages of disease, from 6h preclinical to 4 days later. The viral cycle in the mosquito is 12 days, after which the yellow fever virus reaches the mosquito saliva and remains there for the rest of the mosquito's life.

With every subsequent blood meal the female mosquito transmits virus-contaminated saliva. Infection results, and yellow fever symptoms develop in the host within a week. Urban disease cycles must originate from yellow fever-infected individuals moving from a rural to an urban environment. The disease may persist, leading to prolonged outbreaks in the urban environment.

Thousands of people have died in past epidemics. Some South American monkeys may die of yellow fever, whereas African ones are asymptomatic. Perhaps Neotropical monkeys have had less time to develop tolerance to the disease. The common vector, *Ac. aegypti, is* a mosquito that may have been transported, together with yellow fever, relatively recently from West Africa to South America, perhaps aboard slave ships. The range of *Ae. aegypti is* greater than that of the disease, being present, for example, in southern USA, where it is spreading, and in Australia and much of Asia.

However, only in India are there susceptible but as-yet-uninfected monkey hosts of the disease. Other Flaviviridae affecting humans and transmitted by mosquitoes cause dengue, dengue haemorrhagic fever, and a number of diseases called encephalitis (or encephalitides), because in clinical cases inflammation of the brain occurs.

Each encephalitis has a preferred mosquito host, frequently an *Aedes* (*Stegomyia*) species such as *Ac. aegypti* for dengue, and often a *Culex* species for encephalitis. The reservoir hosts for these diseases vary, and, at least for encephalitis, include wild birds, with amplification cycles in domestic mammals, for example pigs for Japanese encephalitis. Horses can be carriers of togaviruses, giving rise to the name for a subgroup of diseases termed equine encephalitides.

A range of flaviviruses are transmitted by ixodid ticks, including more viruses that cause encephalitis and haemorrhagic fevers of humans, but more significantly of domestic animals. Bunyaviruses may be tick-borne, notably haemorrhagic diseases of cattle and sheep, particularly when conditions encourage an explosion of tick numbers and disease alters from normal hosts (*enzootic*) to epidemic (*epizootic*) conditions. Mosquito-borne bunyaviruses include African Rift Valley fever, which can produce high mortality amongst African sheep and cattle during mass outbreaks.

Amongst the Reoviridae, bluetongue virus is the best known, most debilitating and most significant economically. The disease, which is virtually worldwide and has many different serotypes, causes tongue ulceration (hence 'bluetongue') and an often terminal fever in sheep.

Bluetongue is one of the few diseases in which biting midges of *Culicoides* (Ceratopogonidae) have been clearly established as the sole vectors of an arbovirus of major significance, although many arboviruses have been isolated from these biting flies.

Studies of the epidemiology of arboviruses have been complicated by the discovery that some viruses may persist between generations of vector. Thus, La Crosse virus, a bunyavirus that causes encephalitis in the USA, can pass from the adult mosquito through the egg (transovarial transmission) to the larva, which overwinters in a near frozen tree-hole.

The first emerging female of the spring generation is capable of transmitting La Crosse virus to chipmunk, squirrel or human with her first meal of the year. Transovarial transmission is suspected in other diseases and is substantiated in increasing numbers of cases, including Japanese encephalitis in *Culex tritaenorh ynchus* mosquitoes.

Rickettsias and Plague

Rickettsias are bacteria (Proteobacteria: Rickettsiales) associated with arthropods. The genus *Rickettsia* includes virulent pathogens of humans. *R. prowazekii*, which causes endemic typhus, has influenced world affairs as much as any politician, causing the deaths of millions of refugees and soldiers in times of social upheaval, such as the years of Napoleonic invasion of Russia and those following World War 1.

The vectors of typhus are lice, notably the body louse, *Pediculus humanus*. Infestation of lice indicates insanitary conditions and in western nations, after years of decline, is resurgent in homeless people. Although the head louse (*P. capitis*), pubic louse (*Pthirus pubis*) and some fleas experimentally can transmit *R. prowazekii*, they are of little or no epidemiological significance.

After the rickettsias of *R. prowazekii* have multiplied in the louse epithelium, they rupture the cells and are voided in the faeces. Because the louse dies, the rickettsias are demonstrated to be rather poorly adapted to the louse host. Human hosts are infected by scratching infected louse faeces (which remain infective for up to two months after deposition) into the itchy site where the louse has fed.

There is evidence of low level persistence of rickettsias in those who recover from typhus. These act as endemic reservoirs for resurgence of the disease, and there is some evidence that domestic and some few wild animals may be disease reservoirs.

Lice are also vectors of relapsing fever, a spirochaete disease that historically occurred together with epidemic typhus. Other rickettsial diseases include murine typhus, transmitted by flea vectors, scrub typhus through trombiculid mite vectors, and a series of spotted fevers, termed tick-borne typhus.

Many of these diseases have a wide range of natural hosts, with antibodies to the widespread American Rocky Mountain spotted fever (*Rickettsia rickettsii*) reported from 18 bird and 31 mammal species. Throughout the range of the disease from Virginia to Brazil, several species of ticks with broad host ranges are involved, with transmission through feeding activity alone.

Bartonellosis (Oroya fever) is a rickettsial infection transmitted by South American phlebotomine sand flies, with symptoms of exhaustion, anaemia and high fever, followed by wart-like eruptions on the skin. Plague is a rodent-flea-rodent disease caused by the bacterium *Yersinia pestis*, also known as *Y. pseudotuberculosis var. pestis*.

Plague-bearing fleas are principally *Xenopsylla cheopis*, which is ubiquitous between 35°N and 35°S, but also including X. brasilinesis in India, Africa and South America, and X. astia in southeast Asia. Although other species including *Ctenocephalides felis* and *C. canis* (cat and dog fleas) can transmit plague, they play a minor role at most.

The major vector fleas occur especially on peridomestic (house-dwelling) species of *Rattus*, such as the black rat (*R. rattus*) and brown rat (*R. norvegicus*). Reservoirs for plague in specific localities include the bandicoot, *Bandicota bengalensis*, in India, rock squirrels (*Spermopliilus* spp.) in western USA and related ground squirrels (*Citellus* sp.) in southeast Europe, and gerbils (*Meriones* spp.) in the Middle East and *Tatera spp. in* India and South Africa.

Between plague outbreaks, the bacterium circulates within some or all of these rodents without evident mortality, thus providing silent, long-term reservoirs of infection. When humans become involved in plague outbreaks (such as the pandemic called the '*Black Death*' that ravaged the northern hemisphere during the 14th century) mortality may approach *90%* in undernourished people and around 25% in previously well-fed, healthy people. The plague epidemiological cycle commences amongst rats, with fleas naturally transmitting *Y. pest* is between peridomestic rats.

In an outbreak of plague, when the preferred host brown rats die, some infected fleas move on to and eventually kill the secondary preference, black rats. As *X. cheopis* readily bites humans, infected fleas switch host again in the absence of the rats. Plague is a particular problem where rat (and flea) populations are high, as occurs in overcrowded, insanitary urban conditions.

Outbreak conditions require appropriate preceding conditions of mild temperatures and high humidity that encourage build-up of flea populations by increased larval survival and adult longevity. Thus natural variations in the intensity of plague epidemics relate to the previous years' climate.

Even during prolonged plague outbreaks, periods of fewer cases used to occur when hot, dry conditions prevented recruitment, because flea larvae are very susceptible to desiccation, and low humidity reduced adult survival in the subsequent year. During its infective lifetime the flea varies in its ability to transmit plague, according to internal physiological changes induced by *Y. pestis*.

If the flea takes an infected blood meal, *Y. pestis* increases in the proventriculus and midgut and may form an impassable plug. Further feeding involves a fruitless attempt by the pharyngeal pump to force more blood into the gut, with the result that a contaminated mixture of blood and bacteria is regurgitated.

However, the survival time of *Y. pestis* outside the flea (of no more than a few hours) suggests that mechanical transmission is unlikely. More likely, even if the proventricular blockage is alleviated, it fails to function properly as a one-way valve, and at every subsequent attempt at feeding, the flea regurgitates a contaminated mixture of blood and pathogen into the feeding wound of each successive host.

Protists other than Malaria

Some of the most important insect-borne pathogens are protists (protozoans), which affect a substantial proportion of the world's population, particularly in subtropical and tropical areas. Malaria has been covered in detail above and two important flagellate protists of medical significance remain.

Trypanosoma

Trypanosoma is a large genus of parasites of vertebrate blood that

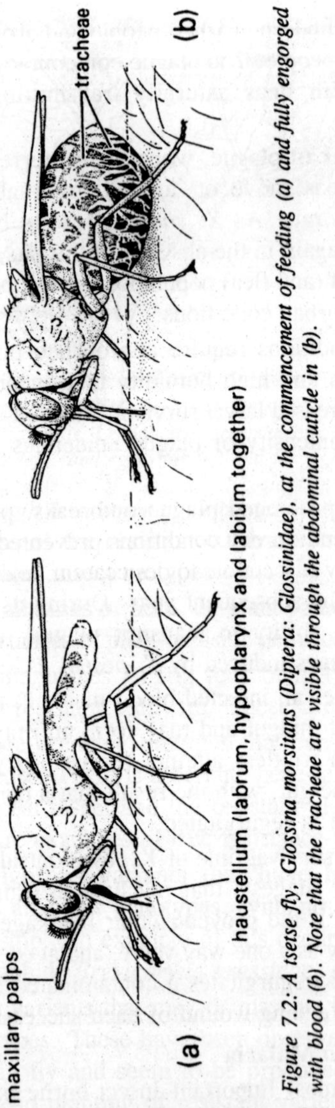

Figure 7.2: A tsetse fly, Glossina morsitans (Diptera: Glossinidae), at the commencement of feeding (a) and fully engorged with blood (b). Note that the tracheae are visible through the abdominal cuticle in (b).

are transmitted usually by bloodfeeding 'higher' flies. However, South American blood-feeding triatomine reduviid bugs ('kissing bugs'), notably *Rhodnius prolixus*, transmit trypanosomes that cause Chagas' disease, which affects 16-18 million people in the Neotropics, with upwards of 50000 deaths each year.

These diseases, termed *trypanosomiases*, include sleeping sicknesses transmitted to African humans and their cattle by tsetse flies (*Glossina* spp.). In this and other diseases, the development cycle of *Trypanosoma* species is complex. Morphological change occurs in the protist as it migrates from the tsetse-fly gut, around the posterior free end of the peritrophic membrane, then anteriorly to the salivary gland.

Transmission to human or cattle host is through injection of saliva. Within the vertebrate, symptoms depend upon the species of trypanosome: in humans, a vascular and lymphatic infection is followed by an invasion of the central nervous system that gives rise to 'sleeping' symptoms, followed by death.

Leishmania

A second group of flagellates belongs to the genus *Leishmania*, which includes parasites that cause internal visceral or disfiguring external ulcerating diseases of humans and dogs. The vectors are exclusively phlebotomines-small to minute sand flies that can evade mosquito netting and, in view of their usual very low biting rates, have impressive abilities to transmit disease.

Most cycles cause infections in wild animals such as desert and forest rodents, canines and hyraxes, with humans becoming involved as their homes expand into areas naturally home to these animal reservoirs.

Filariases

Two of the five main debilitating diseases transmitted by insects are caused by nematodes, namely filarial worms. The diseases are bancroftian and brugian filariases, commonly termed elephantiasis, and onchocerciasis (or river blindness). Other filariases cause minor ailments in humans, and *Dirofilaria immitis* (canine heartworm) is one of the few significant veterinary diseases caused by this type of parasite.

Bancroftian and Brugian Filariasis

Two worms, *Wuchereria banerofti* and *Brugia malayi*, are responsible for upwards of a hundred million cases of filariasis worldwide. The worms live in the lymphatic system, causing debilitation, and oedema, culminating in extreme swellings of lower limbs or genitals called elephantiasis.

Although the disease is less often seen in the extreme form, the number of sufferers is increasing as one major vector, the worldwide peri-domestic mosquito, *Culex quinquefasciatus*, increases. The cycle starts with uptake of small microfilariae with blood taken up by the vector mosquito. The microfilariae move from the mosquito gut through the haemocoel into the flight muscles, where they mature into an infective larva. The 1.5 mm long larvae migrate through the haemocoel into the mosquito head where, when the mosquito next feeds, they rupture the labella and invade the host through the puncture of the mosquito bite.

In the human host the larvae mature slowly over many months. The sexes are separate, and pairing of mature worms must take place before further microfilariae are produced. These microfilariae cannot mature without the mosquito phase. Cyclical (nocturnal periodic) movement of microfilariae into the peripheral circulatory system may make them more available to feeding mosquitoes.

Onchocerciasis

Onchocerciasis actually kills no-one directly but debilitates millions of people by scarring their eyes, which leads to blindness. The common name of 'river blindness' refers to the impact of the disease on people living alongside rivers in West Africa and South America, where the insect vectors, *Sinwlium* black flies (Diptera: Simuliidae), live in flowing waters.

The pathogen is a filarial worm, *Onchoccrea volvulus*, in which the female is up to 50 mm long and the male smaller at 20-30 mm. The adult filariae live in subcutaneous nodules and are relatively harmless. It is the microfilariae that cause the damage to the eye when they invade the tissues and die there.

The major black-fly vector has been shown to be one of the most extensive complexes of sibling species: *'Simulium da,nnosmn'* has more than 40 cytologically determined species known from West and East Africa. The larvae, which are common filter-feeders in flowing waters, are fairly readily controlled, but adults are strongly migratory and re-invasion of previously controlled rivers allows the disease to recur.

FORENSIC ENTOMOLOGY

As seen elsewhere in this book, some flies develop in living flesh, with two waves discernible: primary colonizers that cause initial myiases, with secondary myiases developing in pre-existing wounds. A third wave may follow before death. This ecological *succession* results from changes in the attractiveness of the substrate to different insects.

An analogous succession of insects can be seen in a corpse following death, with a somewhat similar course taken whether the corpse is a pig, rabbit or human. This rather predictable succession in corpses has been used for medico-legal purposes by *forensic entomologists* as a faunistic method to assess the elapsed time (and even prevailing environmental conditions) since death for human corpses. The generalized sequence of colonization is as follows. A fresh corpse is rapidly visited by a first wave of *Calliphora* (blowflies) and *Musca* (house flies), which oviposit or drop live larvae onto the cadaver.

Their subsequent development to mature larvae (which leave the corpse to pupariate away from the larval site) is temperature-dependent. Given knowledge of the particular species, the larval development times at different temperatures, and the ambient temperature at the corpse, an estimate of the age of a corpse may be made, perhaps accurate to within half a day if fresh, but with diminishing accuracy with increasing exposure.

As the corpse ages, larvae and adults of *Dermestes* (Coleoptera: Dermestidae) appear, followed by cheese-skipper larvae (Diptera: Piophilidae). As the body becomes drier, it is colonized by a sequence of other dipteran larvae, including those of Drosophilidae (fruitflies) and *Eristalis* (Diptera: Syrphidae: the rat-tailed maggot, a hover fly).

After some months, when the corpse is completely dry, more species of Dermestidae appear and several species of clothes moth (Lepidoptera: Tineidae) scavenge the desiccated remnants.

This simple outline is confounded by a number of factors including:

- geography, with different insect species (though perhaps relatives) present in different regions, especially if considered on a continental scale;
- variation in ambient temperatures, with direct sunlight and high temperatures speeding the succession (even leading to rapid mummification), and shelter and cold conditions retarding the process;
- variation in exposure of the corpse, with burial, even partial, slowing the process considerably, and with a very different entomological succession;
- variation in cause and site of death, with death by drowning and subsequent degree of exposure on the shore giving rise to a different necrophagous fauna from those infesting a terrestrial corpse, with differences between freshwater and marine stranding.

Despite these difficulties, in several cases entomological forensic evidence has proved crucial to criminal investigations.

8

COLOURATION AND MIMICRY

Although some humans eat insects, many '*western*' cultures are reluctant to use them as food; this aversion extends no further than humans. For very many organisms, insects provide a substantial food source, because they are nutritious, abundant, diverse and found everywhere.

Some animals, termed *insectivores*, rely almost exclusively on a diet of insects; omnivores may eat them opportunistically, and even many herbivores unavoidably consume insects. Insectivores may be vertebrates or invertebrates, including arthropods-insects certainly eat other insects.

Even plants lure, trap and digest insects; for example, pitcher plants (both New World Sarraceniaceae and Old World Nepenthaceae) digest arthropods, predominantly ants, in their fluid-filled pitchers, and the flypaper and Venus flytraps (Droseraceae) capture many flies.

Insects, however, actively or passively resist being eaten, by means of a variety of protective devicesthe *insect* defences-which are the subject of this chapter. Before continuing, some commonly used terms discussed elsewhere in this chapter should be reviewed.

A predator is an animal that kills and consumes a number of prey animals during its life. Animals that live at the expense of another animal but do not kill it are parasites, which may live internally (endoparasites) or externally (ectoparasites). Parasitoids are those that live at the expense of one animal that dies prematurely as a result.

The animal attacked by parasites or parasitoids is a host. All insects are potential prey or hosts to many kinds of predators (either vertebrate or invertebrate), parasitoids or, less often, parasites. Many defensive strategies exist, including use of specialized morphology (as shown for the extraordinary, ant-mimicking membracid bug *Hamma rectum* from tropical Africa in the vignette of this chapter), behaviour, noxious chemicals and responses of the immune system.

This chapter deals with aspects of defence that include death feigning, autotomy, crypsis (camouflage), chemical defences, aposematism (warning signals), mimicry and collective defensive strategies. These are directed against a wide range of vertebrates and invertebrates but, because much study has involved insects defending themselves against insectivorous birds, the role of these particular predators will be emphasized.

Immunological defence against microorganisms is discussed elsewhere in this chapter, and those used against parasitoids are considered elsewhere in this book. A useful framework for discussion of defence and predation can be based upon the time and energy inputs to the respective behaviours.

Thus hiding, escape by running or flight, and defence by staying and fighting involve increasing energy expenditure but diminishing costs in time expended. Many insects will change to another strategy if the previous defence fails: the scheme is not clear cut and it has elements of a continuum.

DEFENCE BY HIDING

Many insects use visual deception to reduce the probability of being found by natural enemies. A well-concealed cryptic insect that either resembles its general background or an inedible (neutral) object may be said to 'mimic' its surroundings.

In this book *mimicry* (in which an animal resembles another animal that is recognizable by natural enemies) is treated separately. However, crypsis and mimicry can be seen as similar in that both arise when an organism gains in fitness through developing a resemblance (to a neutral or animate object) evolved under selection.

In all cases it is assumed that such defensive adaptive resemblance is under selection by predators or parasitoids, but, although maintenance of selection for accuracy of resemblance has been demonstrated for some insects, the origin can only be surmised. Insect crypsis can take many forms. The insect may adopt *camouflage*, making it difficult to distinguish from the general background in which it lives, by:

- resembling a uniform coloured background, such as a green geometrid moth on a leaf;

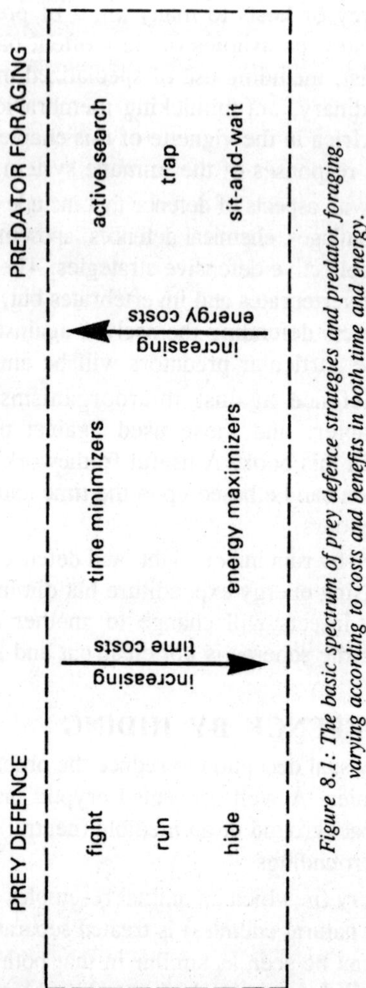

Figure 8.1: The basic spectrum of prey defence strategies and predator foraging, varying according to costs and benefits in both time and energy.

- resembling a patterned background, such as a mottled moth on tree bark;
- being countershaded-light below and dark above-as in some caterpillars and aquatic insects;
- having a pattern to disrupt the outline, as is seen in many moths that settle on leaf litter;
- having a bizarre shape to disrupt the silhouette, as demonstrated by some membracid leafhoppers.

In another form of crypsis, termed *masquerade* or *mimesis* to contrast

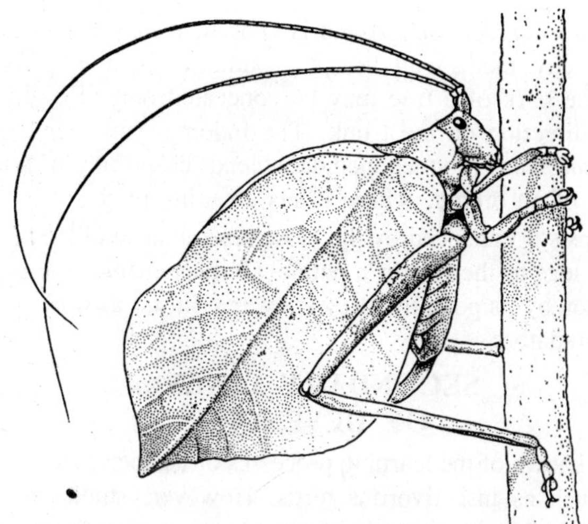

Figure 8.2: A leaf-mimicking katydid, Mimetica mortuifolia (Orthoptera: Tettigoniidae), in which the fore wing resembles a leaf even to the extent of leaf-like venation and spots resembling fungal mottling.

with the camouflage described above, the organism deludes a predator by resembling a object that is a particular specific feature of its environment, but is of no inherent interest to a predator.

This feature may be an inanimate object, such as the bird dropping resembled by young larvae of some butterflies such as *Papilio aegeus* (Papilionidae), or an animate but neutral object-for example, 'looper' caterpillars (the larvae of geometrid moths) resemble twigs, some membracid bugs imitate thorns arising from a stem, and many stick-insects look very much like sticks and may even move like a twig in the wind.

Many insects, notably amongst the lepidopterans and orthopteroids, look like leaves, even to the similarity in venation. These may appear to be dead or alive, mottled with fungus, or even partially eaten as if by a herbivore. Crypsis is a very common form of insect concealment, particularly in the tropics and amongst nocturnally active insects.

It has low energetic costs but relies on the insect being able to select the appropriate background. Experiments with two differently coloured morphs of *Mantis religiosa* (Mantidae), the European praying mantid, have shown that brown and green morphs placed against appropriate and inappropriate coloured backgrounds were fed upon in a highly selectively manner by birds: they removed all 'mismatched' morphs and found no camouflaged ones.

Even if the correct background is chosen, it may be necessary to orientate correctly: moths with disruptive outlines or with striped patterns resembling the bark of a tree may be concealed only if orientated in a particular direction on the trunk. The Indomalayan orchid mantid, *Hymenopus coronatus* (Hymenopodidae) blends beautifully with the pink flower spike of an orchid, where it sits awaiting prey.

The crypsis is enhanced by the close resemblance of the femora of the mantid's legs to the flower's petals. Crypsis enables the mantid to avoid detection by its potential prey (flower visitors) as well as conceal itself from predators.

SECONDARY LINES OF DEFENCE

Little is known of the learning processes of inexperienced vertebrate predators, such as insectivorous birds. However, studies of the gut contents of birds show that cryptic insects are not immune from predation. Once found for the first time (perhaps accidentally), birds subsequently seem able to detect cryptic prey via a 'search image' for some element(s) of the pattern.

Thus, having discovered that some twigs were caterpillars, American blue jays were observed to continue to peck at sticks in a search for food. Primates can identify stick-insects by one pair of unfolded legs alone, and will attack actual sticks to which phasmatid legs have been affixed experimentally. Clearly, subtle cues allow specialized predators to detect and eat cryptic insects.

Once the deception is discovered, the insect prey may have further defences available in reserve. In the energetically least demanding response, the initial crypsis may be exaggerated, as when a threatened masquerader falls to the ground and lies motionless. This behaviour is not restricted to cryptic insects: even visually obvious prey insects may feign death (*thanatosis*).

This behaviour, used by many beetles (particularly weevils), can be successful, as predators lose interest in apparently dead prey or may be unable to locate a motionless insect on the ground. Another secondary line of defence is to take flight and suddenly reveal a flash of conspicuous colour from the hind wings. Immediately on landing the wings are folded, the colour vanishes and the insect is cryptic once more.

This behaviour is common amongst certain orthopterans and underwing moths; the colour of the flash may be yellow, red, purple or, rarely, blue. A third type of behaviour of cryptic insects upon discovery by a predator is the production of a *startle* display. One of the commonest is to open the fore wings and reveal brightly coloured 'eyes' that are usually concealed on the hind wings.

Experiments using birds as predators have shown that the more perfect the eye (with increased contrasting rings to resemble true eyes) the better the deterrence. Not all eyes serve to startle: perhaps a rather poor imitation of an eye on a wing may direct pecks from a predatory bird to a non-vital part of the insect's anatomy. An extraordinary type of insect defence is the convergent appearance of part of the body to a feature of a vertebrate, albeit on a much smaller scale.

Thus the head of a species of fulgorid bug, commonly called the alligator bug, bears an uncanny resemblance to that of a caiman. The pupa of a particular lycaenid butterfly looks like a monkey head. Some tropical sphingid larvae assume a threat posture which, together with false eyespots that actually lie on the abdomen, give a snake-like impression. Similarly, the caterpillars of certain swallowtail butterflies bear a likeness to a snake's head.

These resemblances may deter predators (such as birds that search by 'peering about') by their startle effect, with the incorrect scale of the mimic being overlooked by the predator.

MECHANICAL DEFENCES

Morphological structures of predatory function, such as the modified mouthparts and spiny legs described in the previous chapter, also may be defensive, especially if a fight ensues. Cuticular horns and spines may deter a predator or have use in fighting, for example in defence of territory or in combating a rival. For ectoparasitic insects, which are vulnerable to the actions of the host, one line of defence is given by the body shape and sclerotization.

Fleas are laterally compressed, and biting lice dorsoventrally flattened -shapes that make these insects difficult to dislodge from hairs or feathers. Furthermore, many ectoparasites have resistant bodies, and the heavily sclerotized cuticle of certain beetles must act as a mechanical antipredator device. Many insects construct retreats that can deter a predator that fails to recognize the structure as containing anything edible or that is unwilling to eat inorganic material.

The cases of caddisfly larvae (Trichoptera), constructed of sand grains, stones or organic fragments, may have originated in response to the physical environment of flowing water, but certainly have a defensive role. Similarly, a portable case of vegetable material bound with silk is constructed by the terrestrial larvae of bagworms (Lepidoptera: Psychi-

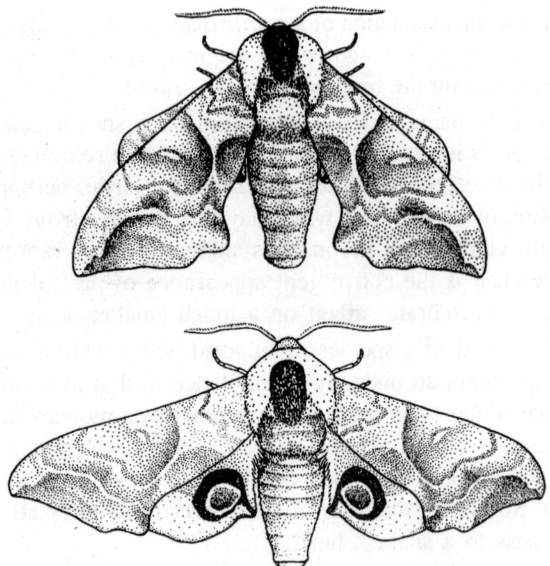

Figure 8.3: The eyed hawkmoth, Smerinthus ocellntus (Lepidoptera: Sphingidae). (a) The brownish fore wings cover the hind wings of a resting moth. (b) When the moth is disturbed, the black and blue eyespots on the hind wings are revealed.

dae). In both caddisflies and psychids, the case serves to protect during pupation. Artificial shields are constructed by some insects; for example, the larvae of certain lacewings cover themselves with the sucked-out carcasses of their insect prey or with lichens, and some larvae of chrysomelid beetles use their faeces for the same purpose.

These may not act as barriers to a determined predator, but will give a first mouthful of inedible material. The waxes and powders secreted by many homopterans (such as scale insects, woolly aphids, whiteflies and fulgorids) may function similarly, and also may entangle the mouthparts of a potential arthropod predator.

Body structures themselves, such as the scales of moths, caddisflies and thrips, can protect as they detach readily to allow the escape of a slightly denuded insect from the jaws of a predator, or from the sticky threads of spiders' webs or the glandular leaves of insectivorous plants such as the sundews.

A mechanical defence that seems at first to be maladaptive is autotomy, the shedding of limbs, as demonstrated by stick-insects (Phasmatodea) and perhaps craneflies (Diptera: Tipulidae). The upper part of the phasmatid leg has the trochanter and femur fused, with no muscles running across the joint. A special muscle breaks the leg at a weakened zone in response to a predator grasping the leg. Immature stick-insects and mantids can regenerate lost limbs at moulting, and even certain autotomized adults can induce an adult moult at which the limb can regenerate.

Secretions of insects can have a mechanical defensive role, acting as a glue or slime that ensnares predators or parasitoids. Certain cockroaches have a permanent slimy coat on the abdomen that confers protection. Lipid secretions from the cornicles (also called siphunculi) of aphids may gum up predator mouthparts or small parasitic wasps.

Termite soldiers have a variety of secretions available to them in the form of cephalic glandular products, including terpenes that dry on exposure to air to form a resin. In *Nasutitermes* (Termitidae) the secretion is ejected via the nozzle-like nasus (a pointed snout or rostrum) as a quick-drying fine thread that impairs the movements of a predator such as an ant.

This defence counters arthropod predators but is unlikely to deter vertebrates. Mechanical-acting chemicals are only a small selection of the total insect armoury that can be mobilized for chemical warfare.

CHEMICAL DEFENCES

Chemicals play vital roles in many aspects of insect behaviour. Chapter 4 dealt with the use of pheromones in many forms of communication, including alarm pheromones elicited by the presence of a predator. Similar chemicals, called allomones, play important roles in the defences of many insects, notably amongst many Heteroptera and Coleoptera.

The relationship between defensive chemicals and those used in communication may be very close, sometimes with the same chemical fulfilling both roles. Thus a noxious chemical that repels a predator can alert conspecific insects to the predator's presence and may act as a stimulus to action. In the energy-time dimensions shown in Figure elsewhere in this chapter, chemical defence lies towards the energetically expensive but time-efficient end of the spectrum.

Chemicallydefended insects tend to have high apparency to predators, i.e. they are usually non-cryptic, active, often relatively large, long-lived and frequently aggregated or social in behaviour. They often signal their distastefulness by *aposematism* -warning signalling usually involving bold colouring but sometimes including odour and even sound production.

Classification by Function of Defensive Chemicals

Amongst the diverse range of defensive chemicals produced by insects, two classes of compounds can be distinguished by their effects on a predator. Class I defensive chemicals are noxious because they irritate, hurt, poison or drug individual predators.

Class II chemicals are innocuous, being essentially antifeedant chemicals that merely stimulate the olfactory and gustatory receptors, or aposematic indicator odours. Many insects use mixtures of the two classes of chemicals and, furthermore, Class I chemicals in low concentrations may give Class II effects.

Contact by a predator with Class I compounds results in repulsion through, for example, emetic (sickening) properties or induction of pain, and if this unpleasant experience is accompanied by odurous Class 11 compounds, predators learn to associate the odour with the encounter.

This conditioning results in the predator learning to avoid the defended insect at a distance, without the dangers (to both predator and prey) of having to feel or taste it. Class I chemicals include both immediate-acting substances, which the predator experiences through handling the prey insect (which may survive the attack), and chemicals with delayed, often systemic, effects including vomiting or blistering.

In contrast to immediate-effect chemicals sited in particular organs and applied topically (externally), delayedeffect chemicals are distributed more generally within the insect's tissues and haemolymph, and are tolerated systemically. Whereas a predator evidently learns rapidly to associate immediate distastefulness with particular prey (especially if it is aposematic), it is unclear how a predator identifies the cause of nausea some time after the predator has killed and eaten the toxic culprit, and what benefits this action brings to the victim.

Experimental evidence from birds shows that at least these predators are able to associate a particular food item with a delayed effect, perhaps through taste when regurgitating the item. Too little is known of feeding in insects to understand if this applies similarly to predatory insects. Perhaps a delayed poison that fails to protect an individual from being eaten, evolved through the education of a predator by a sacrifice, thereby allowing differential survival of relatives.

The Chemical Nature of Defensive Compounds

Class I compounds are much more specific and effective against vertebrate than arthropod predators. For example, birds are more sensitive than arthropods to toxins such as cyanides, cardenolides and alkaloids. Cyanogenic glycosides are produced by zygaenid moths (Zygaenidae), *Leptocoris* bugs (Rhopalidae) and *Acraea* and *Heliconius* butterflies (Nymphalidae). Cardenolides are very widespread, occurring notably in monarch or wanderer butterflies (Nymphalidae), certain cerambycid and chrysomelid beetles, lygaeid bugs, pyrgomorphid grasshoppers and even an aphid.

A variety of alkaloids similarly are acquired convergently in many coleopterans and lepidopterans. Possession of Class I emetic or toxic chemicals is very often accompanied by aposematism, particularly colouration if directed against visual-hunting diurnal predators. However, visible aposematism is of no use at night, and the sounds emitted by nocturnal moths, such as certain Arctiidae when challenged by bats, may be aposematic, warning the predator of a distasteful meal.

Class II chemicals tend to be volatile and reactive organic compounds with low molecular weight, such as aromatic ketones, aldehydes, acids and terpenes. Examples include the stink gland products of Heteroptera and the many low molecular weight substances such as formic acid, emitted by ants.

Bitter-tasting but non-toxic compounds such as quinones are common Class II chemicals. Many defensive secretions are complex mixtures that can involve synergistic effects. Thus the carabid beetle *Heluomorphodes* emits a Class II compound, formic acid, that is mixed with n-nonyl acetate, which enhances skin penetration of the acid giving a Class I painful effect.

The role of these chemicals in aposematism, warning of the presence of Class I compounds, was considered above. In another role, these Class II chemicals may be used to deter predators such as ants that rely on chemical communication. For example, prey such as certain termites, when threatened by predatory ants, release mimetic ant alarm pheromones, thereby inducing inappropriate ant behaviours of panic and nest defence.

In another case, ant-nest inquilines, which might provide prey to their host ants, are unrecognized as potential food because they produce chemicals that appease ants. Class 11 compounds alone appear unable to deter many insectivorous birds. For example, blackbirds (Turdidae) will eat notodontid (Lepidoptera) caterpillars that secrete a 30% formic acid solution; many birds actually encourage ants to secrete formic acid into their plumage in an apparent attempt to remove ectoparasites (so-called 'anting').

Sources of Defensive Chemicals

Many defensive chemicals, notably those of phytophagous insects, are derived from the host plant upon which the larvae, and less commonly, the adults feed. Frequently a close association is observed between

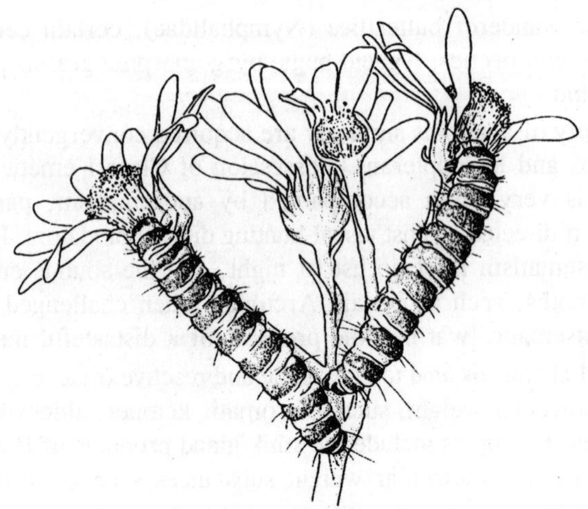

Figure 8.4: The distasteful and warningly coloured caterpillars of the cinnabar moth, Tyria jacobaeae (Lepidoptera: Arctiidae), on ragwort, Senecio jacobaeae.

restricted host-plant use (monophagy or oligophagy) and the possession of a chemical defence. An explanation may lie in a coevolutionary 'arms race' in which a plant develops toxins to deter phytophagous insects. A few phytophages overcome the defences and thereby become specialists able to detoxify or sequester the plant toxins.

These specialist herbivores can recognize their preferred host plants, develop on them and use the plant toxins (or metabolize them to closelyrelated compounds) for their own defence. Although some aposematic insects are closely associated with toxic food plants, certain insects can produce their own toxins.

For example, amongst the Coleoptera, blister beetles (Meloidae) synthesize cantharidin, jewel beetles (Buprestidae) make buprestin, and some leaf beetles (Chrysomelidae) can produce cardiac glycosides. The very toxic staphylinid *Paederus* synthesizes its own blistering agent, paederin. Many of these chemically-defended beetles are aposematic (e.g. Coccinellidae, Meloidae) and will *reflex-bleed* their haemolymph from the femoro-tibial leg joints if handled.

Experimentally it has been shown that certain insects that sequester cyanogenic compounds from plants can still synthesize similar compounds if transferred to toxin-free host plants. If this ability preceded the evolutionary transfer to the toxic host plant, the possession of appropriate bio-chemical pathways may have preadapted the insect to using them subsequently in defence.

Amongst the many unusual means of obtaining a defensive chemical, that used by *Photurus* fireflies (Lampyridae) is one of the most bizarre. Many fireflies synthesize deterrent bufadienolides, but *Photurus* females cannot do so. Instead they acquire their supplies by eating male *Photinus* fireflies, which are lured to their deaths by the *Photurus* females, which mimic the flashing sexual signal of the *Photinus* female.

Defensive chemicals, either manufactured by the insect or obtained by ingestion, are sometimes transmitted between conspecific individuals of the same or a different life stage. Eggs may be especially vulnerable to natural enemies because of their immobility and it is not surprising that some insects endow their eggs with chemical deterrents (Box 13.3). This phenomenon may be more widepread among insects than is currently recognized.

Organs of Chemical Defence

Endogenous defensive chemicals (those synthesized within the insect) are generally produced in specific glands and stored in a reservoir (Box 13.4). Release is through muscular pressure or by evaginating the organ, rather like turning the fingers of a glove inside-out. The Coleoptera have developed a wide range of glands, many eversible, that produce and deliver defensive chemicals.

Many Lepidoptera use urticating (itching) hairs and spines to inject venomous chemicals into a predator. In contrast to these endogenous chemicals, exogenous toxins, derived from external sources such as foods, are usually incorporated in the tissues or the haemolymph. This makes the complete prey unpalatable, but requires the predator to test at close range in order to learn, in contrast to the distant effects of many endogenous compounds.

However, the larvae of some swallowtail butterflies (Papilionidae) that feed upon distasteful food plants concentrate the toxins and secrete them into a thoracic pouch called an *osmeterium*, which is everted if the larvae are touched. The colour of the osmeterium is often aposematic, reinforcing the deterrent effect on a predator. Larval sawflies (Hymenoptera: Pergidae), colloquially called 'spitfires', store eucalypt oils, derived from the leaves that they eat, within a diverticulum of their foregut and ooze this strong-smelling, distasteful fluid from their mouths when disturbed.

DEFENCE BY MIMICRY

The theory of mimicry is an interpretation of the close resemblances of unrelated species and was an early application of the theory of

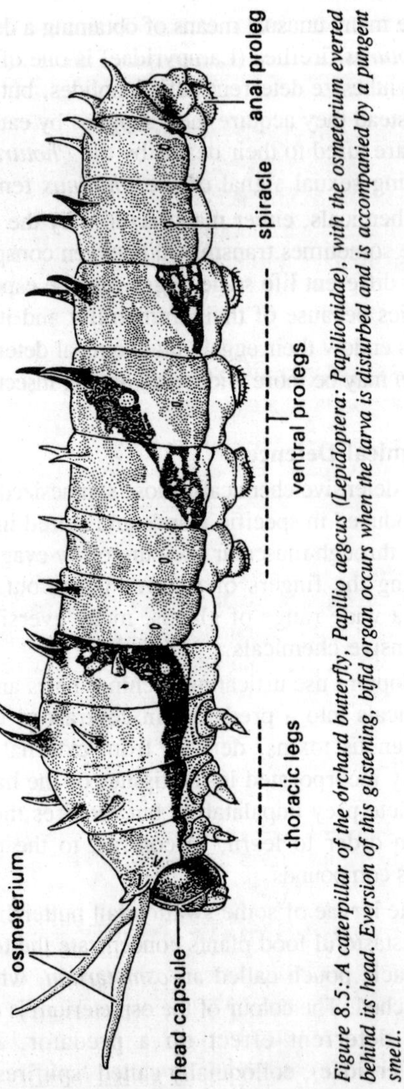

Figure 8.5: A caterpillar of the orchard butterfly, Papilio aegcus (Lepidoptera: Papilionidae), with the osmeterium everted behind its head. Eversion of this glistening, bifid organ occurs when the larva is disturbed and is accompanied by a pungent smell.

evolution. Bates, a naturalist studying in the Amazon in the mid-19th century, observed that many similar butterflies, all slow-flying and brightly marked, seemed to be immune from predators. Although many species were common and related to each other, some were rare, and belonged to fairly distantly related families.

Bates believed that the common species were chemically protected from attack, and this was advertised by their aposematism-high apparency (behavioural conspicuousness) through bright colour and slow flight. The rarer species, he thought, probably were not distasteful, but gained protection by their superficial resemblance to the protected ones.

On reading the views that Darwin had newly proposed in 1859, Bates realized that his own theory of mimicry involved evolution through natural selection. Poorly-protected species gain increased immunity from predation by differential survival of subtle variants that more resembled protected species in appearance, smell, taste, feel or sound.

The selective agent is the predator, which preferentially eats the inexact mimic. Since that time, mimicry has been interpreted in the light of evolutionary theory, and insects, particularly butterflies, have remained central to mimicry studies.

Understanding the defensive systems of mimicry (and crypsis) can be gained by recognizing three basic components: the *model*, the mimic and an *observer* that acts as a *selective agent*. These components are related to each other through signalling and receiving systems, of which the basic association is the warning signal given by the model (e.g. aposematic colour that warns of a sting or bad taste) perceived by the observer (e.g. a hungry predator).

The naive predator must learn of the association between aposematism and subsequent pain or distaste. When learnt, the predator subsequently will avoid the model. The model clearly benefits from this coevolved system, in which the predator can be seen to gain by not wasting time and energy chasing an inedible prey.

Once such a mutually beneficial system has evolved, it is open to

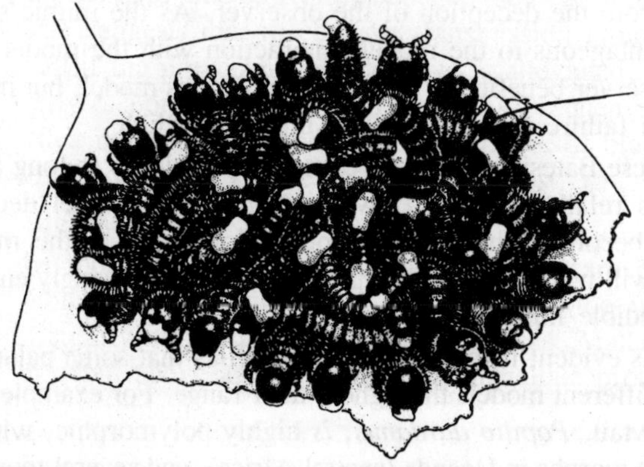

Figure 8.6: An aggregation of sawfly larvae (Hymenoptera: Pergidae: Perga) on a eucalypt leaf. When disturbed, the larvae bend their abdomens in teh air and exude droplets of sequestered eucalypt oil from their mouths.

manipulation by others. The third component is the mimic: an organism that parasitizes the signalling system through deluding the observer, for example by false warning colouration.

If this provokes a reaction from the observer similar to true aposematic colouration, the mimic is dismissed as unacceptable food. It is important to realize that the mimic need not be perfect, but only must elicit the appropriate avoidance response from the observer. Only a limited subset of the signals given by the model may be required.

For example, the black and yellow banding of venomous wasps is an aposematic colour pattern that is displayed by countless species from amongst many orders of insects. The exactness of the match, at least to our eyes, varies considerably.

This may be due to subtle differences between several different venomous models, or it may reflect the inability of the observer to discriminate: if yellow and black banding is all that is required to deter a predator, then there may be little or no selection to refine the mimicry more fully.

Batesian Mimicry

In these mimicry triangles, each component has a positive or negative effect on each of the others. In *Batesian mimicry* an aposematic inedible model has an edible mimic. The model suffers by the mimic's presence because the aposematic signal aimed at the observer is diluted as the chances increase that the observer will taste an edible individual and fail to learn the association between aposematism and distastefulness.

The mimic gains from the presence of the protected model and gains from the deception of the observer. As the mimic's presence is disadvantageous to the model, interaction with the model is negative. The observer benefits by avoiding the noxious model, but misses a meal through failure to recognize the mimic as edible.

These Batesian mimicry relationships hold up as long as the mimic remains relatively rare. However, should the model decline (or the mimic become abundant), the protection given to the mimic by the model will wane because the naive observer increasingly encounters and tastes edible mimics.

It is evident from studies of butterflies that some palatable mimics adopt different models throughout their range. For example, the mocker swallowtail, *Papilio dardanus*, *is* highly polymorphic, with up to five mimetic morphs in Uganda (central Africa), and several more throughout the wide range of the species. This polymorphism allows a larger total population of *P. dardanus* without prejudicing (diluting) the successful mimetic system, as each morph can remain rare relative to its Batesian model. In this case, and for many other mimetic polymorphisms, the males retain the basic colour pattern of the species and only amongst females in some populations does mimicry of such a variety of models occur.

The conservative male pattern may result from sexual selection to ensure recognition of the male by conspecific females of all morphs for mating, or by other conspecific males in territorial contests. An additional consideration concerns the effects of differential predation upon females (by virtue of slower flight and conspicuousness at host plants)—meaning females may gain more by mimicry relative to the differently behaving males.

Larvae of the Old World tropical butterfly *Danaus chrysippus* (Nymphalidae: Danainae) feed predominantly on milkweeds (Asclepiadaceae) from which they can sequester cardenolides, which are retained to the aposematic, chemically-protected adult stage. A variable but often high proportion of *D. chrysippus* develop on milkweeds lacking bitter and emetic chemicals, and the resulting adult is unprotected.

These are intraspecific Batesian *automimics* of their protected relatives. Where there is an unexpectedly high proportion of unprotected individuals, this situation may be maintained by parasitoids that preferentially parasitize noxious individuals, perhaps using cardenolides as kairomones in host finding.

The situation is further complicated, because unprotected adults, as in many *Danaus* species, actively seek out sources of pyrrolizidine alkaloids from plants to use in production of sex pheromones; these alkaloids also may render the adult less palatable.

Mullerian Mimicry

In a contrasting set of relationships, called *Mullerian mimicry*, the model(s) and mimic(s) are all distasteful and warningly-coloured and all benefit from coexistence, as observers learn from tasting any individual. Unlike Batesian mimicry, in which the system is predicted to fail as the mimic becomes relatively more abundant, Mullerian mimicry systems gain through enhanced predator learning when the density of component distasteful species increases.

'Mimicry rings' of species may develop, in which organisms from distant families, and even orders, acquire similar aposematic patterns, although the source of protection varies greatly. In the species involved, the warning signal of the co-models differs markedly from that of their close relatives, which are non-mimetic.

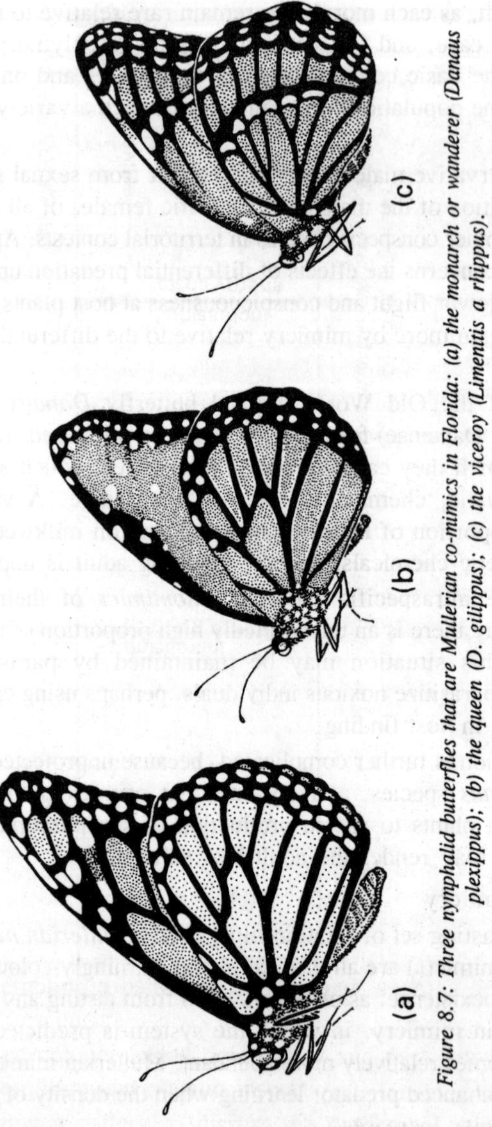

Figure 8.7: Three nymphalid butterflies that are Mullerian co-mimics in Florida: (a) the monarch or wanderer (Danaus plexippus); (b) the queen (D. gilippus); (c) the viceroy (Limenitis a rhippus).

Interpretation of mimicry may be difficult, particularly in distinguishing protected from unprotected mimetic components. For example, a century after discovery of one of the seemingly strongest examples of Batesian mimicry, the classical interpretation seems flawed.

The system involves two North American danaine butterflies, *Dana us plexippus*, the monarch or wanderer, and *D. gilippus*, the queen, which are chemically-defended models each of which is mimicked by a morph of the nymphaline viceroy butterfly (*Limenitis archippus*).

Historically, larval food plants and taxonomic affiliation have suggested that viceroys were palatable, and therefore Batesian mimics. This interpretation was overturned by experiments in which isolated butterfly abdomens were fed to natural predators (wild-caught redwing blackbirds).

The possibility that feeding by birds might be affected by previous exposure to aposematism was excluded by removal of the aposematically patterned butterfly wings. Viceroys were found to be at least as unpalatable as monarchs, with queens least unpalatable. At least in the Florida populations and with this particular predator, the system is interpreted now as Mullerian, either with the viceroy as model, or with the viceroy and monarch acting as comodels, and the queen being a less well chemicallyprotected member that benefits through the asymmetry of its palatability relative to the others.

Few such appropriate experiments to assess palatability, using natural predators and avoiding problems of previous learning by the predator, have been reported and clearly more are required. If all members of a Mullerian mimicry complex are aposematic and distasteful, then it can be argued that an observer (predator) is not deceived by any member- and this can be seen more as shared aposematism than mimicry.

More likely, as seen above, distastefulness is unevenly distributed, in which case some specialist observers may find the least well-defended part of the complex to be edible. Such ideas suggest that true Mullerian mimicry may be rare and/or dynamic and represents one end of a spectrum of interactions.

Mimicry as a Continuum

The strict differentiation of defensive mimicry into two forms—Mullerian and Batesian—can be questioned, although each gives a different interpretation of the ecology and evolution of the components, and makes dissimilar predictions concerning life histories of the participants. For example, mimicry theory predicts that in aposematic species there should be:

- limited numbers of co-modelled aposematic patterns, reducing the number that a predator has to learn;
- behavioural modifications to 'expose' the pattern to potential predators, such as conspicuous display rather than crypsis, and diurnal rather than nocturnal activity;

- long postreproductive life, with prominent exposure to encourage the naive predator to learn of the distastefulness on a postreproductive individual.

All of these predictions appear to be true in some or most systems studied. Furthermore, theoretically there should be variation in polymorphism with selection enforcing aposematic uniformity (monomorphism) in Mullerian cases, but encouraging divergence (mimetic polymorphism) in Batesian cases.

Sex-limited (female-only) mimicry and divergence of the model's pattern away from that of the mimic (evolutionary escape) are also predicted in Batesian mimicry Although these predictions are met in some mimetic species, there are exceptions to all of them. Polymorphism certainly occurs in Batesian mimetic swallowtails (Papilionidae), but is much rarer elsewhere, even within other butterflies; furthermore, there are polymorphic Mullerian mimics such as the viceroy.

It is suggested now that some relatively undefended mimics may be fairly abundant relative to the distasteful model and need not have attained abundance via polymorphism. It is argued that this can arise and be maintained if the major predator is a generalist that requires only to be deterred relative to other more palatable species.

A complex range of mimetic relationships are based on mimicry of lycid beetles, which are often aposernatically odoriferous and warningly coloured. The black and orange Australian lycid *Metriorrhynchus rhipidius is* protected chemically by odorous methoxyalkylpyrazine, and by bitter principles and acetylene antifeedants.

Species of *Metriorrhynchus* provide models for mimetic beetles from at least six distantly-related families (Buprestidae, Pythidae, Meloidae, Oedemeridae, Cerambycidae and Belidae) and at least one moth. All these mimics are convergent in colour; some have nearly identical alkylpyrazines and distasteful chemicals; others share the alkylpyrazines but have different distasteful chemicals; and some have the odorous chemical but appear to lack any distasteful chemicals.

These aposematically-coloured insects form a mimetic series. The oedemerids are clearly Mullerian mimics, modelled precisely on the local *Metriorrhynchus* species and differing only in using cantharidin as an antifeedant. The cerambycid mimics use different repellent odours, whereas the buprestids lack warning odour but are chemically protected by buprestins. Finally, pythids and belids are Batesian mimics, apparently lacking any chemical defences.

After careful chemical examination, what appears to be a model with many Batesian mimics, or perhaps a Mullerian ring, is revealed to demonstrate a complete range between the extremes of Mullerian and Batesian mimicry.

Although the extremes of the two prominent mimicry systems are well studied, and in some texts appear to be the only systems described, they are but two of the possible permutations involving the interactions of model, mimic and observer. Further complications ensue if model and mimic are the same species, as in automimicry, or in cases where there is sexual dimorphism and polymorphism.

All mimicry systems are complex, interactive and never static, because population sizes change and relative abundances of mimetic species fluctuate so that density-dependent factors play an important role. Furthermore, the defence offered by shared aposematic colouring, and even shared distastefulness, can be circumvented by specialized predators able to learn and to cue on the warning, overcome the defences and eat selected species in the mimicry complex.

Evidently, consideration of mimicry theory demands recognition of the role of predators as flexible, learning, discriminatory, coevolving and coexisting agents in the system.

COLLECTIVE DEFENCES IN GREGARIOUS AND SOCIAL INSECTS

Chemically-defended, aposematic insects are often clustered rather than uniformly distributed through a suitable habitat. Thus unpalatable butterflies may live in conspicuous aggregations as larvae and as adults; the winter congregation of migratory adult monarch butterflies in California and Mexico is an example.

Many chemicallydefended hemipterans aggregate on individual host plants, and some vespid wasps congregate conspicuously on the outside of their nests. Orderly clusters occur in the phytophagous larvae of sawflies and some chrysomelid beetles that form defended circles (cycloalexy). Some larvae lie within the circle and others form an outer ring with either their heads or abdomens directed outwards, depending upon which end secretes the noxious compounds.

These groups often make synchronized displays of head and/or abdomen bobbing, which increase the apparency of the group. Formation of such clusters is sometimes encouraged by the production of aggregation pheromones by early arriving individuals, or may result from the young failing to disperse after hatching from one or several egg batches. Benefits to the individual from the clustering of chemicallydefended insects may relate to the dynamics of predator training.

However, these also may involve kin selection in subsocial insects, in which aggregations comprise relatives that benefit at the expense of an individual 'sacrificed' to educate a predator. This latter scenario for the origin and maintenance of group defence certainly seems to apply to the eusocial Hymenoptera (ants, bees and wasps), elsewhere in this chapter.

In these insects, and in the termites (Isoptera), defensive tasks are undertaken usually by morphologically modified individuals called soldiers. In all social insects, excepting the army ants, the focus for defensive action is the nest, and the major role of the soldier caste is to protect the nest and its inhabitants.

Nest architecture and location is often a first line of defence, with many nests buried underground, or hidden within trees, with a few, easily defendable entrances. Exposed nests, such as those of savanna-zone termites, often have hard, impregnable walls.

Termite soldiers can be male or female, have weak sight or be blind, and have enlarged heads (sometimes exceeding the rest of the body length). Soldiers may have well-developed jaws, or be *nasute*, with small jaws but an elongate 'nasus' or rostrum.

They may protect the colony by biting, by chemical means or, as in *Cryptoterines*, by phragmosis-the blocking of access to the nest with their modified heads. Amongst the most serious adversaries of termites are ants, and complex warfare takes place between the two.

Termites soldiers have developed an enormous battery of chemicals, many produced in highly elaborated frontal and salivary glands. For example, in *Pseudacanthotermes spiniger* the salivary glands fill nine-tenths of the abdomen, and *Globitermes sulphurous* soldiers are filled to bursting with sticky yellow fluid used to entangle the predator -and the termite, usually fatally.

This suicidal phenomenon is seen also in some *Camponotus* ants, which use hydrostatic pressure in the gaster to burst the abdomen and release sticky fluid from the huge salivary glands. Some of the specialized defensive activities used by termites have developed convergently amongst ants.

Thus the soldiers of some formicines, notably the subgenus *Colobopsis*, and several myrmecines show phragmosis, with modifications of the head to allow the blocking of nest entrances. Nest entrances are made by minor workers and are of such a size that the head of a single major worker (soldier) can seal it; in others such as the myrmecine *Zacryptocerus*, the entrances are larger, and a formation of guarding

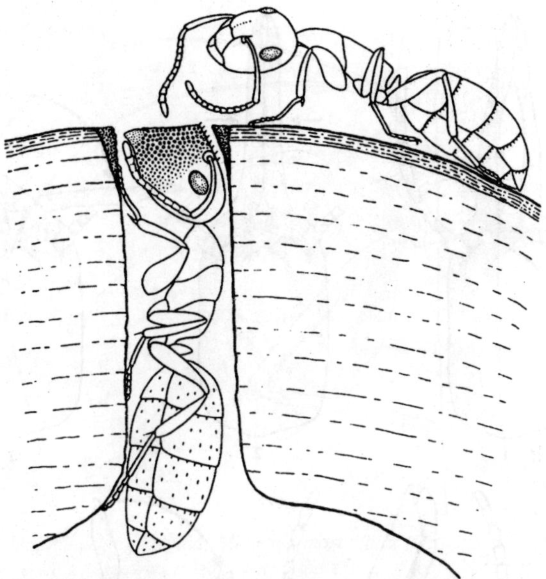

Figure 8.8: Nest guarding by the European ant Camponotus (Colobopsis) truncatus: a minor worker approaching a soldier that is blocking a nest entrance with her plugshaped head.

blockers may be required to act as 'gatekeepers'. A further defensive strategy of these myrmecines is for the head to be covered with a crust of secreted filamentous material, such that the head is camouflaged when it blocks a nest entrance on a lichen-covered twig.

Most soldiers use their strongly developed mandibles in colony defence as a means of injuring an attacker. A novel defence in termites involves elongate mandibles that snap against one another, as we might snap our fingers. A violent movement is produced as the pent-up elastic energy is released from the tightly appressed mandibles.

In *Capritermes* and *Homallotermes*, the mandibles are asymmetric and the released pressure results in the violent movement of only the right mandible; the bent left one, which provides the elastic tension, remains immobile. These soldiers can only strike to their left!

The advantage of this defence is that a powerful blow can be delivered in a confined tunnel, in which there is inadequate space to open the mandibles wide enough to obtain conventional leverage on an opponent. Major differences between termite defences and those of social hymenopterans are the restriction of the defensive caste to females in Hymenoptera, and the frequent use of venom injected through an ovipositor modified as a sting.

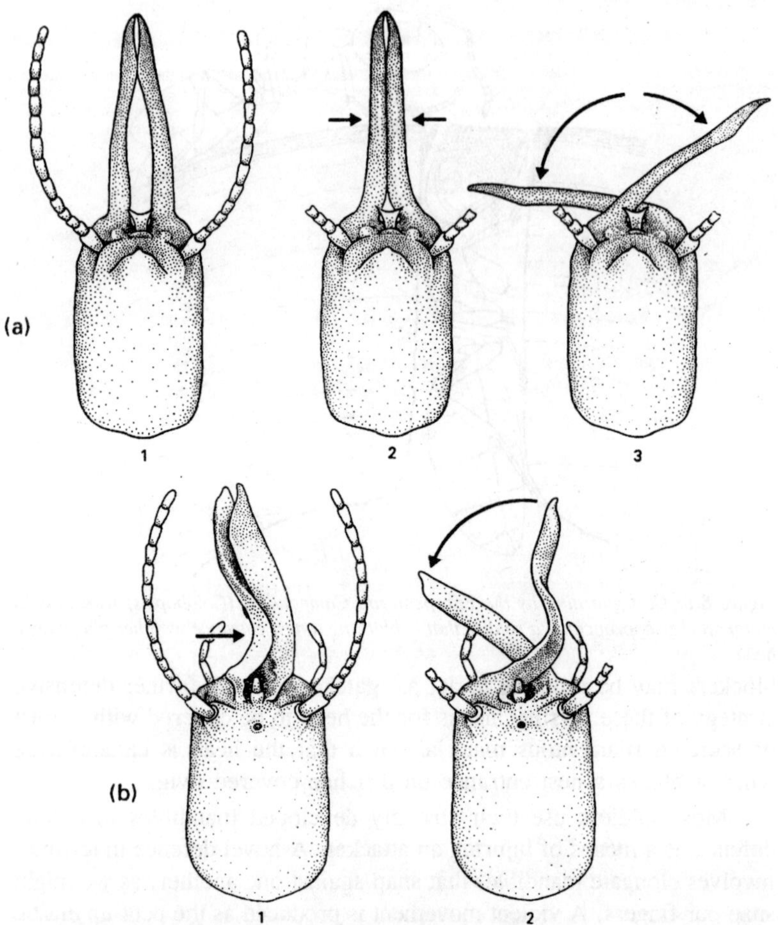

Figure 8.9: Defence by mandible snapping in termite soldiers. (a) A symmetric snapping soldier of Termes in which the long thin mandibles are pressed hard together (1) and thus bent inwards (2) before they slide violently across one another (3). (b) An asymmetric snapping soldier of Hoinellotermes in which force is generated in the flexible left mandible by being pushed against the right one (1) until the right mandible slips under the left one to strike a violent blow (2).

Whereas parasitic hymenopterans use this weapon to immobilize prey, in social aculeate hymenopterans it is a vital weapon in defence against predators. Many subsocial and all social hymenopterans co-operate to sting an intruder *en masse*, thereby escalating the effects of an individual attack and deterring even large vertebrates.

The sting is injected into a predator through a lever (the furcula) acting on a fulcral arm, though fusion of the furcula to the sting base in some ants leads to a less manoeuvrable sting. Venoms include a wide variety of products, many of which are polypeptides. Biogenic amines such as any or all of histamine, dopamine, adrenaline and noradrenaline (and serotonin in wasps), may be accompanied by acetylcholine, and several important enzymes including phospholipases and hyaluronidases (which are highly allergenic).

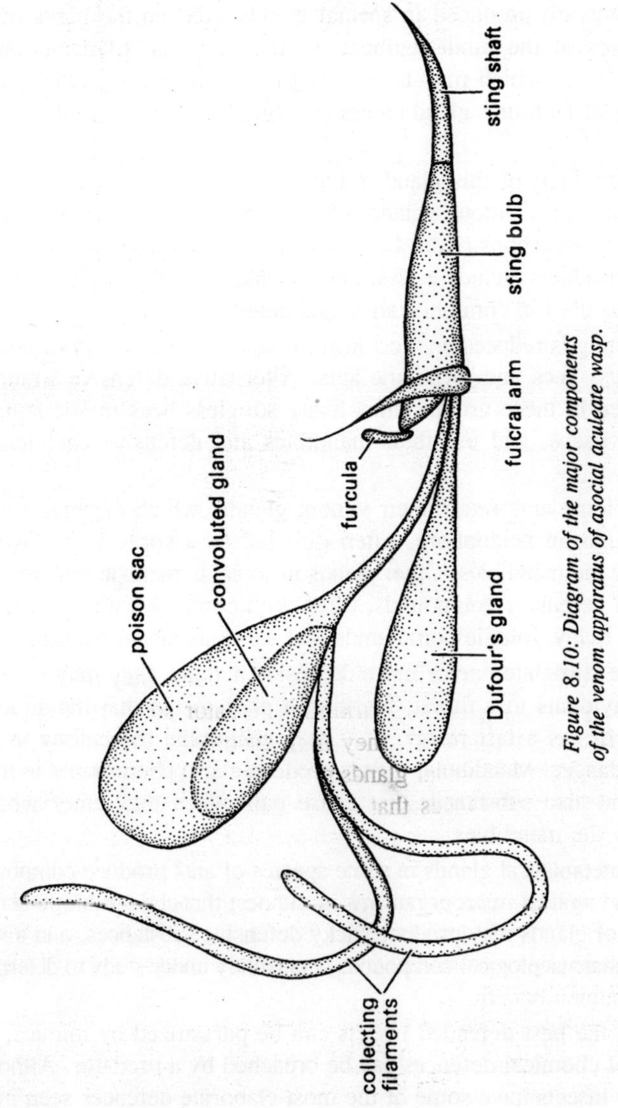

Figure 8.10: Diagram of the major components of the venom apparatus of asocial aculeate wasp.

Wasp venoms have a number of vasopeptides-pharmacologically active kinins that induce vasodilation and relax smooth muscle in vertebrates. Nonformicine ant venoms comprise either similar materials of proteinaceous origin or a pharmacopoeia of alkaloids, or complex mixtures of both types of component. In contrast, formicine venoms are dominated by formic acid.

Venoms are produced in special glands sited on the bases of the inner valves of the ninth segment, comprising free filaments and a reservoir store, which may be simple or contain a convoluted gland. The outlet of Dufour's gland enters the sting base ventral to the venom duct.

The products of this gland in eusocial bees and wasps are poorly known, but in ants Dufour's gland is the site of synthesis of an astonishing array of hydrocarbons (over 40 in one species of *Camponotus*). These exocrine products include esters, ketones and alcohols, and many other compounds used in communication and defence.

The sting is reduced and lost in some social hymenopterans, notably the stingless bees and formicine ants. Alternative defensive strategies have arisen in these groups; thus many stingless bees mimic stinging bees and wasps, and use their mandibles and defensive chemicals if attacked.

Formicine ants retain their venom glands, which disperse formic acid through an acidophore, often directed as a spray into a wound created by the mandibles. Other glands in social hymenopterans produce additional defensive compounds, often with communication roles, and including many volatile compounds that serve as alarm pheromones.

These stimulate one or more defensive actions: they may summon more individuals to a threat, marking a predator so that the attack is targeted, or, as a last resort, they may encourage the colony to flee from the danger. Mandibular glands produce alarm pheromones in many insects and also substances that cause pain when they enter wounds caused by the mandibles.

The metapleural glands in some species of ants produce compounds that defend against microorganisms in the nest through antibiotic action. Both sets of glands may produce sticky defensive substances, and a wide range of pharmacological compounds is currently under study to determine possible human benefit.

Even the best-defended insects can be parasitized by mimics, and the best of chemical defences can be breached by a predator. Although the social insects have some of the most elaborate defences seen in the

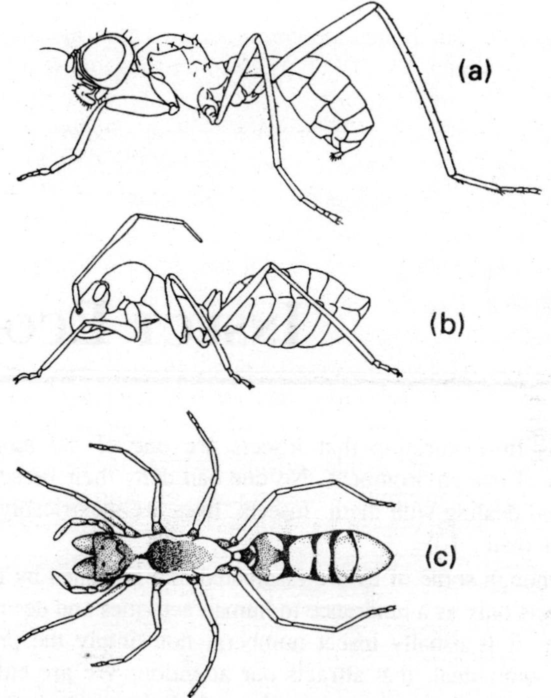

Figure 8.11: Three ant mimics: (a) a fly (Diptera: Micropezidae: Badisis); (b) a bug (Hemiptera: Miridae: Phylinae); (c) a spider (Araneae: Clubionidae: Sphecotypus).

Insecta, they remain vulnerable. For example, many insects model themselves on social insects, with representatives of many orders converging morphologically on ants, particularly with regard to the waist constriction and wing loss, and even kinked antennae.

Some of the most extraordinary ant-mimicking insects are tropical African bugs of the genus *Hamma* (Membracidae), as exemplified by *H. rectum* depicted in both side and dorsal view in the vignette for this chapter.

The aposematic yellow-and-black patterns of vespid wasps and apid bees provide models for hundreds of mimics throughout the world. Not only are these communication systems of social insects parasitized, but so are their nests, which provide many parasites and inquilines with a hospitable place for their development.

Defence must be seen as a continuing coevolutionary process, analogous to an 'arms race', in which new defences originate or are modified and then are selectively breached, stimulating improved defences.

9

INSECT ECOLOGY

There is little question that insects are one of the most prevalent features of our environment. No one can deny their presence; no one can avoid dealing with them. Insects' lives are inextricably intertwined with our own.

Although some of us are fascinated and intrigued by them, others see insects only as a hindrance to human activities and desires. In either instance, it is usually insect numbers, not simply the presence of a solitary individual, that attracts our attention. We are either appalled or in awe at seeing insects virtually explode in numbers as the growing season develops. We question why they can be so abundant in one area and not in another or why they are numerous one year and not the next. To understand insect numbers is to understand their inherited traits and the particular environment of their life cycles.

The interaction between inherited traits and environment results in given numbers of individuals, and because these aspects are constantly changing, insect numbers also are dynamic. A major objective of insect ecology is to explain the dynamics of insect numbers in time and space. For this explanation, insect ecology relies on an understanding of physiology and behavior of insects as affected by their environment.

The focal point of study can be the individual, collections of individuals of the same species, or interactions between or among species. In addition to the dynamics of insect numbers, environment also affects timing of biological events in insects (phenology) and the diversity of species in an area. These additional topics addressed by insect ecology are no less important than the question of abundance.

By providing explanations of how environment (including the

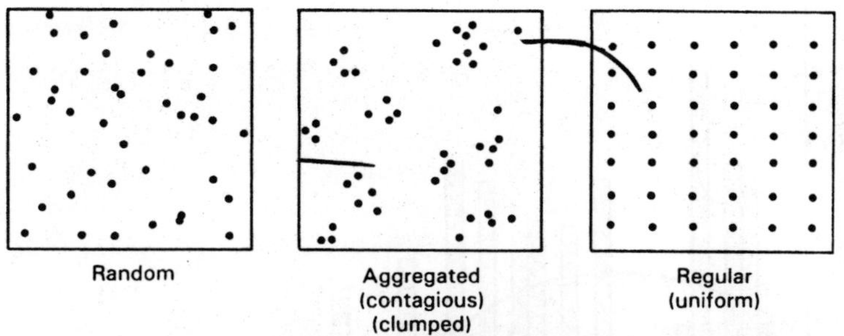

Figure 9.1: Diagrams showing types of spatial dispersions among insects and other organisms.

agricultural environment) affects abundance, timing, and diversity of insects, ecology forms the very basis of pest management. Because pest problems usually develop from too many insects occurring at inappropriate times, dealing with them necessitates a knowledge of ecological processes.

With this knowledge, the occurrence and severity of potential problems can be predicted and appropriate management activities formulated. In this chapter, we consider the ecological role of pests in agricultural environments and survey the major determinants of insect abundance. Then we learn how environmental factors affect timing of seasonal events and function to regulate insect numbers.

THE ECOLOGICAL ROLE OF INSECT PESTS

The Idea of Populations

Insect populations are groups of individuals set in a frame limited in time and space. Often the boundaries of time and space for a population are somewhat vague and are fixed for convenience by the ecologist. Therefore, it is not uncommon (or inappropriate) to speak of, for example, the black cutworm population in Boone County, Iowa, in 1995.

The aspects of time and space are of utmost importance in studying the population and need to be defined for any consideration of population dynamics. Every insect population has unique characteristics; to understand population dynamics, it is necessary to define and quantify these. The characteristics of a population are group attributes not possessed by single individuals in the group.

These population attributes include: density, dispersion, natality, mortality, age distribution, and growth form. Density and dispersion are complementary attributes. *Density* is the number of individuals per some unit of measure (for example, number of redlegged grasshoppers

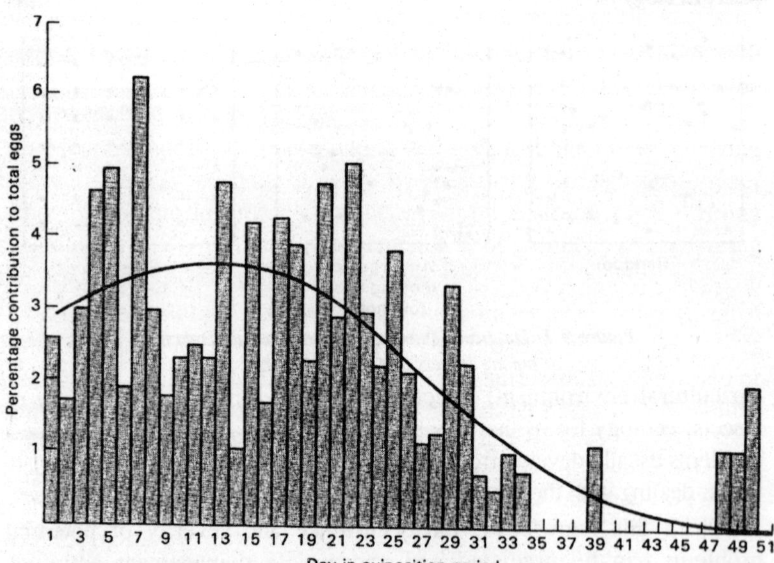

Figure 9.2: Pattern of egg laying (natality) found in the green cloverworm, Playthypena scabra. The curve in the graph is a fit to the data points, represented by bars. Such natality patterns are typical of many insect populations.

per square meter), whereas *dispersion* is the spatial arrangement of those numbers.

Most insect populations are said to have clumped or aggregated dispersions, although in relatively uniform habitats (for example, grain fields with even terrain) dispersion may seem random. Randomness means that an insect is as likely to be found in one place as another.

Natality and mortality are rate processes. *Natality* is birth rate, often measured as the total number of eggs or eggs per female laid per unit time. *Mortality* is the death rate, or numbers dying per unit of time. These processes act in concert, natality adding numbers and mortality subtracting them, in determining population density and dispersion.

Age distribution is the particular proportions of individuals in different age groups at a given time. For instance, in early season the age distribution of an insect population may be adults, 75 percent; eggs, 20 percent; first-stage larvae, 5 percent. This distribution would change to mostly eggs and larvae as time progressed, and so on.

Growth form of a population refers to the particular shape of the density curves during a season or over a longer time period. Growth curves of many insect populations in temperate climates are J-shaped;

the population grows exponentially, then falls off abruptly with the advent of winter. The particular shape of growth curves determines in part the amount of overlap between numbers of different life stages within a generation and between generations.

Ecosystems and Agroecosystems

When studying insect populations in a locale, one very quickly discovers that no population exists as an isolated entity. Individuals not only interact among themselves for mating, feeding, and other purposes, but also interact with individuals of other animal and plant populations.

At the very least, individuals in a population feed upon and, in turn, are fed upon by individuals of other populations. This interacting "web" of populations in an area is called a *community*. The interaction of populations in a community is strongly influenced by the physical

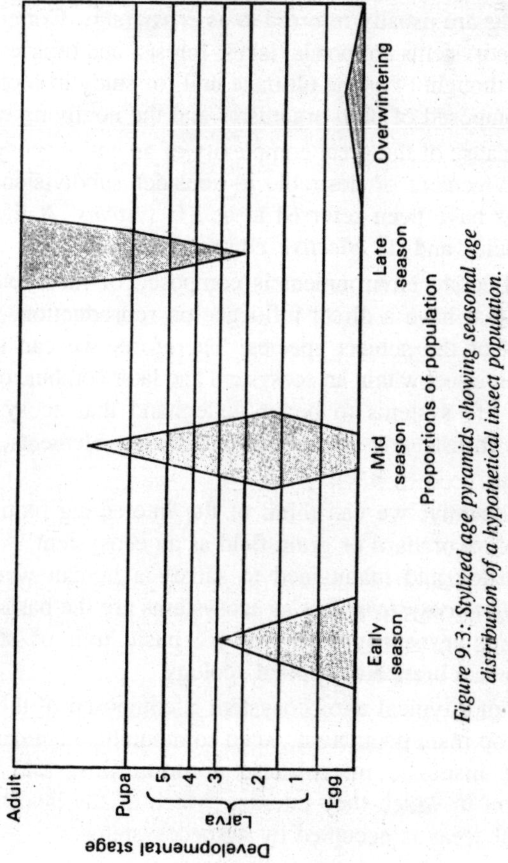

Figure 9.3: Stylized age pyramids showing seasonal age distribution of a hypothetical insect population.

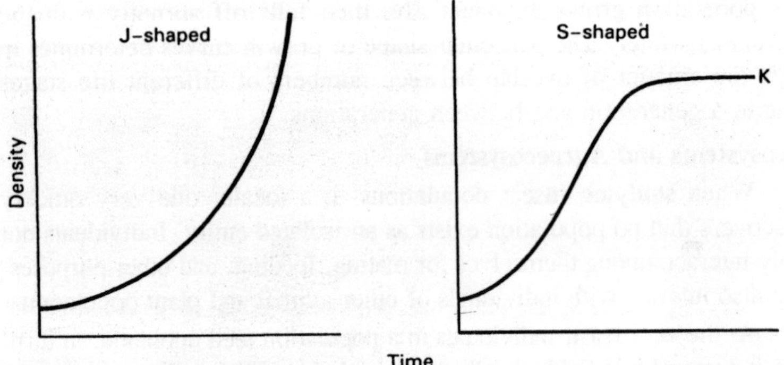

Figure 9.4: Simplified growth curves, J-shaped and S-shaped, found in animal populations. K in the S-shaped curve is the upper asymptote, or limit of growth.

environment. These assemblages of elements, communities, and physical environments are usually referred to as *ecosystems*. Common examples of natural ecosystems are ponds, lakes, forests, and prairies. Ecosystems are usually thought of as the ultimate unit for study in ecology, because they are composed of both organisms and the nonliving environment.

But because of the great complexity of an entire ecosystem, it may be more convenient or desirable to consider subdivisions of it. Such subdivisions have been referred to as *life systems*. A life system is a subject species and its *effective environment*.

The effective environment is composed of those elements in an ecosystem that have a direct influence on reproduction, survival, and movements of the subject species. Therefore, we can study the life system of an insect within an ecosystem and later combine our knowledge of several life systems to better understand that ecosystem. Just as ponds and forests are systems of interacting elements, so are crop areas.

Consequently, we can think of the interacting biotic and abiotic elements of an orchard or grain field as an ecosystem. Any ecosystem largely created and maintained to satisfy a human want or need is called an *agroecosystem*. Just as ecosystems are the basic unit of study for ecology, agroecosystems are the basic unit of study for pest management, a branch of applied ecology.

Much of a typical agroecosystem is composed of the more or less uniform crop-plant population, weed communities, animal communities (including insects), microbiotic communities, and the physical environment in which they interact. Much of the land mass in major agricultural areas is occupied by agroecosystems.

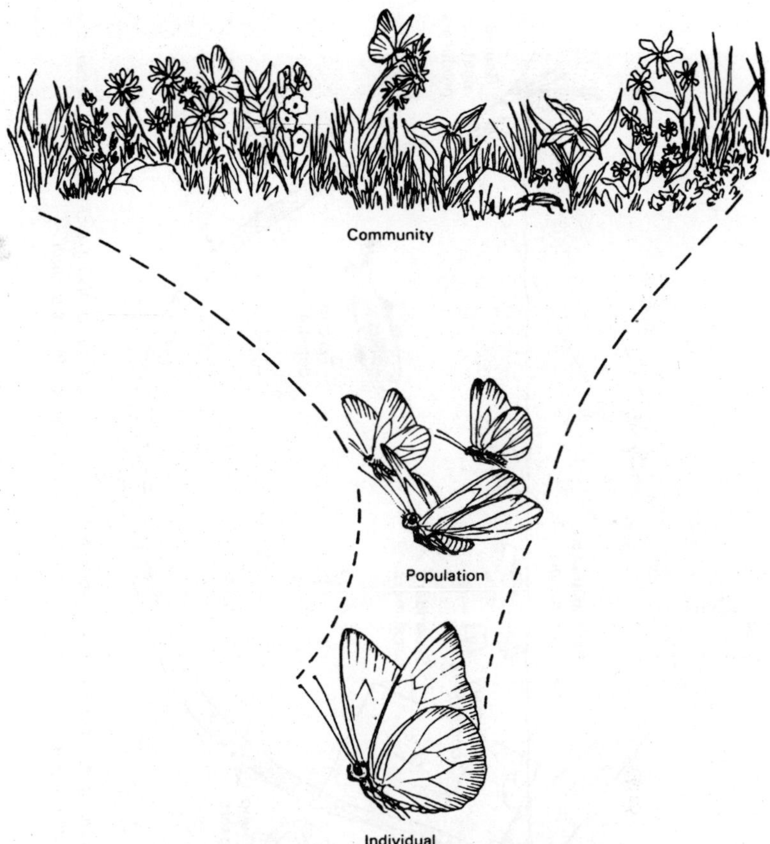

Figure 9.5: Diagram of the relationship between the individual, the population, and the community.

Although the theory of ecosystems extends to agroecosystems, several features make plant-based agroecosystems unique:

1. Agroecosystems often lack temporal continuity. Their existence may be of limited duration and may undergo immense, abrupt changes in microclimate because of cutting, plowing, disking, burning, chemical application, and other cultural practices.
2. Agroecosystems are dominated by plants selected by humans, many consisting of imported genetic material. Other crop plants not from imported material have been in protective cultivation so long that they hardly resemble the parent stock from which they were derived.
3. Most agroecosystems have little species diversity, and the

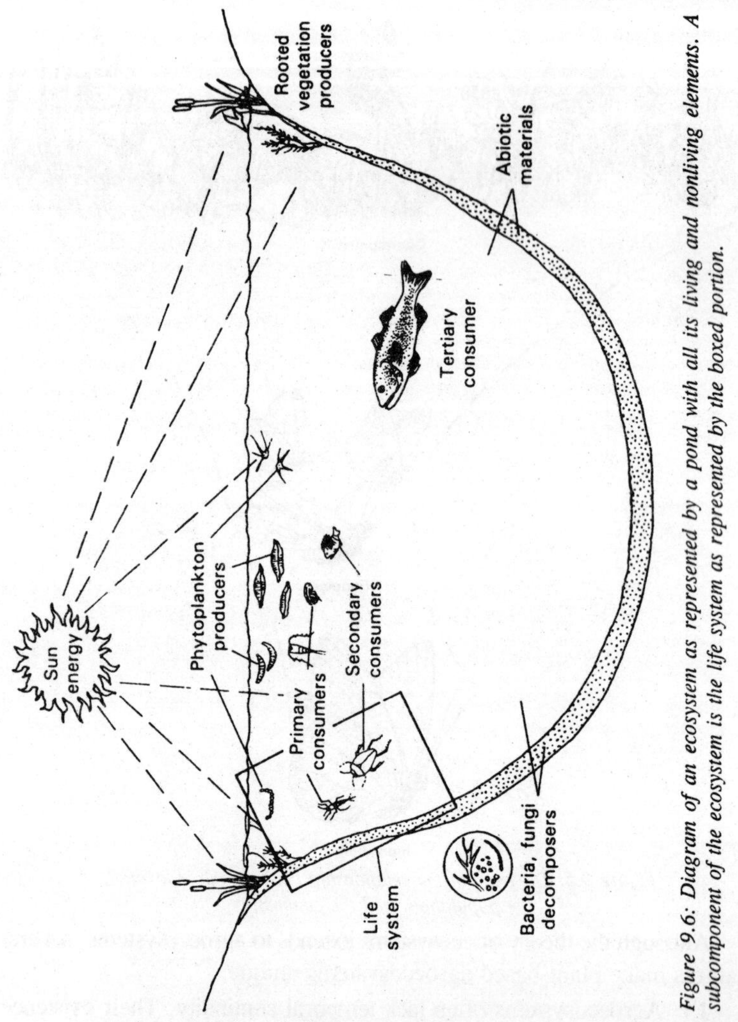

Figure 9.6: Diagram of an ecosystem as represented by a pond with all its living and nonliving elements. A subcomponent of the ecosystem is the life system as represented by the boxed portion.

crop species has little intraspecific diversity; in other words, the crop tends to be genetically uniform. Usually a single species dominates an agroecosystem, and the elimination of weed species further simplifies the environment.

4. With crop plants of similar type and age in the system, the vegetative structure is uniform, and a given phenological event (for example, flowering or podding) occurs in almost all the plants at the same time.
5. Nutrients usually are added to agroecosystems, which results

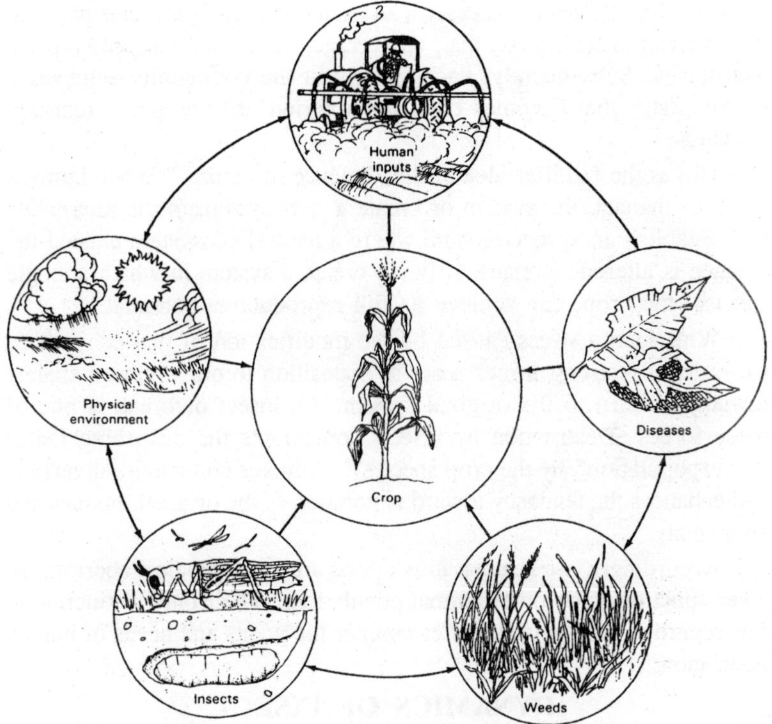

Figure 9.7: Diagram showing the major interacting elements of an agroecosystem.

in crop plants with uniformly succulent, nutrient-rich tissues.

6. Agroecosystems often have frequently occurring insect, weed, and disease outbreaks.

The last feature, pest outbreaks, largely results from the preceding five features. With insects, only a small fraction of the entire community finds the crop environment optimal, but those species that do can reproduce and survive very well, creating populations that can cause devastating losses.

The Ecological Role of Insect Outbreaks

We often ask, why do we have insects that cause damage to our crops? What is the real role of damaging insects in the great plan of nature? Of course, an answer to these questions is teleological.

However, a consideration of the ecological mechanisms operating in natural ecosystems may give some insights. Some ecologists believe that in unmanaged ecosystems, a state of balance exists or will be reached; that is, species interact with each other and with their physical environment in such a way that, on average, individuals can only replace themselves. Subsequently, each species in the community achieves a certain status that becomes fixed for a period of time and is resistant to change.

This is the familiar idea of the "balance of nature." When humans begin to manage the system or create a new system in the area-when they establish an agroecosystem where a natural ecosystem existed-the balance is altered. Humans strive to create a system in which a single species, the crop, can achieve its full reproductive potential.

With such a stress caused by the modification of that ecosystem, exceptionally strong forces react in opposition to our imposed change toward a return to the original system. An insect outbreak is one of those forces. Destruction by insects counteracts the disturbing factor ("overpopulation" by the crop species), promotes community diversity, and enhances the tendency toward restoration of the original, unmanaged community.

Accordingly, we see that insect pests are not ecological aberrations. They function as do other animal populations. Their only distinction in this regard is that their activities counter the wants and needs of human populations.

DYNAMICS OF INSECT LIFE SYSTEMS

Determinants of Insect Abundance

The determinants of insect abundance are found within a species' life system. They comprise the inherited properties of individuals in the species and attributes of the effective environment. These factors operate either to reduce or to promote insect numbers.

Together, they explain differences in abundance among habitats and numerical change over time in the same habitat. Inherited properties involve characteristics transferred genetically from individuals of one generation to those of the next. The inherited properties of individuals in a population combine to give the population its unique characteristics and mainly affect their ability to reproduce and survive. Reproductive ability is often expressed as potential natality.

Potential natality is the reproductive rate of individuals in an optimal environment. Potential natality varies greatly among insects. For example, house flies, *Musca domestica*, have a potential natality of approximately 500 eggs per female, whereas in sheep keds, *Melophagus*

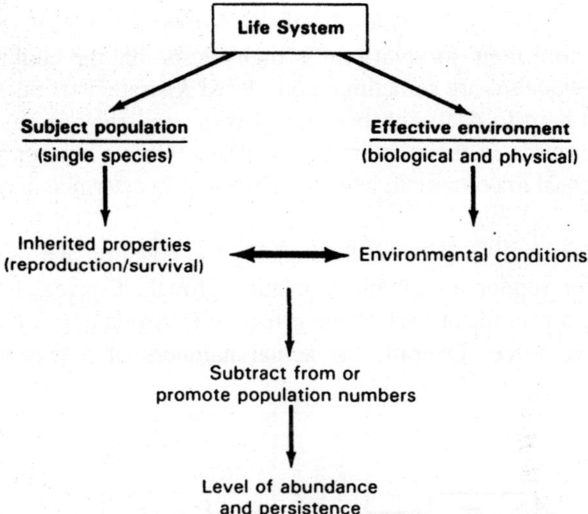

Figure 9.8: Diagram of the determinants of insect abundance in a life system.

ovinus, potential natality is only about 15 eggs per female. Survival rate also varies widely among insect species and depends much on feeding habits and protection of young. Insects that feed on a wide variety of food sources and protect their young to a degree have greater survival potential.

In the latter instance, viviparous and ovoviviparous birth types generally have less mortality of newborns than oviparous birth types. This is because the offspring are in a protected environment, inside the females, much longer than are those of oviparous species. Reproductive rate and survival rate are usually related in that species with high potential natalities tend to have relatively low survival rates and vice versa.

Insect pests with high reproductive rates and low survival rates are called ***r strategists***, named after the statistical parameter *r*, the symbol for the growth-rate coefficient. Such pests may overwhelm the environment with new individuals, and although their losses are great, they can succeed because of sheer numbers.

These pests, for example, aphids (Homoptera: Aphididae), increase astronomically in a favourable environment and can rebound quickly after environmental catastrophes. In contrast, ***K strategists***, named after the symbol for the asymptote or flattened portion of a population growth curve, reproduce slowly.

However, they compete effectively for environmental resources, and therefore their survival rate is high. Pests like the codling moth, *Cydia pomonella*, are sometimes considered *K* strategists. Such species are often hard to deal with because of their resiliency to induced and natural hazards in their environment. The effective environment is a force of equal importance to inherited properties in determining population numbers.

Factors such as weather, food quality and quantity, and living space may either support or inhibit population growth. Conversely, natural enemies, a prominent part of the effective environment, are strictly a subtractive force. Overall, the actual numbers of a population are

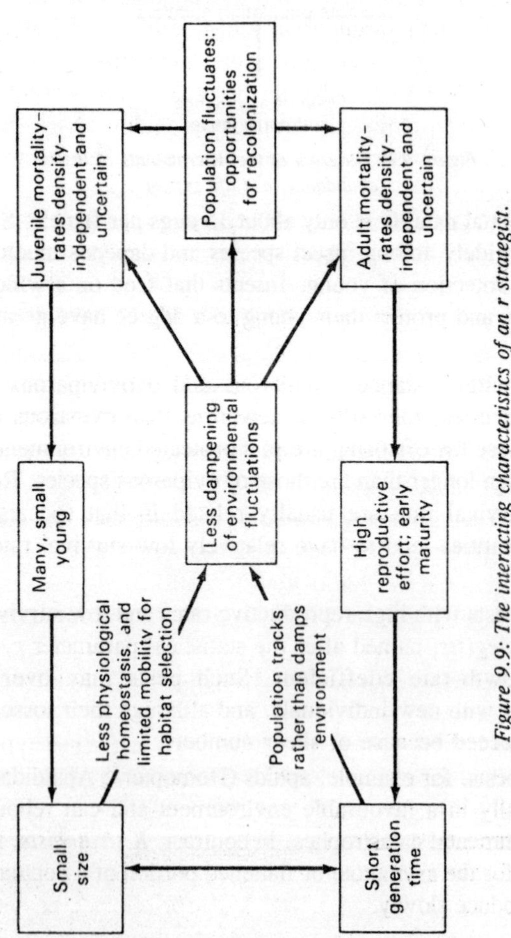

Figure 9.9: The interacting characteristics of an r strategist.

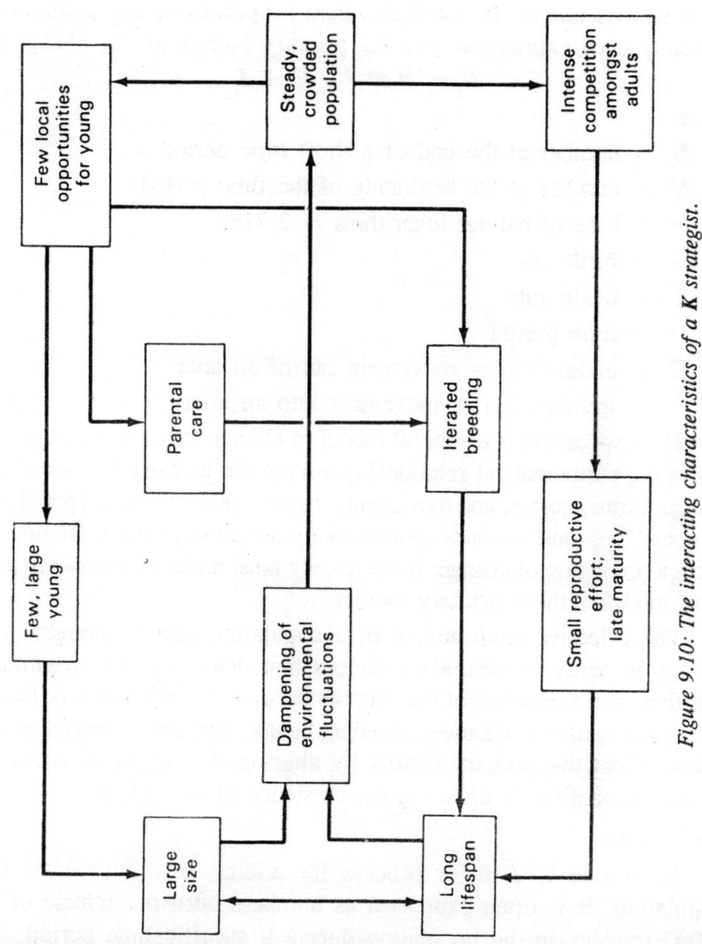

Figure 9.10: The interacting characteristics of a K strategist.

sometimes thought of as a sort of algebraic sum of the innate ability of the population to reproduce and survive and the degree of restraint imposed by the environment. R. N. Chapman, an early ecologist, referred to this innate ability as biotic potential and the restraint as environmental resistance.

He reasoned that populations grow at a rate determined by the dynamic power of a species pitted against the subtractive forces of the environment. His idea can be shown as

Actual Abundance = Biotic Potential – Environmental Resistance

Population Change

Change in numbers from one time to the next and from one place to the next is one of the most prevalent properties of any population. A widely used expression with the primary factors of this change is

$$N_t = N_0e^{(b-d)t} - E_t + I_t$$

where

N_t = number at the end of a short time period

N_o = number at the beginning of the time period

e = base of natural logarithms = 2.7183

b = birth rate

d = death rate

t = time period

E = emigration = movement out of an area

I = immigration = movement into an area

The expression is a general model of change in any population and shows the mathematical relationship among the primary factors of this change: births, deaths, and movements. In attempting to explain population numbers, we must account quantitatively for these primary factors. To attempt prediction of change, however, we must understand how environment modifies these primary factors.

The effective environment of a population can be thought of as having an array of secondary factors that determine the magnitude, duration, and frequency of the primary factors. Some secondary factors are weather, natural enemies, breeding habitat, and overwintering space. These affect the primary factors by altering the supply of necessary resources or directly affecting the existence of individuals.

Birth Rate

Birth rate is a major process for adding new individuals to a population. It is often expressed as numbers born per female or per 1,000 females in the population during a specific time period. The major factors determining birth rate are fecundity, fertility, and sex ratio.

Fecundity is the rate at which females produce ova, whereas *fertility* is the rate at which they produce new individuals, for example, fertilized eggs. With fecundity, the focus is strictly on female capability to produce reproductive units. Fertility focuses on the mating and fertilization process, or the production of zygotes. *Sex ratios* in most populations are 1:1, male to female.

Exceptions to this ratio are most common in parasitic Hymenoptera and, of course, parthenogenetic species. Overall, changes in birth rate may be caused by changes in the average production of eggs per female,

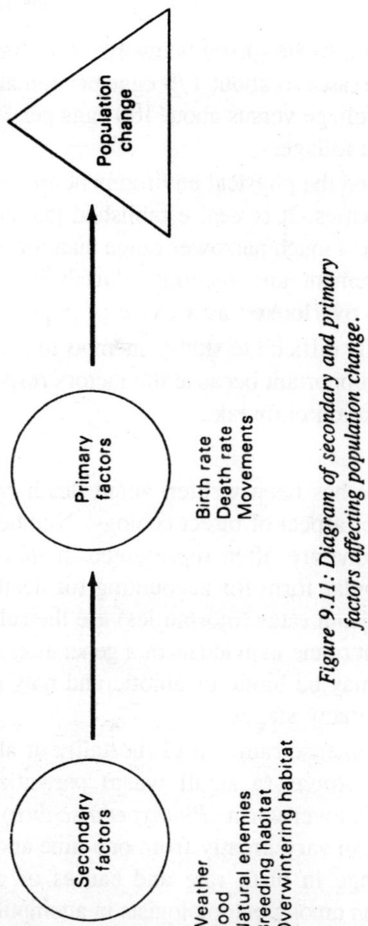

Figure 9.11: Diagram of secondary and primary factors affecting population change.

changes in mating success, changes in the proportion of female individuals in the population, or a combination of these. Both fecundity and fertility may vary greatly for an insect population. Secondary factors like temperature, moisture, and food may strongly influence the number of eggs produced by a female.

For instance, in controlled experiments with the European corn borer, *Ostrinia nubilalis*, 708 fertile eggs were produced per female at a temperature of 21 °C, but only 533 were produced at 32 °C. Likewise, female egg production can be greatly influenced by nutrition during the immature stage. For example, egg production by the Colorado potato beetle, *Leptinotarsa decemlineata*, depends on the variety of potato on which the larvae feed. In the spruce budworm, *Choristoneura fumiferana*, egg production increases to about 170 eggs per female when larvae are fed succulent new foliage versus about 100 eggs per female when larvae consume lateseason foliage.

Also, habitat and the physical environment are especially important during mating activities. It is well established that conditions essential to reproduction have a much narrower range than for other life functions, for example, movement and feeding. Variability in birth rate of a population is often overlooked as a cause of population change.

Although usually difficult to study, attempts to document and explain this variability are important because the factors responsible may be the essence of a population outbreak.

Death Rate

Probably more has been written about death rates and causes of death than any other aspect of insect ecology. Numbers of insects dying over a period of time are often represented in *survivorship curves* or in *life tables*, a tabular form for accounting for deaths. In many insect populations, high death rates (mortalities) are the rule, with sometimes fewer than 1 percent of the individuals of a generation reaching adulthood. Mortality factors may be biotic or abiotic and may operate in a single life stage or over many stages.

For example, intense rain causes mortality of all stages of aphids, but the parasitoid *Rogas* (a small wasp) parasitizes and kills only middle-aged green cloverworm (*Plathypena scabra*) larvae. Like birth rates, death rates can vary greatly from one time and place to the next. Documenting change in birth rate and causes of death have been a major preoccupation among entomologists in attempting to explain insect numbers.

Indeed, in many instances, relaxation of an important mortality factor may be the primary cause of a population outbreak.

L. R. Clark and his colleagues conveniently grouped the causes of mortality of insects into seven major categories.

Aging

Aging and death from old age is sometimes referred to as "physiological death." In most insect populations, only a small percentage of individuals live to achieve their longevity potentials-a "ripe old age."

Exceptions are many of the social insects (for example, Hymenoptera), where there is elaborate care of the young and a highly protected nest, and adults can effectively defend themselves. As a rule,

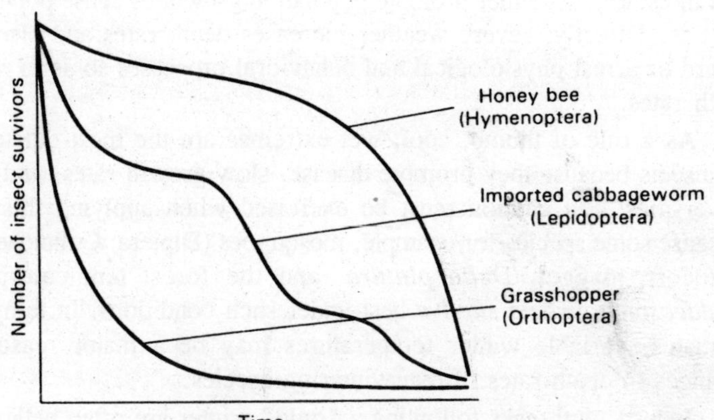

Figure 9.12: Graph of stylized survivorship curves found in insect populations.

physiological death is probably not highly variable and is most important in populations with relatively low reproductive rates.

Low Vitality

One of an insect's characteristics is the ability to survive, the inherent trait to resist adverse environmental factors. Individuals of a population vary in this ability, and sometimes the average vitality of a population may change because of the proportions of certain types of individuals.

Therefore, unusually heavy mortality may be caused by an environmental factor-for example, rainfall-acting on a population with an unusually high proportion of susceptible individuals. Rather than being credited to the rainfall, this unusual mortality may be credited to low vitality, à genetic trait.

Accidents

Accidents encompass abnormal events in the insect life cycle resulting in death. Such events range from the physiological (for example, inability to completely shed the old larval skin or failure to expand wings after molting) to the purely ecological (for example, leaf-feeding insects being eaten along with lcavcs by a browsing dccr). Thc proportion of individuals dying from accidents may be fairly constant in a population.

Physicochemical Conditions

Physicochemical conditions involve the physical and chemical conditions of air, water, and substrates in or on which the insect population lives. A particular feature with which we are concerned for most pest insects is weather. Components of weather, mainly temperature and moisture, can either promote population growth or cause population decline. Directly, severe weather increases death rates and also may retard or arrest physiological and behavioral processes so as to reduce birth rates.

As a rule of thumb, cool, wet extremes are the most deleterious to insects because they promote disease, slow growth rates, and other adversities. But caution must be exercised when applying this rule, because some species-for example, mosquitoes (Diptera: Culicidae), the seedcorn maggot, *Delia platura*, and the forest tent caterpillar, *Malacosoma disstria-survive* best under such conditions. In temperate climates, variable winter temperatures may be a major reason for changes in death rates of overwintering species.

Indeed, outbreaks following a "mild" winter are often believed to be the result of lower death rates. Again, however, caution is the rule when correlating these events because some "mild" winters may cause more mortality than "harsh" winters. This condition can occur because during the "mild" winter abnormally warm days may cause some species to become active early.

If this early activity is followed by days of normally cold temperatures, unusually high mortality may result because the insects are no longer protected by their previous state of dormancy. The long-term influence of weather on insect mortality ultimately results in a particular geographical distribution of a species. However, this distribution may change during the course of a year, with some species occupying regions during the growing season that will not allow survival during the winter.

Wellknown examples of pest species that cannot survive winters of the upper midwestern United States but invade this area during the growing season include the potato leafhopper (*Empoasca fabae*), corn earworm (*Helicoverpa zea*), and black cutworm (*Agrotis ipsilon*). Many more pests probably exhibit this behavior than are known to exist today. Because of its omnipotence, weather also affects death rate indirectly. For instance, rainfall can affect plant phenology and nutrient quality for insects.

Moreover, asynchrony between a flowering or podding event of a plant and occurrence of a particular stage of the insect also can result in unusually heavy mortality. Asynchrony occasionally occurs with the apple blossom weevil, *Anthonomus pomorum*, which lays its eggs in flower buds and suffers high mortalities when blossoms open early in relation to egg hatch. In this instance, new larvae fall out of the

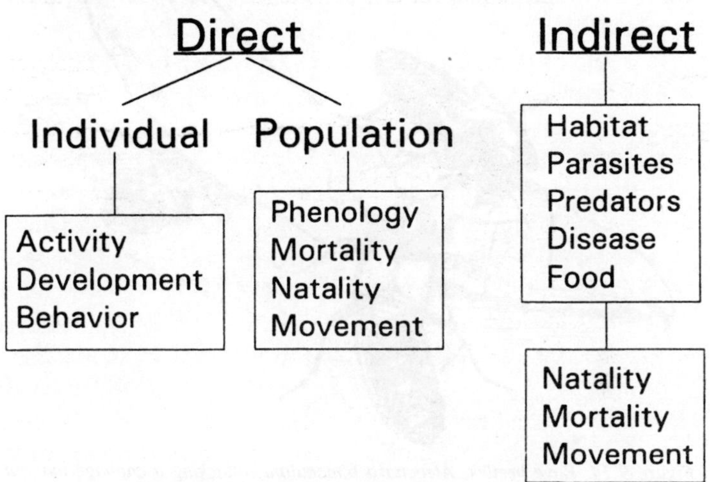

Figure 9.13: Diagram showing direct and indirect effects of meteorological factors on insects.

blossom before they have time to tie the petals together. Another indirect effect of weather is on natural enemies.

Here, high humidities are known to enhance the growth and virulence of disease-causing organisms such as fungi, and these in turn form widespread epidemics in insect populations.

Conversely, abnormally low mortalities from parasitism may result in insect host populations (for example, some Diptera) because of unusually low summer temperatures; in other words, low temperature has a more deleterious effect on the parasite species than on the host species.

Natural Enemies

Organisms that prey upon insects or parasitize them are called natural enemies. Natural enemies can be grouped, for convenience, as predators, parasites, and pathogenic microorganisms. These are discussed in greater detail elsewhere in this book, but a brief mention here will allow their orientation among the other mortality factors. Natural enemies are a very important component in the population dynamics of insect species.

They have a strictly subtractive influence on total insect numbers, and sometimes their impact is related to the density of their prey or host; their action is *density-dependent*. Therefore, in some life systems

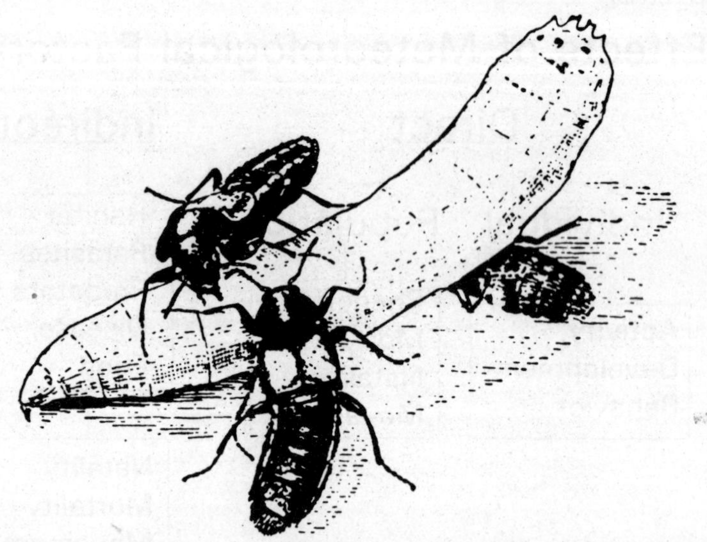

Figure 9.14: Rove beetles, Aleochara bimaculata, attacking a cabbage maggot (Diptera: Anthomyiidae). Such insect predators are important natural enemies.

they become an all-important part of insuring the stability of insect numbers.

In these instances, when numbers become large, death rate from natural enemies is great, and when numbers are small, death rate is low. Because all pest species have natural enemies, understanding mortality caused by these enemies is critical to managing the pest. Indeed, the primary principle of all pest management systems is to conserve natural enemies in the system. We return to this principle several times throughout the book.

Food Shortage

Food for insects largely depends on prevailing conditions in the ecosystem. In agroecosystems, the major food source, at least for plantfeeding insects, is the crop species, and to a major extent, supply of this food is determined by the grower. Except when weather seriously limits crop production, lack of food is not a major cause of insect pest mortality in agroecosystems.

This is not true, however, for many insects that prey on or parasitize other insects. These insect natural enemies must search through the habitat for prey or hosts of select species and often select age. Particularly when physicochemical conditions limit numbers of prey or hosts or the natural enemy decimates its own food source, starvation can be widespread.

The latter phenomenon (growth of the natural enemy population when its host is abundant, subsequent decline of the host, followed by a decline of the natural enemy) is the very basis for classical biological control. Here competition for food and starvation (or reduced reproduction) in natural enemy populations are the mechanisms by which regulation of some host populations is achieved.

Lack of Shelter

Lack of shelter influences death rate indirectly. Protective habitats allow insects to avoid exposure to weather extremes and natural enemies; the absence of such may produce considerable mortality in the population. For example, Colorado potato beetles succumb to winter temperatures below -12°C. In sandy soils, beetles burrow to depths of 36 to 91 cm, thereby escaping the lethal temperatures.

In some soils, an impervious layer of clay, a hardpan, occurs at 20 cm, preventing beetles from reaching required shelter. Unless adequate snow cover insulates the soil and moderates temperatures, widespread beetle mortality occurs. The effect of overwintering sites on insect mortality is discussed in detail by Leather et al..

Movements

Knowledge of movements into an area (*immigration*) and out of an area (*emigration*) is vital to understanding population dynamics. Indeed, movements, rather than births or deaths, may be the main cause of rapid population change within a season; that is, predictable movement

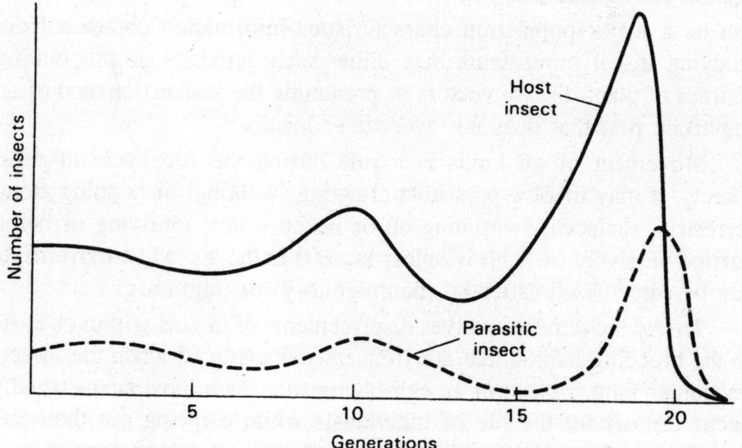

Figure 9.15: Hypothetical relationship between numbers of a parasite and those of its host, showing density-dependent action.

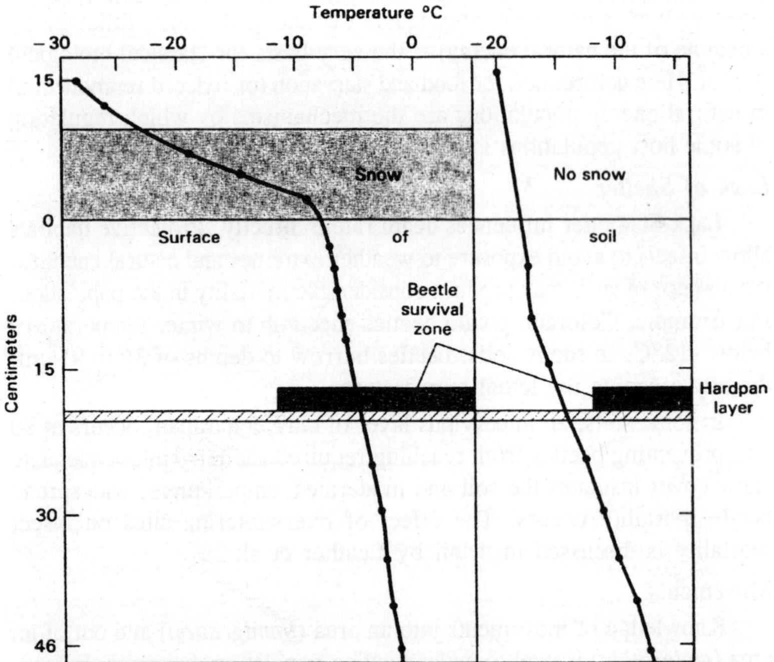

Figure 9.16: Graph showing soil temperatures relative to snow cover and level of a "hardpan." Overwintering Colorado potato beetles, Leptinotarsa decemlineata, cannot burrow through the hardpan, and survival in these soils is possible only in years and locations with adequate snow cover.

can be a major population characteristic. Information obtained from studying insect movements may allow such activities as pinpointing sources of plant-disease vectors or predicting the seasonal arrival of an important pest that does not overwinter locally.

Movement of all kinds is a rule during the life cycle of most insects. It may involve persistent crawling, walking, or hopping along terrestrial surfaces; swimming on or in the water; or flying or being carried passively (as with wingless insects) in the air. Most movements can be categorized as trivial (nonmigratory) or migratory.

Trivial movement involves displacements of insects within or close to the breeding habitat that are frequently interrupted when the insects encounter food, mates, or an egg-laying site. Such movements usually occur throughout the life of individuals while carrying out their life functions, except during egg and pupal stages and during dormancy.

An example of trivial movement is when a butterfly flits from flower to flower, sometimes moving among several habitats, feeding on nectar. Such movements are termed trivial because of the distances involved, not because they are trivial to the ecology and survival of the insect. Conversely, *migratory* movements may involve great distances, perhaps hundreds of kilometers, during which time locomotion is not inhibited by food, mates, or oviposition sites. Migration is usually accomplished by flight.

Migratory flights are composed of individuals which are predisposed to fly and are undistracted from this behavior for a lengthy period. This peculiar type of flight is an adaptation to periodically transport insects beyond the boundaries of their old reproductive sites and into new ones. During migratory flights, great mortality may occur, because many individuals are deposited in areas where they cannot survive, including open seas, lakes, glaciers, and snow fields.

However, a portion of the migrants (perhaps a minute fraction) locate suitable habitats, often fortuitously, where they can reproduce. According to C. G. Johnson, the surface of the earth is scanned very effectively by millions of insects flying on air currents, who continuously encounter suitable and unsuitable situations.

They stop temporarily in suitable habitats and reproduce, and offspring migrate in directions determined either by the wind or by themselves. The height of migration flights above the surface can vary from only a few meters (for example, some butterflies) to hundreds of meters (some leafhoppers, aphids, and moths). Migrating butterflies, flower flies, and dragonflies flying at lower levels are readily seen by the casual observer and appear to maintain a steady course.

These insects are said to migrate within their *boundary* layer. The insect boundary layer (not to be confused with meteorologists' use of the term) is the layer of air that extends from ground level upward through increasing wind speeds to a height where wind speed and insect flight speed are equal.

Within this level insects determine their own flight track. Insects migrating at higher altitudes, above their boundary layer, may not be seen. The flight track of these insects is determined by the flight orientation of the insect and wind direction; in other words, they are largely transported by the wind. One of the most famous insect migrations in North America is that of the monarch butterfly, *Danaus plexippus*.

This migration occurs each spring when butterflies fly northward from overwintering sites in Mexico, California, and other southern locations. They reach destinations in the northern United States and Canada in May and June, repopulating more than 1 million square miles in 2 months. Reproduction occurs, and two generations usually develop by September. The second generation then migrates back, often in large aggregations, to overwintering sites.

By marking, releasing, and recapturing butterflies in the southerly migration, researchers have determined that between 18 and 109 days are required to make the return flight, which may cover as many as 3,465 kilometers (2,153 miles). The difference in time is probably determined by the distance that individuals travel to their destination and weather along the migration route.

During the southern migration, butterflies aggregate (roost) in trees at night and during poor weather. Another famous example of migration is that of the desert locust, *Schistocerca gregaria*. This insect occurs across north and central Africa to the Middle East, Arabia, and India, causing plagues that have been reported since biblical times.

Vast swarms may occur across hundreds of kilometers and may be composed of as many as 10 billion individuals, with a weight of 15,000 tons. Such a swarm is estimated to have the same daily consumption as 1.5 million people. When they alight, the locusts consume all aboveground vegetation.

The insect has both solitary and migratory phases, with phase determined by degree of crowding of nymphs and their mothers. The migratory swarm appears as a mass flying purposively in a fixed direction. However, orientation of individuals in the swarm is random, and members at the swarm's edge move toward the center of the swarm.

This flight behavior is adaptive, because the whole swarm is displaced downwind toward zones of wind convergence. One such area is the Intertropical Convergence Zone, where winds of both sides of the equator meet. Borne on these winds, locusts accumulate in the convergence zone, and swarm displacement ends there.

The environment in the convergence zone is favourable for the locusts because rising air here causes rainfall. The rainfall in turn allows the growth of vegetation, and locusts in these areas find environments appropriate for successful reproduction.

The Intertropical Convergence Zone moves back and forth across the equator once each year, and because of individual flying behavior and meteorological conditions, locust swarms follow and take advantage of the resulting favourable environments. The desert locust example shows that crowding and subsequent shortage of food can be an important stimulus for insects to migrate.

Other important stimuli may include photoperiod (usually long day length) and weather factors. In particular, weather factors may be important in determining the exodus flight. Convection caused by warming of the earth's surface provides thermal updrafts that transport some migrants to altitudes required for horizontal transport by the wind; the opportunity for night-flying insects to take advantage of such updrafts is not as great, and these insects often must gain altitude by their own flight activity.

Rapid changes in atmospheric pressure may also stimulate migratory flight and allow insects to take advantage of certain wind movements; for example, many aphids and flies are known to increase their takeoff with decreasing barometric pressure. Once aloft, migrants seemingly respond to weather forces like wind speed and direction, temperature, barometric pressure, and dew point. These factors change with altitude, and migrant insects may actively find an altitude where conditions are favourable.

Finding the proper altitude, insects may continue to fly or assume a flight attitude and be carried for hundreds of kilometers with the wind. Transport by the wind continues for hours or days, until the migrant becomes grounded. Deposition may be gradual or abrupt. Gradual deposition, grounding of the migrants over a period of time and over a considerable area, often is caused by factors intrinsic to the population.

These include changes in neurophysiological state, inefficient flight in cold air, exhaustion, or flight inhibition triggered by light intensity. Sudden deposition of migrants probably occurs as a result of atmospheric conditions. Such may include downdrafts in cold fronts or cooling of the insect to the point that it cannot support itself in the air.

Of all possible weather conditions, cold fronts seem to be the most important in deposition. We thus see that migration is an important adaptive characteristic of insects, one that can strongly influence their population dynamics. As the study of insect migration continues, it seems that many more insect species than heretofore believed use wind flow to relocate and colonize favourable habitats.

Some insect pests whose migration patterns are well known are the potato leafhopper, black cutworm, velvetbean caterpillar (*Anticarsia gemmatalis*), fall armyworm (*Spodoptera frugiperda*), and spruce budworm. It is particularly important that we recognize this potential when predicting pest outbreaks, because rapid population increase may well be caused by migration alone.

EFFECTS OF ENVIRONMENT ON INSECT DEVELOPMENT

Like other organisms, a given insect species is capable of survival only within certain environmental limits, and when possible, individuals actively seek out preferred temperatures, humidities, and light intensities. Within this favourable range, these environmental factors usually influence rate responses of activities such as feeding, dispersal, egg laying, and development.

In recent years, an understanding of insect developmental rates has played a particularly important role in insect pest management. Timing of management activities is crucial to implementation of pest management tactics.

Knowing or predicting that an insect population is in the egg stage or larval stage, for example, may be one of the cues to begin insect sampling, initiate spraying, destroy crop residues, or plant a crop. Of the environmental factors, temperature probably has the greatest affect on insect developmental rates. Primarily, this is because insects are *poikilothermic*, or cold-blooded.

Within certain limits the higher the temperature, the faster the development of the insect. Developmental rate increases with temperature because chemical reactions occur more frequently and proceed more rapidly at higher temperatures. As temperature increases, diffusion rates for substrates and enzymes also increase, resulting in greater formation of enzyme-substrate complexes. In addition, higher temperatures provide more thermal energy for the requirements of biochemical reactions.

Predicting Biological Events: The Degree-day Method

Because temperature is crucial to biochemical reactions, it can be used to predict rates of insect development. The idea of using temperature and time to describe development of cold-blooded animals is more than 250 years old, and several methods have been advanced to utilize the relationship for prediction.

Of these, the most prevalent method of measuring and estimating this socalled physiological time is the *degree-day* method. Degree days represent the accumulation of heat units above some temperature for a 24-hour period. Below this minimum, no development takes place, but above it, heat units are accumulated toward development.

For degree-day accumulation, if the *developmental minimum*, or

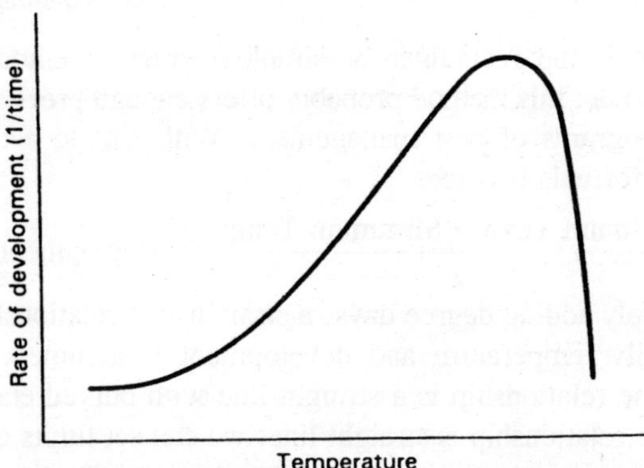

Figure 9.17: Graph of the relationship between rate of development (1/time) in insects and temperature.

threshold, of an insect is 15°C and the average temperature for the day is 27°C, then 12 degree days, (symbolized as DD or °D) would have accumulated on that day.

To predict the stage of development from degree days, the thermal constant for an event must have been established. This *thermal constant* is the number of degree days required for an event to occur. By accumulating degree days each day and relating these to the thermal constant for an event, one can estimate whether or not the event occurred on the day in question.

The most common events for which insect thermal constants are established are hatching, each larval or nymphal molt, pupation, and adult emergence. Both thermal constants and developmental thresholds vary among different species of insects. For instance, the thermal constant for egg to adult development of the painted lady butterfly, *Vanessa cardui, is* 440 Celsius degree days, but for the seedcorn maggot, it is 376 Celsius degree days.

Developmental thresholds for these insects are 12°C and 4°C, respectively. Because of significant differences, threshold values must be determined for each species of interest.

The following formula has been devised to calculate degree days (DD) for a specific date:

DD = Average Daily Temperature – Developmental Threshold

The main difference among workers in making degree-day calculation is in computing average daily temperature. Although four basic procedures have been developed to estimate average daily temperature (rectangle method, sinewave method, cosine curve, and triangle method), the most widely used is the rectangle, or simple-average, method. Although somewhat crude, this method probably offers enough precision for most practical programs of pest management. With simple averaging, the degree-day formula becomes

$$DD = \frac{\text{Maximum Texp.} + \text{Minimum Temp.}}{2} - \text{Development Threshold}$$

By simply adding degree days, a straight-line relationship between average daily temperature and development is assumed. In reality, however, the relationship is a straight line with curved ends. Because much of the relationship is straight line, we can set limits on the upper curve and ignore minor deviations caused by the lower curve. In so doing, we gain simplicity but introduce error.

Several conventions or rules are used in making degree-day calculations, mostly for the purpose of reducing this error. These rules can be listed as follows:

1. If the maximum temperature did not exceed the developmental threshold, no degree days are accumulated. For example,

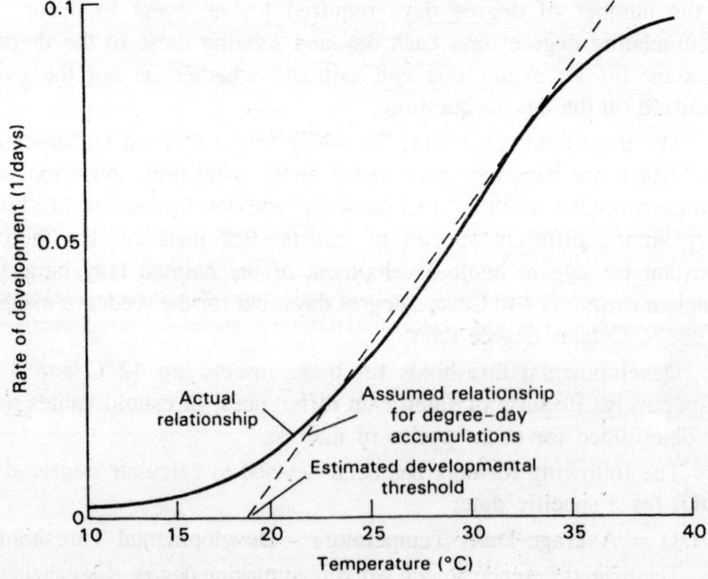

Figure 9.18: Graph showing the actual relationship of insect development and temperature (solid line) and the assumed relationship used with degree-day accumulations (broken line). Although some error is introduced in its use, the straight-line relationship is practical for predicting insect development. Slope and intercept of the straight line are calculated from data of the curved line.

Developmental Threshold = 10°C
Maximum Temperature = 9°C
Minimum Temperature = 4°C
DD = 0

2. If the maximum temperature was above the developmental threshold, but the minimum temperature is below it, the minimum is set equal to the developmental threshold in calculating the average. For example,

   Developmental Threshold = 10°C
   Maximum Temperature = 20°C
   Minimum Temperature = 8°C
   Transformed Minimum = 10°C
   DD = 5

3. If the maximum temperature exceeded that of the developmental optimum (the temperature at which developmental rate is highest), it is set equal to the optimum. For example,

   Developmental Threshold = 10°C
   Developmental Optimum = 27°C
   Maximum Temperature = 29°C
   Transformed Maximum = 27°C
   Minimum Temperature = 21°C
   DD =14

Rule number 1 is always applied in calculating degree days, and rules number 2 and 3 are applied when so instructed by the particular degree-day program. Degree-day programs for insect species are usually developed by research entomologists who record rate of development of insects placed in laboratory growth chambers, each set at a different temperature.

Time required for development of the egg stage, each larval or nymphal stage, and pupal stage are recorded for each temperature. The reciprocal of time (1/days) for an event to occur is plotted for each temperature, and a straight line is fitted to these points using a statistical procedure called linear regression analysis.

The point at which this line crosses the horizontal axis is the developmental threshold. As can be seen, this point is a statistical estimation of development and not a true biological point; in other words, some development can occur below the estimated developmental thresh old, but usually it is trivial for the purpose of estimation. Once

Table 9.1: Degree-day Requirements (Thermal Constants) for Certain Activities of the European Corn Borer.

Stage	*Activity*	*Degree Days*
	First Generation	
Egg	Peak egg hatch	100
1st-2nd instars	Leaf feeding	200+
3rd instar	Stalk boring	350+
4th instar	Stalk boring	400+
5th instar	Stalk boring	550+
Pupa	Peak pupation	900+
Adult	Egg laying	1150-1700
	Second Generation	
Egg	Peak egg hatch	1260
1st instar	Sheath feeding	1350+
2nd instar	Sheath feeding	1500+
3rd instar	Sheath feeding	1600+
3rd instar	Initial stalk boring	1650

a developmental threshold is determined, the experimental data can be used further to establish thermal constants for important events in the insect life cycle.

In addition to manual calculations for degree-day accumulations, several programs have been written for computer calculation. One such program, DEGDAY, is functional on personal computers and derives degree-day accumulations by rectangle, sine-wave, and triangle methods.

Degree-day Programs in Insect Pest Management

As mentioned previously, degree-day programs are a basic component of many insect pest management programs. In most programs, degree-day accumulations are made from the beginning of a growing season and are continuously compared with thermal constants that indicate time of potential crop injury.

Thereafter, samples are taken, density estimates are compared with economic threshold levels, and decisions are made as to whether suppression is necessary or not. Although the degree-day method has been useful in the management of many insect pests, it is not always applicable.

For such pests as corn rootworms, *Diabrotica* species, developmental time can be predicted best by date, without considering temperature. In such instances, some factor other than temperature may be more important, or temperatures in the microhabitat are relatively uniform, making them unimportant in prediction.

Additionally, research information on degree-day requirements is not yet available for many insect species. Other limitations of the degree-day method relate to accuracy. Accuracy of degree-day accumulations depends on temperature measurements used in the calculations.

Consequently, degree days should be calculated with temperatures that represent environments where the species is present. Also, temperatures at one site give only a rough estimate of insect development at another site several miles away.

REGULATION OF INSECT POPULATIONS

Anyone who has seen hundreds of aphids crowded on a single plant leaf or witnessed the swarms of pomace flies hovering over ripened fruit will not doubt the reproductive capabilities of insects. Indeed, it would seem that population growth might cause numbers to overrun their food supply and thus cause their complete destruction from starvation.

Likewise, at certain times of the year or at certain locations, the numbers of a species may seem so small that extinction would be imminent. Neither of these catastrophes usually occurs to a species, at least in the duration of a human lifetime. Rather, population numbers fluctuate within certain bounds for long periods of time, neither increasing (overrunning resources) nor wasting away to extinction.

The natural phenomenon of numbers being arrested short of extinction has been called *regulation*. Therefore, it might be said that all existing populations are regulated in one way or another. This regulation may occur at levels not bothersome to humans or at levels that are inconvenient to them, as with pests. How regulation occurs or, indeed, if it occurs at all has been the subject of much biological debate. Some popular theories to explain how animal regulation occurs or, in some instances, simply why numbers change have been advanced by W. R. Thompson, A. J. Nicholson, H. G. Andrewartha and L. C. Birch, D. Chitty, V. C. Wynne-Edwards, D. Pimentel, A. Milne, and T. R. E. Southwood.

In particular, Milne's theory provides a useful way of looking at natural regulation in insect populations, and data from many studies seem to support his tenets. As Milne's theory goes, there are basically three types of natural factors acting to regulate population numbers: (1) perfectly density-dependent factors, (2) imperfectly density-dependent factors, and (3) density-independent factors.

According to Milne, a *perfectly density-dependent factor* would be one that never fails to control the increase in population numbers. Such a factor acts strongly to subtract numbers from a population when density is high and increasing, and the factor reduces its pressure when density is low and decreasing.

The only natural factor influenced solely by numbers in the subject population is intraspecific competition. *Intraspecific competition* is a phenomenon whereby individuals in a population vie for a resource in limited supply, such as food. As population growth occurs, more and more of the resource is eliminated, causing greater and greater intraspecific competition.

As individuals compete, some are eliminated, in this case from starvation, and density is reduced. With falling numbers, competition is relaxed and the rate of decrease drops. An *imperfectly density-dependent factor* functions similarly to a perfectly density-dependent factor, except that the imperfect factor may sometimes fail to limit numerical increase. Agents in this category include predators, parasites, and pathogenic microorganisms that cause insect death.

Because the lives of these organisms are influenced by many environmental factors, one or more may limit their influence on a prey or host population. For example, a population of parasitic wasps may be very effective in limiting the size of a caterpillar population, and the action of the parasite acts in a density-dependent manner; it causes a greater proportion of deaths when the host population is large than when that population is small.

Occasionally, however, wet, cool weather has a severe effect on the parasite and not on its host. Therefore, the density-dependent action of the parasite fails, and the host population increases. Density-dependent factors do not vary in their impact on a population according to its density. The primary example of this kind of factor is weather.

Weather factors, including rainfall, temperature, and humidity, may have a strong effect on insect survival, but the size of the population has no significant influence on the degree of impact from these factors. Milne visualizes annual numbers as fluctuating within three zones. Zone I is a level of very low numbers, and populations seldom fall here from Zone II.

When they do, it is because of an unusual occurrence (duration and/

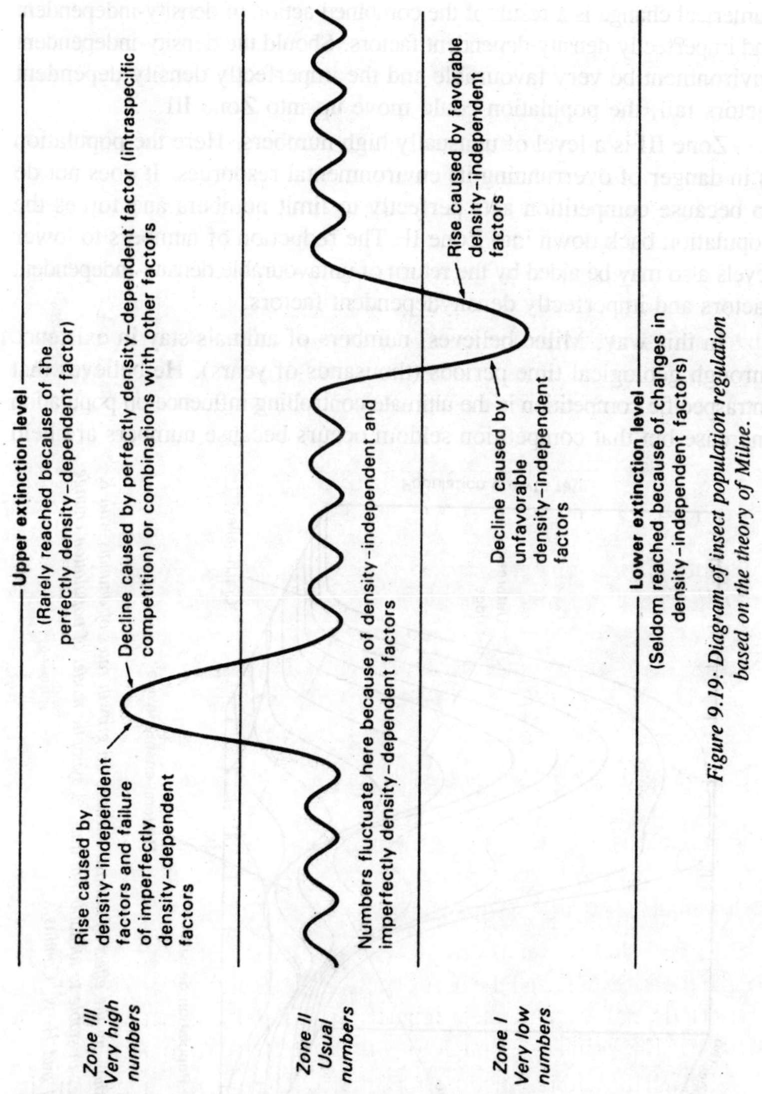

Figure 9.19: Diagram of insect population regulation based on the theory of Milne.

or intensity) of unfavourable *density-independent factors*. Extinction from being in this zone usually does not occur in a human lifetime because density-independent factors, acting in random fashion, are not sufficiently deleterious long enough for this catastrophe to occur.

On the return of favourable density-independent factors, the population moves back into Zone II. Zone II is the level of usual numbers. Population density fluctuates within this zone for long periods of time. Here numerical change is a result of the combined action of density-independent and imperfectly density-dependent factors. Should the density-independent environment be very favourable and the imperfectly density-dependent factors fail, the population could move up into Zone III.

Zone III is a level of unusually high numbers. Here the population is in danger of overrunning its environmental resources. It does not do so because competition acts perfectly to limit numbers and forces the population back down into Zone II. The reduction of numbers to lower levels also may be aided by the return of unfavourable density-independent factors and imperfectly densitydependent factors.

In this way, Milne believes, numbers of animals stay in existence through geological time periods (thousands of years). He believes that intraspecific competition is the ultimate controlling influence on population increase but that competition seldom occurs because numbers are held

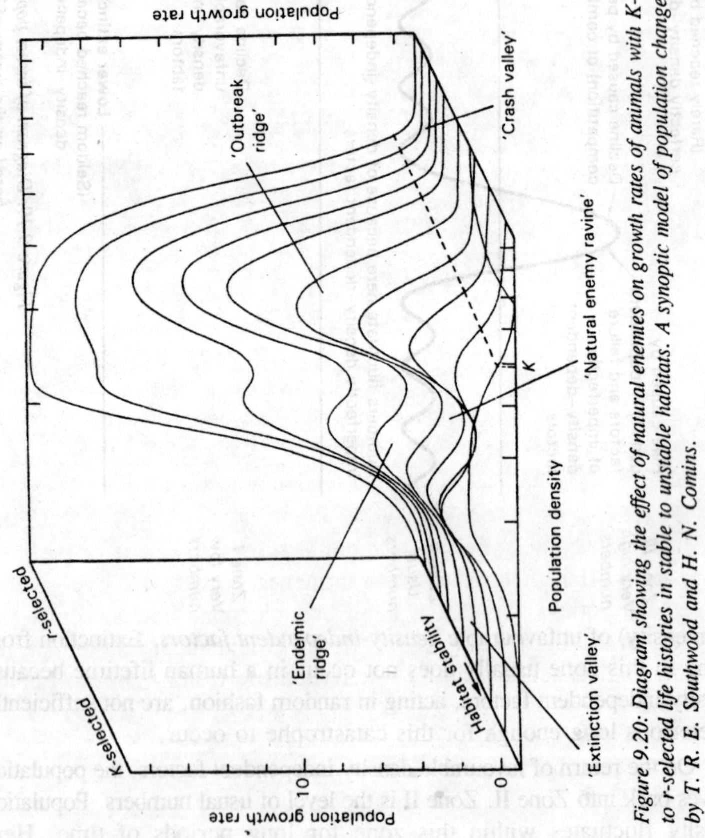

Figure 9.20: Diagram showing the effect of natural enemies on growth rates of animals with K- to r-selected life histories in stable to unstable habitats. A synoptic model of population change by T. R. E. Southwood and H. N. Comins.

at lower levels by factors such as weather and natural enemies. As useful as Milne's theory is in explaining the functional aspects of environmental factors, it does not tell us much about the importance of species life history and habitat in population dynamics. Ecologists T. R. E. Southwood and H. N. Comins present the idea that most natural enemies have little or no impact on growth rate of populations with r-selected life histories (rapid colonization and high reproduction) in unstable habitats (for example, many annual crops).

Here, they believe that biotic factors may have little influence in preventing outbreak growth. In such instances, abnormally rapid growth rates are believed brought down by food shortages, disease, and emigration. However, the ecologists feel that populations in stable habitats (for example, some perennial crops) that tend toward K-selected life histories (poor colonizers and low reproduction) are more influenced by natural enemies.

These extremes can be seen in Figure elsewhere in this chapter, which shows a graph with curves responding to three axes, population density, population growth, and a combined axis, representing *K/r* selection and habitat stability. The shapes of the curves are controlled largely by the power of natural enemies to counteract growth.

Therefore, a major feature of the graph shows a natural enemy "ravine," or depression in growth rates, that occurs at moderate population densities in most curves. Note that the growth-rate curve of strongest r-selection in an unstable habitat is very large and has no natural enemy ravine. Outbreak growth is intense in these populations, indicating a sort of "boom or bust" situation, and natural enemies can seldom prevent outbreaks from occurring. However, an ever-deepening natural enemy ravine and lower intensity of outbreak growth occurs with increasing habitat stability and tendency toward a K-selected life history.

In the most stable habitat, the curve shows no ravine or outbreak ridge at all. Here natural enemies influence growth rate over a wide range of densities. This theory helps us understand how insect species may differ in their response to density dependent factors of the environment, depending on their inherited life history. It also implies that these factors may operate differently within a species, depending on the habitat occupied.

In practical terms, the theory might suggest that the utility of at least some biological control agents will depend on a pest's life history and the particular habitat occupied by the pest at a given time. As can be seen, these population theories give a general explanation of the mechanism of population regulation.

As such, they play an important role in pest management by orienting researchers and practitioners in the study of individual problems. As a primary benefit, detailed analyses of specific insect life systems based on such theory allow prediction of outbreaks. Ultimately, knowing the specifics of how numbers fluctuate gives clues to how insect life systems can be manipulated for the benefit of humankind.

10

Plant Resistance to Insects

One of the most promising ways to reduce dependence on pesticides in agriculture is to plant insect-resistant crops. Planting resistant cultivars when available is one of our most effective, economical, and environmentally safe management tactics.

The concept of using host resistance to our advantage comes from the knowledge that most plants and animals are resistant to most potential insect attackers. Certain physiological, morphological, and/or behavioral characteristics inherited by organisms form a core of defense against species that would otherwise attack them.

These defenses are the result of natural selection. In nature, crosses that produce highly susceptible plants and animals are not repeated because resultant progeny do not survive to reproduce. However, although resistant to most attacks, even well-adapted survivors are susceptible to a few forms with the ability to overcome their defenses.

Therefore, attackers sustain their populations at the expense, though not usually the complete elimination, of the host. These successful attackers on wild hosts are equivalent to what we would call pests on domesticated hosts. Just as wild plants and animals have degrees of susceptibility to enemies, so do domestic species.

From the gene pool of a crop species, certain crosses produce *phenotypes* (visible expressions of the crosses) that vary from complete susceptibility to high levels of resistance. Susceptibility is the underlying cause of a pest problem, and the degree of it in a species forms the basis of developing useful, pest-resistant types. By definition, pest resistance is any inherited characteristic of a host that lessens the effects of attack.

From an evolutionary standpoint, such characteristics are preadaptive traits that have allowed the organism to overcome the pressures of insects and disease organisms and thereby increased the organism's chances of survival and reproduction. The technology of plant and animal breeding is aimed, in part, at discovering these preadaptive traits and using them to develop pest-resistant cultivars and breeds. Breeding for pest resistance is only one of many objectives of total breeding programs.

Indeed, usually yield and quality are the two most important aims, with pest resistance an important complementary objective. Breeding for pest resistance may focus on any type of pest, but particular emphasis is placed on pathogenic microorganisms, nematodes, and arthropods. Breeding programs emphasizing resistance to insects and other arthropods are some of the most important in agriculture.

Presently, breeding for insect resistance in plants is far more advanced than that for domesticated animals. Seemingly, this is because of the lower costs, shorter time, and greater opportunity for hybridization involved in plant breeding. Because of its significance in plant pest management and lesser importance in animal production, only plant resistance is discussed here.

BRIEF HISTORY

Some of the earliest observations of plant resistance to insects were recorded in the late eighteenth and early nineteenth centuries. As early as 1792, "Underhill" variety wheat resistant to the introduced Hessian fly, *Mayetiola destructor*, was reported in the United States by J. N. Havens. This is generally considered the earliest documented report of an insectresistant plant variety.

Somewhat later, in 1831, "Winter Majetin" apples were reported resistant to the woolly apple aphid, *Eriosoma lanigerum*. The first dramatic example of the value of plant resistance against insects occurred in the late 1800s. An insect species, the grape phylloxera, *Daktulosphaira vitifoliae*, was inadvertently introduced into French vineyards and spread across Europe.

The effect was catastrophic, and by 1880, the pest threatened to wipe out the French wine industry. Earlier, it had been found that American grapes were resistant to the phylloxera, and this knowledge led to the grafting of susceptible European grapevine scions to resistant American rootstocks. This produced vines resistant to grape phylloxera

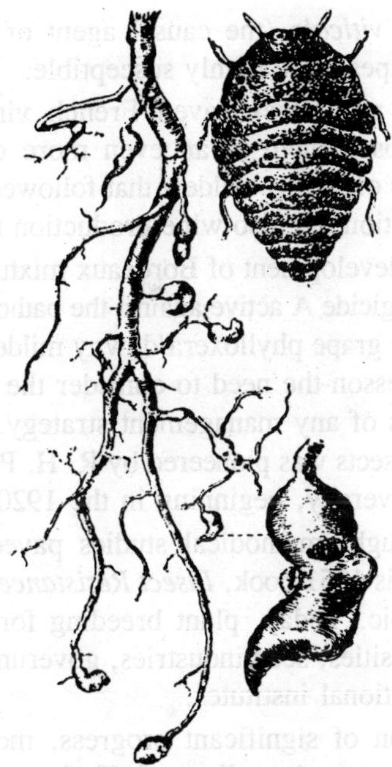

Figure 10.1: Grape phylloxera, Daktulosphaira vitifoliae, female (upper right) and galls on terminal roots of grape caused by the pest. Gall at lower right is enlarged to show size relative to the insect.

and yet allowed quality European wine grapes to be grown. Satisfactory insect control occurred by 1890, thereby saving the French wine industry.

An American entomologist, C. V Riley, was awarded a gold medal by the French government for making this recommendation. Resistant grapevines have been the major means of preventing grape phylloxera injury for 100 years. However, grape phylloxera problems began to reoccur in Sonoma and Napa County, California, in the 1980s.

It seems that a new biotype of the phylloxera (an asexual, totally root-inhabiting mutant) has developed there that can overcome plant resistance. The previously resistant root stocks currently are being replaced by new resistant varieties, which growers hope will be effective for the next 100 years.

An important lesson in this story is that insect pests have the ability to overcome nearly any single management tactic used against them. Although the grape phylloxera example is often cited to illustrate the value of plant resistance, there is even more to the story. Ironically, plants introduced into France from North America carried the pathogenic fungus *Plasmopara viticola* (the causal agent of downy mildew), to which European grapes were highly susceptible.

The American root stock saved French vineyards from grape phylloxera but exposed them to an even more dangerous risk. The devastating epidemic of downy mildew that followed threatened not only French wine production but also wine production throughout Europe.

Ultimately the development of Bordeaux mixture (lime plus copper sulfate), an early fungicide A active against the pathogen, saved European vineyards. Thus, the grape phylloxera/downy mildew episode offers yet another important lesson-the need to consider the whole pest complex and the implications of any management strategy. Modern work with plant resistance to insects was pioneered by R. H. Painter and colleagues at Kansas State University, beginning in the 1920s.

Painter's thorough, methodical studies paved the way for later achievements, and his 1951 book, *Insect Resistance in Crop Plants*, was the first on this topic. Today, plant breeding for insect resistance is conducted by universities, seed industries, governments, and numerous national and international institutes.

As an indication of significant progress, more than 400 insect-resistant cultivars or germplasm lines of alfalfa, cotton, corn, sorghum, and wheat have been developed and released to the public in the past 15 years alone. Moreover, resistant varieties have become a crucial element in the success of many ongoing insect pest management programs.

INSECT AND HOST-PLANT RELATIONSHIPS

To understand the mechanisms of plant resistance to insects, it is important to understand some of the basic relationships between these organisms. Such relationships, commonly referred to as insect/plant interactions, are usually couched with heavy emphasis on insects and plant response to attack.

The Insect Aspect

The insect aspect of the insect/plant interaction is often described as a series of steps, in time and space, that lead to suitability of a plant for the insect. The major steps usually recognized by authorities include (1) finding the general habitat, (2) finding the host plant, (3) acepting the plant as a proper host, and (4) sufficiency of the plant for survival and successful reproduction of the insect population.

Finding the General Habitat

Insects locate the general area of the host by means usually unrelated to the plant. Physical stimuli such as light, wind, gravity, and perhaps temperature and humidity may help orient dispersing insects to the overall location of the host. This step is most important when a species does not reside in an area yearround, as with many migrating forms.

Finding the Host Plant

Once in the general area the insect next must find a proper host. Most insects rely on vision and/or smell to locate a host plant. Remote factors in locating the plant include colour, size, and shape. Much of the information on colour in host finding is limited mainly to aphids (Homoptera: Aphididae) and whiteflies (Homoptera: Aleyrodidae), which are attracted to yellow-green surfaces.

Colour usually cannot be used in plant resistance because changing it affects fundamental physiological processes. In a few instances, however, red cultivars of cotton, cabbage, and oats have been shown less attractive to insects, and yet they have retained good agronomic characteristics. In addition to colour, some insects, like fruit flies, *Ragoletis* species, are known to associate shape and size of trees in locating hosts.

Once insects are in contact with the plant, short-range stimuli arrest further movement. These stimuli are both physical, exciting tactile receptors, and chemical, exciting chemoreceptors on tarsi, antennae, and mouthparts.

Accepting the Plant as a Proper Host

Subsequent to host finding, insects may take test bites, as do some caterpillars, to confirm host recognition. Continuous feeding seemingly is governed by the stimulation from various chemicals. In a monophagous insect, the silkworm (*Bombyx mori*), a series of substances are perceived in mulberry leaves that seem to mediate biting, swallowing, and continued feeding.

Feeding to satiation then follows in the presence of appropriate chemicals. Major physical factors involved in acceptance of a host may include such factors as leaf and stem toughness, leaf surface waxes, and pubescence (density and types of hairs). These factors may be important in relation to feeding and/or oviposition.

Sufficiency of the Plant for Requisites

Sufficiency of the plant as a host is finally determined during feeding. If nutrients are adequate and no toxicity occurs, the insect completes development within a normal time period and becomes an adult. Also, sufficiency is indicated in normal adult longevity and fecundity (the production of male and female gametes).

The Plant Aspect

As the supplier of physical and chemical stimuli, the plant itself becomes an important participant in the insect and host-plant relationship. Both morphological and physiological characteristics of a plant elicit given insect responses.

Morphological Characteristics

Plant morphological features may produce physical stimuli or bar insect activity. Variations in foliage size, shape, colour, and presence or absence of glandular secretions may determine degree of acceptance or utilization by insects. Pubescence and tissue toughness sometimes limit insect mobility and feeding.

Physiological Characteristics

Physiological characteristics influencing insects usually involve chemicals that are the products of plant metabolism. Such chemicals are the result of primary and secondary metabolic processes. Primary metabolic processes in plants produce substances to catalyze reactions, build tissues, and supply energy.

The plant requires inorganic ions and produces enzymes, hormones, carbohydrates, lipids, proteins, and phosphorus compounds for energy transfer. Together, these *primary metabolites* promote growth and reproduction of the plant. For insects, some of these primary metabolites are feeding stimulants, nutrients, and toxicants.

Other primary metabolites are inert as far as an insect is concerned. Secondary metabolic processes in plants seem to be coincidental to primary metabolism. The chemicals produced, *secondary metabolites*, vary widely among plants and are believed nonessential in primary metabolism.

Some of these secondary metabolites are thought to have arisen as mechanisms for chemical defense against plant eating. They may be stored in any convenient place in the plant structure and often are exuded from outer layers of plant tissues. Here, they may be sensed by insects and function as *token stimuli*.

A token stimulus elicits a response initially and afterward has no effect. This relationship between plant chemical stimuli and insect response is a form of chemical communication between these organisms. Such chemicals are called *semiochemicals*. Among semiochemicals are *pheromones*, which promote communication between members of the same species, and *allelochemics*, which promote communication between members of different species.

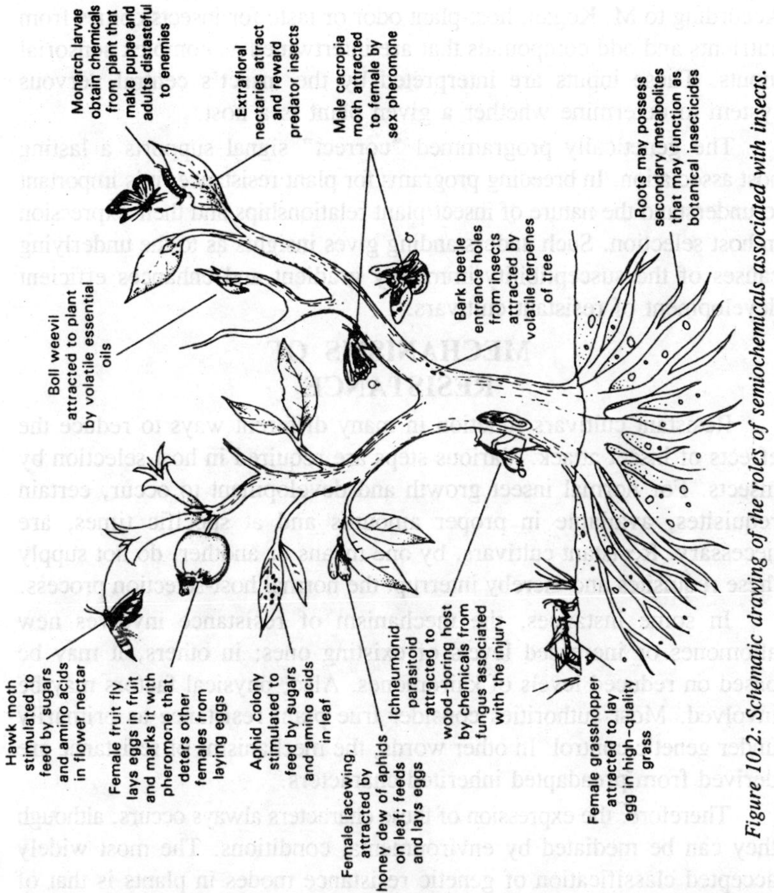

Figure 10.2: Schematic drawing of the roles of semiochemicals associated with insects.

Metabolites in plants that stimulate responses are kinds of allelochemics. Allelochemics can be subdivided further into allomones and kairomones. *Allomones* are mostly defensive chemicals, producing negative responses in insects and reducing chances of contact and utilization. They include repellents, oviposition and feeding deterrents, and toxicants. Conversely, *kairomones* are advantageous to an insect, promoting host finding, oviposition, and feeding. They include attractants, arrestants, excitants, and stimulants.

Host-Plant Selection

Host-plant selection by insects usually involves both primary and secondary metabolites. Some theorists emphasize secondary metabolites in this process; however, many contend that both play an important role.

According to M. Kogan, host-plant odor or taste for insects comes from nutrients and odd compounds that are intertwined as complex sensorial inputs. These inputs are interpreted by the insect's central nervous system to determine whether a given plant is a host.

The genetically programmed "correct" signal supports a lasting host association. In breeding programs for plant resistance, it is important to understand the nature of insect/plant relationships and their expression in host selection. Such understanding gives insights as to the underlying causes of the susceptibility/immunity gradient and enhances efficient development of resistant cultivars.

MECHANISMS OF RESISTANCE

Resistant cultivars function in many different ways to reduce the effects of insect attack. Various steps are required in host selection by insects. For normal insect growth and development to occur, certain requisites, available in proper amounts and at specific times, are necessary. Resistant cultivars, by one means or another, do not supply these requisites and thereby interrupt the normal host-selection process.

In some instances, the mechanism of resistance involves new allomones or increased levels of existing ones; in others, it may be based on reduced levels of kairomones. Also, physical factors may be involved. Most authorities consider true plant resistance as primarily under genetic control. In other words, the mechanisms of resistance are derived from preadapted inherited characters.

Therefore, the expression of these characters always occurs, although they can be mediated by environmental conditions. The most widely accepted classification of genetic resistance modes in plants is that of R. H. Painter. These modes or mechanisms include nonpreference, antibiosis, and tolerance.

Nonpreference

Nonpreference refers to plant characteristics that lead insects away from a particular host; it includes activities of both plant and insect. Another, perhaps more appropriate, term suggested for nonpreference is *antixenosis*. *Xenosis* is Greek for "guest"; therefore, antixenosis means against or expelling guests.

With nonpreference, normal insect behavior is impaired in such a way as to lessen chances of the insect's using a plant for oviposition, food, or shelter. Nonpreference can be expressed in a cultivar through either allelochemic or morphological characteristics.

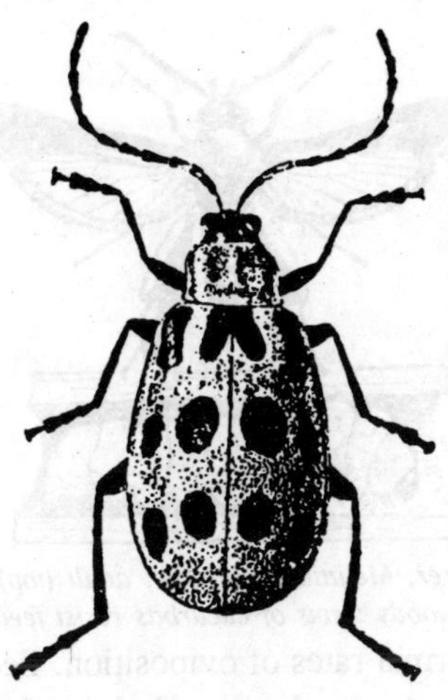

Figure 10.3: Spotted cucumber beetle, also referred to as the southern corn rootworm, Diabrotica undecimpunctata howardi, adult (top) and larva. Beetles are attracted to cucurbits and incited to feed by cucurbitacins.

Allelochemic Nonpreference

This form of nonpreference is common among plants, sometimes causing them to be totally rejected by insects. Allelochemic nonpreference occurs with insects like the spotted cucumber beetle, *Diabrotica undecimpunctata howardi*, and other *Diabrotica* species on cucurbits.

In this insect/plant relationship, cucurbitacins (a class of tetracyclic terpenes) produced by cucurbits act as attractants and feeding incitants for the beetles. Cultivars that lack or display low levels of specific cucurbitacins attract fewer beetles and receive much less damage than those with the feeding requisite.

Morphological Nonpreference

This form of nonpreference results from plant structural characteristics that disrupt normal behavior by physical means. As an example, the corn earworm, *Helicoverpa zea*, an important pest of many field and garden crops, prefers to oviposit on pubescent surfaces.

Experiments involving cotton genotypes that lack hairs have shown that these genotypes suffer much less damage by many insect species

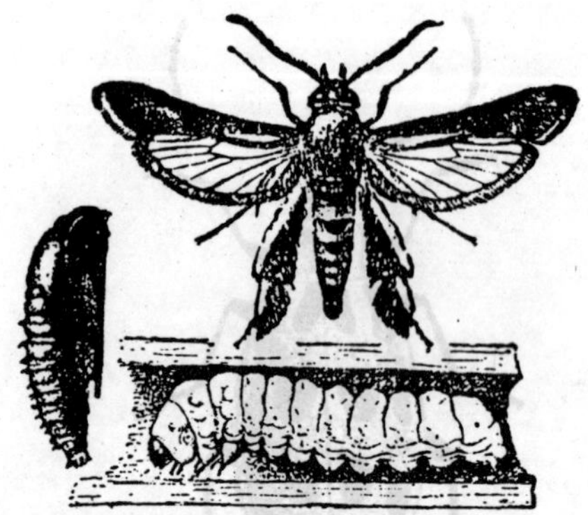

Figure 10.4: Squash vine borer, Melittia cucurbitae, adult (top), pupa (bottom left), and larva in stem. Hard, woody stems of cucurbits resist feeding by this insect.

because of lower than normal rates of oviposition. Feeding activity also is diminished in many instances by morphological factors, including pubescence, tissue characteristics, and gummy exudates.

As examples, husk tightness in corn resists damage from corn earworms, stem den- density of pith and node tissues in wheat resists damage by the wheat stem sawfly (*Cephus cinctus*), and hard, woody stems with closely packed vascular bundles in cucurbits resist feeding of the squash vine borer, *Melittia cucurbitae.*

Use of Nonpreference

In a practical sense, the use of some nonpreference characteristics may be limited by given cultural environments. Many cultivars may show nonpreference if alternate hosts are in the vicinity, but in the absence of alternate hosts, the nonpreference may break down.

The insect species does not particularly prefer the cultivar, but if nothing else is available, it will accept it. Because of the widespread practice of monocropping and the breakdown of resistance, allelochemic nonpreference is not a primary goal in plant breeding programs.

On the other hand, forms of morphological nonpreference that impair feeding behavior are very important and may be a first line of defense against many pests.

This is partly because morphological nonpreference provides longlasting effectiveness, compared with most chemically based resistance; that is, insect populations have a difficult time overcoming this form of resistance.

Antibiosis

By far, antibiosis is the most widely sought after objective of plant breeders. This mechanism usually impairs an insect's metabolic processes and often involves consumption of plant metabolites. As with nonpreference, both insect and plant factors are involved in the antibiosis mechanism.

Allelochemics frequently are associated with antibiosis. Some of the bestdocumented allelochemics include the cyclic hydroxamic acids in corn (DIMBOA), gossypol and related compounds in cotton, steroidal glycosides in potato, and saponins in alfalfa.

Quantity and quality of primary metabolites also may be important in conferring antibiosis. Particularly significant in this regard are imbalances of sugars and amino acids that result in nutritional deficiencies for insects feeding on the plant.

For example, pea cultivars with low amino acid levels and increased sugar content show resistance to the pea aphid, *Acyrthosiphon pisum*, and rice cultivars deficient in asparagine (an amino acid) cause reduced fecundity in the brown planthopper, *Nilaparvata lugens*.

Symptoms of insects affected by antibiosis include:

1. Death of young immatures
2. Reduced growth rate
3. Increased mortality in pupal stage
4. Small adults with reduced fecundity
5. Shortened adult life span
6. Morphological malformations
7. Restlessness and other abnormal behavior

Tolerance

Unlike nonpreference and antibiosis, only a plant response is involved in tolerance. The plant has the ability to give satisfactory yields in spite of injury levels that would debilitate nonresistant plants. This is the least dramatic resistance mechanism, and some plant scientists do not consider it a form of resistance.

Many factors are involved in plant tolerance, yet the overall mechanisms are poorly understood. Known components of this form of resistance include general vigor, compensatory growth in individual plants and/or the plant population, wound healing, mechanical support in tissues and organs, and changes in photosynthate partitioning.

An important advantage of tolerance is that it places no selective pressure on insect populations, as do nonpreference and antibiosis mechanisms. Without selection pressure, variants do not develop that can overcome the resistance. Its disadvantage is that insect populations may be allowed to sustain epidemics in an area, causing problems in other crops. Also, producers are wary of recommendations that allow large populations of seemingly injurious species to build up. Another, perhaps more important, disadvantage is that tolerance is more strongly affected by environmental extremes than are other forms of resistance.

An example of tolerance is found in several corn genotypes that have the ability to repair and replace roots fed upon by the western corn rootworm, *Diabrotica virgifera.* Such tolerance allows the plants adequate water and nutrient uptake and anchorage despite heavy feeding. Surprisingly, tolerant genotypes developed greater root volume with rootworm feeding than without.

In addition to corn, tolerant cultivars have been observed in many crops including alfalfa, barley, cassava, cotton, rice, sorghum, and wheat.

Apparent Resistance

Apparent resistance, sometimes called ecological resistance or pseudoresistance, usually is not considered true resistance. This is because expression of apparent resistance relies more heavily on environmental conditions than on genetics.

The characteristics of this resistance are temporary, and cultivars involved are potentially susceptible. Apparent resistance is important in insect pest management, but its use must be carefully synchronized with prevailing environmental conditions for effectiveness. The three types of apparent resistance recognized by most authorities include host evasion, induced resistance, and host escape.

Host Evasion

With host evasion, the plant passes through a susceptible stage quickly or at a time such that its exposure to potentially injurious insects is reduced. Often, host evasion is accomplished by planting early maturing varieties.

A good example is the planting of fast-fruiting, short-season cotton varieties in Texas to provide a long, host-free period for populations of the boll weevil, *Anthonomus grandis*, and pink bollworm, *Pectinophora gossypiella.* The same varieties also give considerable evasion from populations of corn earworm and tobacco budworm, *Helicoverpa virescens.*

Sometimes evasion with early maturing varieties is confused with true resistance. To test early varieties for true resistance, they can be planted later than usual and inspected for late-season injury.

Induced Resistance

Induced resistance is a form of temporary resistance derived from plant condition or the environment. Factors like fertilization or changes in soil moisture levels may make plants more tolerant of insects than under other circumstances. For instance, nitrogen and potassium levels are known to affect aphid populations on plants.

High nitrogen levels usually allow increases in survival, but the opposite may occur for high levels of potassium. Providing a proper balance of these nutrients in fertilizers has been suggested as a means of inducing resistance to aphids. Recently, some attention has been given to the role of *phytoalexins* in inducing plant resistance to insects. Phytoalexins are phenolic compounds produced by plants when they become diseased or are attacked by insects.

These compounds enable plants, once fed upon, to resist further damage by the pests. The mechanism involved results from an accumulation of allomones triggered by the injury or some other environmental factor. For example, phytoalexin production in laboratory soybeans has been induced by inoculation with a fungus, *Phytophthora megasperma* variety *sojae*.

Subsequently, phytoalexin levels in cotyledons increased and functioned as feeding deterrents against larvae of the Mexican bean beetle, *Epilachna varivestis*. The potential of induced-resistance is shown in research with spider mites that infest grapevines in the San Joaquin Valley of California. Leaves are injured both by the Pacific spider mite (*Tetranychus pacificus*) and the Willamette mite (*Eotetranychus willametti*).

The Pacific spider mite is by far the most injurious. Researchers found that when vines were infested with Willamette mites early in the season, Pacific mite densities were much lower. Experiments confirmed that "vaccinating" vines with the less injurious species early could effectively reduce effects of the more injurious species, at least in some situations. Research is continuing on this "inoculation" approach.

Host Escape

This category explains the lack of infestation of susceptible plants in a population of otherwise infested plants. The principle of host escape recognizes that the presence of an uninfested plant may not mean that it is resistant and emphasizes that escapes occur in most plant populations, even with heavy insect infestations. The reason for escapes is rarely understood.

GENETIC NATURE OF RESISTANCE

Plant breeding activities aimed at developing resistance rely heavily on a knowledge of genetic background for the resistance. Such knowledge provides a quantitative basis for designs to recombine genes and select for proper characters. It also allows the identification of stable resistance factors that are least likely to be overcome by a pest population.

Epidemiological Types of Resistance

This classification of resistant types has been advanced by plant pathologists to express effectiveness and stability against a population of pests. Effectiveness and stability of resistant varieties are determined by the plant genes that confer resistance and the insect genes that allow the resistance to be overcome.

The Gene-for-Gene Relationship

Many pest populations include individuals with *virulent genes*, which allow a pest species to overcome resistance and once more attack a plant. One or more virulent genes may be present that allow an individual pest to overcome the effects of one or more plant genes responsible for resistance.

This principle has been called the *gene-for-gene* relationship. In the gene-for-gene relationship, plant cultivars are resistant because they have a resistant allele at a gene locus that corresponds to an avirulent (susceptible) allele at an equivalent locus in the insect.

Even though the resistant cultivar is effective against most insects in the population, an occasional insect may have a virulent allele instead of the normally avirulent allele. For example, the resistance gene in the host plant may code for a protein toxic to the insect, and a corresponding virulent gene in the insect may code for an enzyme that detoxifies the toxic protein of the plant.

This circumstance allows virulent individuals to attack the otherwise resistant plant, and over a period of time, the virulent genotype can replace the avirulent genotype. Eventually, the effectiveness of the resistant cultivar would decrease. Different populations of an insect species that vary in their virulence to a cultivar are referred to as *biotypes*.

Some species of insects like the Hessian fly, *Mayetiola destructor*, are known to have several biotypes. The term biotype is frequently used for certain insect populations that overcome plant resistance. To date, most insect biotypes have developed among aphid pests. Prominent examples include spotted alfalfa aphid, *Therioaphis maculata*, on alfalfa; greenbug, *Schizaphis graminum*, on wheat; corn leaf aphid, *Rhopalosiphum maidis*, on sorghum and corn; and pea aphid, *Acyrthosiphon pisum*, on peas and alfalfa.

Other homopterans with biotypes include grape phylloxera on grapes and brown planthopper on rice. However, one of the best understood and most famous examples of biotypes is with a dipteran, the Hessian fly. To date, nine biotypes of this pest have been discovered.

Vertical and Horizontal Types of Resistance

Judging from the range of effectiveness of a resistant plant variety, J. E. van der Plank recognized two types of resistance, vertical and horizontal. In entomological terms *vertical resistance* refers to cultivars with resistance limited to one or a few pest genotypes.

Horizontal resistance describes cultivars that express resistance against a broad range of genotypes. Some authorities have argued against vertical resistance in breeding programs because of the potential development of biotypes. But it has been successful in many instances, as with the Hessian fly on wheat, and is easier to incorporate into new varieties than horizontal resistance.

To manage insects by using vertical resistance, it has been suggested that resistant plant genes need to be identified and incorporated into varieties that are held, then released when biotypes appear. Improvement in crops with horizontal resistance is a building process based on stepwise accumulation of genes with favourable additive effects.

At present, the only known way to accumulate these favourable genes is by selective breeding over several generations, involving genetic recombinations (recurrent selection). Horizontal resistance has low heritability and is difficult for plant breeders to incorporate.

Nevertheless, some success with insects has been possible, for example, cultivars of corn with high resistance to both generations of the European corn borer, *Ostrinia nubilalis*. Furthermore, horizontal resistance may be the most desirable type of resistance to use in pest management because of its stability.

Resistance Classes Based on Mode of Inheritance

Classes of plant resistance also can be distinguished according to the mode by which the resistance is inherited. In this regard, P R. Day recognized three major resistance categories: oligogenic, polygenic, and cytoplasmic.

Oligogenic Resistance

Oligogenic resistance is also called "major-gene resistance" and is conferred by one or only a few genes. This type usually produces vertical resistance against insects and may be inherited through dominant or recessive genes. Single-gene dominant resistance has been incorporated into varieties of such crops as apple, cotton, raspberry, rye, rice, and sweet clover. Single-gene recessive resistance can be found in corn lines resistant to the western corn rootworm and wheat resistant to the greenbug.

Wheats resistant to Hessian fly probably also should be considered oligogenic; in this instance, however, resistance is conferred by a series of dominant or partially dominant genes, as well as by several recessive genes.

Resistance is often considered oligogenic in this instance because a well-understood gene-for-gene relationship exists between resistance genes in wheat and the corresponding virulence genes in the Hessian fly.

Polygenic Resistance

Polygenic resistance is conferred by many genes, each contributing to the resistance effect. For this reason, it is also called "minor-gene resistance." Resistance inherited through the polygenic mode is usually very complex and may be associated with such quantitative traits as plant vigor and yield.

Horizontal resistance is usually polygenic. An example of polygenic resistance, as already mentioned, occurs in corn varieties resistant to the European corn borer.

Cytoplasmic Resistance

Cytoplasmic resistance is conferred by mutable (capable or liable to mutation) substances in cell cytoplasm. Cytoplasmic inheritance is maternal because most cytoplasm of the zygote comes from the ovum. Although cytoplasmic inheritance is very important in resistance to pathogenic microorganisms, it has not been a factor in resistance to insects.

FACTORS MEDIATING THE EXPRESSION OF RESISTANCE

Although resistance is governed primarily by genetics, physical and biotic elements of the environment often influence its expression. Indeed, abnormal deviations of environmental factors can have profound effects on the performance of many resistant cultivars.

Physical Factors

Weather, soil, plant architecture, and cultural practices are some of the most important influences on the plant's physical environment. These factors can affect plant resistance by influencing such elements as temperature, light intensity, and soil fertility. Changes in these elements cause fundamental changes in plant physiological processes and can alter levels of allelochemics or cause imbalances in basic nutrients.

Temperature

Abnormally high or low temperatures for a period of time may cause loss of resistance. As an example, exceptionally low temperatures have caused the loss of resistance of some alfalfa genotypes to spotted alfalfa aphid and pea aphid and of some sorghum genotypes to greenbug. Loss of resistance to the Hessian fly has been found in some wheats at temperatures above 18°C.

Light Intensity

Shade-induced loss of resistance has been found in several instances. These include wheats resistant to the wheat stem sawfly, *Cephus cinctus;* sugar beets resistant to the green peach aphid, *Myzus persicae;* and potatoes resistant to the Colourado potato beetle, *Leptinotarsa decemlineata.* With potatoes, shading was found associated with reduced levels of steroidal glycosides in leaves. These substances are known to retard feeding and development of the beetle.

Soil Fertility

Changes in soil-nutrient levels also may mediate the expression of resistance in some plants, but little is known about the mechanisms involved. In an example of this phenomenon, clones of alfalfa resistant to the spotted alfalfa aphid were found to have reduced resistance if deficient levels of calcium or potassium or excess levels of magnesium or nitrogen were present. In the same example, resistance was increased by deficiency of phosphorus.

Biological Factors

Just as physical factors can influence expressions of resistance, so can biological ones. The most significant biological factors are the selection of biotypes and changes in resistance with plant age.

Biotypes

Increases in the proportion of resistance-breaking biotypes already has been discussed. When resistant cultivars are grown widely, selection pressure is imposed by these hosts on the insect population. When capable, the insect population responds with genotypes having virulence to overcome the resistance.

As time passes, the virulent genotypes with superior fitness increase in number, displacing the avirulent types. The result is a situation of

Figure 10.5: Colourado potato beetle, Leptinotarsa decemlineata, showing striped adult, larvae (center), pupa (lower left), and eggs (far left and far right). Shading has been found associated with reduced levels of steroidal glycosides in potato leaves. These compounds are known to retard development of the beetle.

growing ineffectiveness of the resistant cultivar. Presently, there are more than 70 documented insect biotypes.

Biotypes occur in all kinds of pests. In plant pathology biotypes are called "races," or in instances of plant-parasitic nematodes, "pathotypes."

G. E. Russell distinguishes among four main types of genotypic variants in relation to resistant cultivars. These are:

1. True resistance-breaking biotypes that can attack previously resistant varieties. There is a definite gene-for-gene relationship between the pest insect and the resistant plant. Most Hessian fly biotypes are examples of true resistance-breaking biotypes.
2. Unusually vigorous variants that have high reproductive potentials on all plant genotypes, with no definite gene-for-gene relationship. An example of this occurs with biotypes of the cabbage aphid, *Brevicoryne brassicae*, on rape.
3. Geographical variants that may or may not be true resistance-breaking biotypes. These have been observed among biotypes of the Hessian fly and seem to be produced by factors other than widespread planting of resistant varieties.
4. Mistaken identities believed to be biotypes that really are different species for which resistance was never developed. Examples here are often difficult-to-identify forms like some nematodes.

It is important to distinguish among these forms of "biotypes" in developing a proper counter-response to the problem. The time required for breakdown in resistance may be only a few years, as for example, brown planthopper resistance in rice. However, it has not been uncommon for a resistant cultivar to remain effective for 8 to 10 years.

During this period, time is available to search for new resistant genes and incorporate them into new varieties, anticipating the next appearance of another biotype. As an example of excellent stability, some cotton cultivars in Africa with vertical leafhopper resistance have remained effective for more than 50 years. Other than aphids, the development of biotypes has occurred infrequently in most insect groups. The frequent occurrence of aphid biotypes is partly the result of aphid reproduction, which has a parthenogenetic mode during parts of the seasonal cycle.

Consequently, only one individual mutant, capable of feeding on a resistant variety, can produce a new biotype. Even including aphids, however, resistance-breaking insect biotypes have occurred much less frequently than have those among fungal and bacterial plant pathogens.

Plant Age

Physiological responses in plants vary with age, and these can lead to changes in the expression of cultivar resistance. For instance, resistance in corn to the European corn borer results from the presence of the cyclic hydroxamic acid *DIMBOA* (2,4-dihydroxy-7-methoxy-1,4-benzoxazine-3-one). DIMBOA levels are highest early in the growing season (midwhorl growth stage), thus offering maximum resistance to first-generation corn borers.

DIMBOA levels decline as the season progresses (more rapidly in susceptible than in resistant cultivars), and many commercial cultivars have very little resistance to second-generation corn borers. The expression of resistance corresponding to plant age also has been reported in alfalfa resistant to spotted alfalfa aphid and some tobacco resistant to green peach aphid.

TRADITIONAL DEVELOPMENT OF INSECT RESISTANT VARIETIES

It is beyond the scope of this discussion to describe the many activities and details of resistant-plant development. But a brief overview of the major steps traditionally involved may be of value in obtaining a perspective of the process. According to W M. Tingey, these major steps include:

1. Review pest problems of the crop with an interdisciplinary

group composed of entomologists, plant breeders, plant pathologists, and other crop production specialists.

2. Determine the economic need for management of insect pests and define the nature of plant damage. Review the biology and ecology of the target pests and the crop host.
3. Collect adapted and wild germplasm for evaluation of resistance.
4. Determine methodology appropriate in mass screening for resistance and initiate the screening program.
5. Intermate parental germplasm and select resistant progeny. Recycle germplasm for recombination as long as reasonable progress is made each generation. Initiate selection for desired properties.
6. Initiate studies of plant traits conferring resistance, their influence on pest performance, mechanisms of reducing damage, and inheritance.
7. Determine the permanence and stability of resistance by evaluation of advanced genotypes in diverse cultural and environmental conditions.
8. Evaluate the influence of resistance traits on key predators and parasitoids of the cropping system.
9. Determine the vulnerability of advanced resistant germplasm by using infested versus noninfested comparisons.
10. Determine the economic value of resistance in elite germplasm by using infested versus noninfested comparisons.
11. Multiply seed of elite resistant germplasm and release to public and commercial organizations.
12. Monitor postrelease performance of resistant cultivars to determine the appearance of host-specific biotypes and varietal reaction to other commercial production hazards and practices.
13. Publicize the economic and environmental benefits of insect-resistant cultivars to grower groups using demonstration plots, press releases, and other extension information devices.
14. Continue breeding and selection programs for intensified levels and alternate modalities of resistance.
15. Publish research findings to familiarize the scientific community with progress and to establish a formal reference base for justification of continued financial support.

Crop resistance programs are based on the involvement of specialists from several disciplines. With plant resistance to insects, the programs require input from plant geneticists, plant breeders, and entomologists. The actual crossing, genetic analysis, and evaluation of agronomic characteristics are the responsibilities of plant scientists.

Entomologists contribute by identifying resistance sources, characterizing mechanisms of resistance, and performing laboratory and field assays on resistance sources.

BIOTECHNOLOGY AND RESISTANT-VARIETY DEVELOPMENT

Today, much excitement is being generated over rapid advances in biotechnology and its possible use in solving many of our most difficult insect pest problems. One major use of biotechnology in insect pest management is in the development improved insect-resistant cultivars. With its newfound popularity in the media, the term *biotechnology* has had many different meanings and is represented in different ways.

The Office of Technology Assessment (United States Congress) defines biotechnology as "any technique that uses living organisms, or substances from those organisms, to make or modify a product, to improve plants or animals, or to develop microorganisms for specific uses."

In this sense biotechnology is not a new technology since it includes methodology for brewing, food fermentation, conventional animal vaccine production, and many other traditional endeavors. Usually, however, biotechnology is perceived as a new technology that encompasses (1) genetic engineering for producing vaccines and improving plants and animals, (2) monoclonal antibodies for diagnosis of cell proteins, and (3) new cell and tissue culture techniques for rapid propagation of living cells.

Particularly, genetic engineering has created much excitement in agriculture because it can allow for the manipulation and control of genes in heretofore unimaginable ways. However, all three aspects of modern biotechnology are very important to agriculture and can be used to aid in the development of new plant cultivars resistant to insect pests.

Basics of Genetic Engineering

An understanding of how plants are "engineered" begins with elementary information about molecular biology and proceeds with manipulations of genetic material to arrive at a transformed plant.

DNA: The Blueprint of Life

All living organisms can be subdivided into several functional

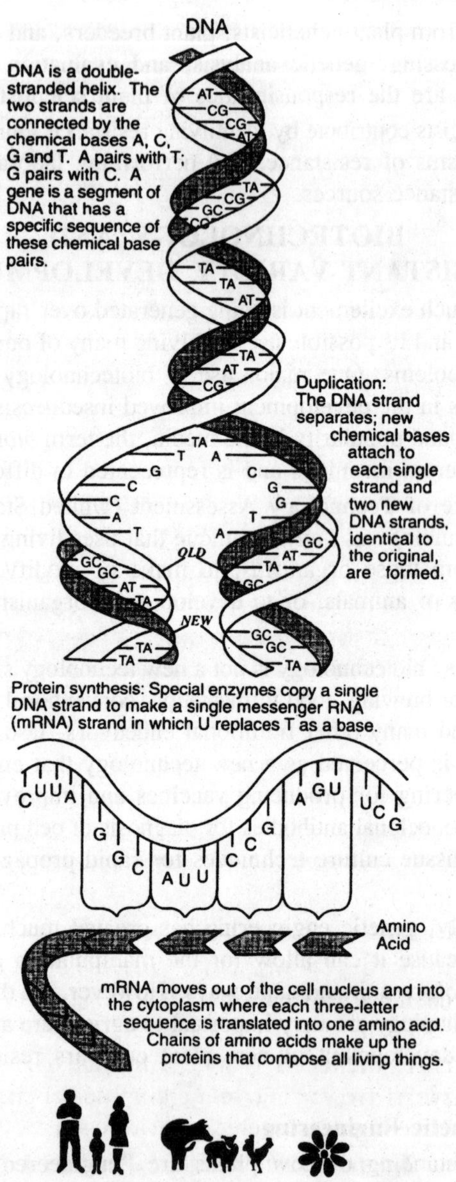

Figure 10.6: A DNA molecule (top) showing double stranded helix and paired bases, A, C, G, and T. Duplication is occurring in the bottom portion of the helix. Protein synthesis (middle) occurs when special enzymes copy a single DNA strand and produce messenger RNA. Here U replaces the T base. The messenger RNA produces sequences of amino acids (bottom) which build proteins and subsequently whole organisms.

components beginning with organ systems, organs, tissues, cells, and, ultimately, cell contents. Of particular interest here is the nucleus of the cell, which contains a slightly acid substance, deoxyribonucleic acid, or DNA.

This substance controls every biochemical process within cells and, consequently, the whole organism. Moreover, DNA possesses all information necessary for all phases of an organism's development, and this information is passed on to offspring from parents through a sophisticated process of replication. The structure of DNA resembles a helix with two strands.

The two strands are attached by the chemical bases A, C, G, and T, which occur in pairs. In these pairs, A occurs with T and G occurs with C. A portion of a DNA strand that encodes sufficient information to make a single protein is called a gene. The gene passes instructions to the cell through a complex decoding process. To accomplish this, the DNA double helix separates. New bases then pair with the open DNA strands to form a molecule like DNA, called messenger RNA (ribonucleic acid) or mRNA.

Finally, the messenger RNA commands the cell to assemble amino acids in certain ways to make proteins. The proteins give rise to new cells, and, subsequently, to tissues, organs, organ systems, and the whole organism.

Cutting and Splicing Chromosomes

Molecular biologists now understand the relationships between the A's, C's, G's, and T's of genes and the specific order and type of amino acids in proteins. In knowing this, they proceeded to change the DNA in cells for making new proteins, with the goal of conferring novel and useful properties in domesticated plants and animals.

The process of inserting new DNA along the DNA strand chromosome involves cutting and splicing procedures referred to as *recombinant DNA (rDNA) technology*. To cut DNA into reproducible pieces at specific locations, chemicals called *restriction enzymes* are used. Restriction enzymes are specific to a chromosomal site, and many of such enzymes have been discovered and cataloged.

By selecting the appropriate restriction enzyme, biologists can cut a DNA molecule at just the right location to obtain a desired gene from the donor and open another DNA molecule of the recipient for insertion. In this process, the cut ends of the fragments are chemically "sticky" and attach to one another (recombine) to form a new molecule.

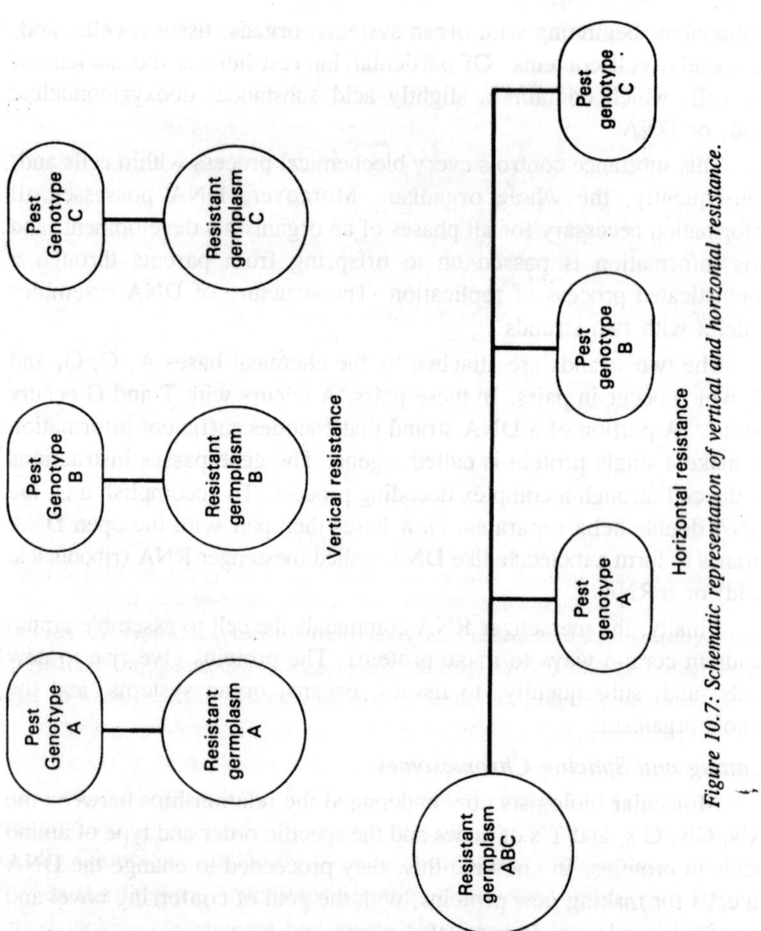

Figure 10.7: Schematic representation of vertical and horizontal resistance.

Resistant Plants from Recombinant DNA Technology

At present, rDNA technology to develop resistant plants mostly has involved inserting the gene responsible for producing delta endotoxin from the insect pathogen, *Bacillus thuringiensis* (*Bt*), into plant genomes. With this approach, the transformed or *transgenic* plant has the power to produce the toxic protein in its tissues, consequently killing feeding insects and protecting the plant.

In most instances the transgenic plants are developed with the use of a vector bacterium, *Agrobacterium tumefaciens*. This is a natural soil-born bacterium that causes "crown gall" disease in plants. *A. tumefaciens is* an efficient vector of DNA because it has the ability to transmit a fragment of its large plasmid (a closed loop of DNA in bacteria) into the nuclear genome of an infected cell. The fragment, called T-DNA, transferred contains genes, known as "oncogenes," that induce tumors in the plant tissue.

With the ability to insert its own DNA in a host, *A. tumefaciens* has been referred to as a natural "genetic engineer." By understanding the site of the T DNA, a fragment of DNA controlling delta endotoxin production from a Bt cell is inserted into the *A. tumafaciens* plasmid. The transgenic *Agrobacterium* then is used to transfer the delta endotoxin protein into the plant-cell chromosome.

Subsequently, the plant cell is cultured and grown into a whole plant whose cells contain the toxic protein. These transgenic resistant plants then produce seed expressing the insectresistant trait, which can be commercialized. This procedure has been used to transfer Bt delta endotoxin gene to many plants, most notably cotton, tobacco, tomato, and potato.

The new transgenic cottons resistant to the tobacco budworm and cotton bollworm are among the most developed, with commercial seed expected for marketing in the late 1990s. Although the *A. tumafaciens* method of gene transfer has been a good and flexible system, it has not worked very well with cereals. Even still, techniques are being developed which will allow transformation, such as biolistics ("gene gun" technology).

Using this method, tiny particles coded with the new gene are propelled by a burst of helium gas through plant-cell walls. A case in point is corn, where several seed companies have used this technology to develop Bt delta endotoxin cultivars for use against the European corn borer. These resistant cultivars currently are being field tested and have given outstanding results.

Although the transfer of Bt genes has been most prevalent in resistance development, genes that confer other modes of resistance also are being investigated. Most notable among these are genes that control the production of protease inhibitors.

In this area, resistance of tobacco to tobacco budworm has been conferred by introduction of a gene from cowpea, coding for the production of a trypsin inhibitor. Proteinase inhibitors have relatively low acute toxicities compared to Bt and may require higher levels of expression for effectiveness.

However, since their mode of action is more complex than Bt, the trait may be more resilient to the formation of biotypes.

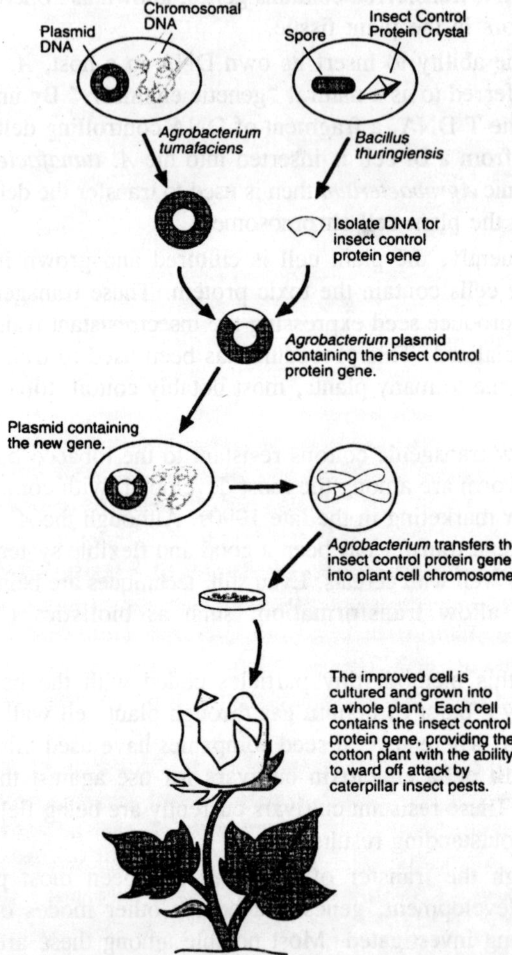

Figure 10.8: The process of developing a transgenic plant using Agrobacterium tumafaciens as a vector of delta-endotoxin-expressing DNA from Bacillus thuringiensis.

Deployment of Engineered Resistant Plant Varieties

The future looks very bright for the development of transgenic resistant plants. We can expect the early release of plant varieties with both Bt and proteinase inhibiting traits in many crops. However, there is considerable concern about the durability of these varieties because of the potential for resistancebreaking biotypes.

This potential is heightened because of their effectiveness, which produces strong selective pressures on pest insect populations, and the nature of the inheritance. Since resistance in most transgenic plants has been monogenic or oligogenic, it can be overcome more easily than polygenic traits.

For sustainability, the deployment of the engineered resistance factor should involve strategies to avoid the development of resistance-breaking biotypes early on. Some of these strategies include (1) mixes of resistant and susceptible plants in the plant stand, leaving refugia for some individuals, (2) sublethal doses that make insects more vulnerable to other environmental factors, and (3) expression of the resistance factor only in the plant part needing protection, usually reproductive structures.

In all of these strategies, the objective is to reduce total insect mortality, thereby reducing selection pressures. An alternative strategy is to deploy the resistance factor in very high titer, thereby causing very high mortality and consequently leaving no individuals to reproduce. Of course, none of these strategies is new; all have been suggested previously for avoiding resistance to insecticides.

Clearly, with continued advances in biotechnology, we are on the threshold of a new era, marked by effective new tools for managing pests. However, the most significant challenge ahead is not the development of new transgenic plants but finding ways to deploy resistance factors to help these plants remain effective in the long term.

SUCCESSFUL USES OF INSECT-RESISTANT CULTIVARS

Since the first major successes of grapes resistant to grape phylloxera in the late 1800s, many other outstanding accomplishments in plant resistance to insects have been achieved. Major developments have taken place particularly in grain and forage crops, including wheat, rice, corn, sorghum, sugarcane, beans, barley, and alfalfa. Progress, with varying degrees of success, also has occurred in vegetables, flowers, and other field crops.

According to a survey of G. F. Sprague and R. G. Dahms, more than 100 cultivars resistant to more than 25 insect species had been released to commercial production by 1972. Many more could be added to this total today.

Many specific examples of success with plant resistance against insects could be mentioned; in the United States, however, five stand out as having provided significant monetary gains to users. These include

Table 10.1: Summary of Inheritance of Resistance and Presence of Resistantbreaking Biotypes by Insect and Crop.

Inheritance	*Insect*	*Crop*	*Biotypes*
Oligogenic	Greenbug	Sorghum	Yes
		Wheat	Yes
		Barley	Yes
	Aphids	Raspberry	Yes
	Planthoppers	Rice	Yes
	Leafhoppers	Cotton	No
	Pea aphid	Alfalfa	No
	Wheat stem sawfly	Wheat	No
	Hessian fly	Wheat	Yes
	European corn borer	Corn	No
Polygenic	Cereal leaf beetle	Oats	No
	Stem borers	Rice	No
	Corn leaf aphid	Corn	?
	Corn earworm	Corn	No
	Spotted alfalfa aphid	Alfalfa	No
	Aphids	Brassicae	Yes

wheats resistant to Hessian fly and wheat stem sawfly, corn resistant to the European corn borer, alfalfa resistant to the spotted alfalfa aphid, and barley resistant to the greenbug.

Resistance to Hessian Fly

The search for wheat resistant to the Hessian fly began in 1914 in Kansas. An early variety, Kawvale, developed from a soft-wheat variety, Indiana Swamp, was released as resistant in 1928. Subsequently, Kawvale was superseded by higher-quality and more resistant varieties like Pawnee and, later, Ponca.

In Kansas, growing resistant varieties has resulted in the virtual disappearance of the insect, except where susceptible varieties are present. Annual savings from growing resistant varieties has been estimated at $238 million, produced from reductions in fly populations of 95 percent.

Resistance to European Corn Borer

The release of corn varieties resistant to the European corn borer began in the 1940s, and by the 1950s, workers in Iowa and Minnesota had developed more than 40 insect-resistant lines and hybrids.

Subsequently, many other varieties have been bred and released that have significantly reduced the threat of this introduced pest.

One of the more popular varieties, CI31A, has shown good resistance to the European corn borer in the United States, Romania, Canada, Yugoslavia, Hungary, and Russia. Although many resistant cultivars do not show activity against second-generation borers, one line, B52, offers a degree of resistance.

B52 has been successfully transferred to sweet corn, where second-generation injury is particularly important. However, heavy infestations can seriously impede development of the primary ear of B52 and other resistant lines, signifying the need for higher levels of resistance.

Two other cultivars, B86 and BS9C5, also are resistant to both generations of borers, and B86 has been successfully transferred to popcorn, which suffers injury from both generations.

Today, many commercial field corn hybrids possess genes for resistance to the European corn borer. It has been estimated that resistant cultivars are grown on about one-third of the corn area of the United States, resulting in annual savings of approximately $150 million.

Resistance to Spotted Alfalfa Aphid

The spotted alfalfa aphid was introduced into the United States probably about 1954. Shortly after the introduction of this insect, the alfalfa variety Lahontan, along with three of its five parental clones, were discovered to have resistance to the insect in Kansas.

Further work allowed the development of the alfalfa variety Cody, which possessed even higher levels of resistance and was well adapted to Kansas growing conditions.

Other varieties developed with good resistance and adapted to regional growing conditions include Mopa in California and Zia in New Mexico. Reselection within existing varieties is continuing, and yearly savings from growing resistant cultivars are estimated at $60 million.

Resistance to Wheat Stem Sawfly

One of the most dramatic instances of success in host-plant resistance has occurred with the wheat stem sawfly. This insect was a very destructive pest of wheat grown in the western United States and Canada until the use of flyresistant wheat, beginning in 1946.

At that time the solid-stemmed resistant variety, Rescue, was developed and released in Canada. Subsequently, the variety has been grown extensively in Canada and areas of the northern States. Rescue has continued to offer protection against wheat stem sawfly since its introduction, and biotypes have not been known to develop. However, relatively low-quality agronomic characteristics have prompted recommendations of Rescue's rotation with susceptible varieties in some instances. Nevertheless, savings of $4 million per year have been estimated because of the use of plant resistance.

Resistance to the Greenbug

Much plant-breeding activity has been invested in developing greenbug resistance in both wheat and barley. More than 7,000 wheat genotypes have been screened by the (United States Department of Agriculture) in Kansas and Oklahoma, and eight spring wheat cultivars have shown substantial levels of resistance.

Triticale, a hybrid cross of wheat and rye, also is significantly resistant. However, barleys have shown the highest levels of resistance. These include the American varieties Dicktoo and Will, as well as other varieties developed in China, South Korea, and Japan.

Although resistance in barley is controlled by a single dominant gene, biotypes have not been a major problem. The savings from growing greenbug-resistant barley in the United States are estimated at $500,000 annually.

USE OF PLANT RESISTANCE IN INSECT PEST MANAGEMENT

In insect pest management, plant resistance is used as a preventive, and most resistant cultivars have been developed for severe pests where economically significant populations are probable. When varieties providing nonpreference, or antibiosis, are grown, the carrying capacity of the agroecosystem is reduced and the general equilibrium position of the pest population drops.

The use of tolerant varieties does not reduce environmental carrying capacities; instead, loss is managed by insuring yield output. In the first two instances selective pressure is placed on the pest population, and in the third it is not.

Plant Resistance as the Sole or Primary Tactic

Resistant plants have been used as the primary management tactic where losses are heavy and economics will not allow such curative measures as pesticides. In dealing with most plant diseases, it is the only feasible approach because curative tactics are usually absent and other preventive measures generally lack effectiveness.

Considerable success using resistant varieties as the sole or primary tactic against several insects has shown the approach worthy of continued development. But because of the threat of resistance-breaking biotypes (particularly with vertical resistance), continual monitoring of the pest's status is necessary, as are dynamic breeding programs and transgenic plant development to provide timely supplies of new resistant varieties when needed. The use of horizontal resistance seems not to present these dangers; however, continued pest population assessment is still advisable.

Plant Resistance Integrated with other Tactics

A basic principle of insect pest management is that long-lasting solutions to pest problems depend on several harmonious tactics. Plant resistance can serve as an excellent component tactic, because it is usually compatible with pesticides and sometimes with biological agents.

One of the most important combinations is plant resistance and insecticides. Quite often, levels of plant resistance alone are not sufficient to avoid economic losses from insect pests. Combining plant resistance with welltimed low dosages of insecticides sometimes can achieve adequate suppression while reducing otherwise high insecticide inputs.

Such was the case with using resistant sweet corn (471-U6 × 81-1) and insecticides against the corn earworm in Georgia. Here, the resistant cultivar plus insecticide resulted in about 93 percent protection, compared with 86 percent for an insecticide-treated susceptible cultivar and 78 percent for the untreated resistant cultivar.

Although plant resistance and natural enemies are not always compatible, integrating them has been effective in certain instances. Theoretical studies have indicated that even small reductions in the growth rate of a pest population feeding on a resistant plant would allow significant increases in the action of a natural enemy.

This has been established with resistant varieties of sorghum and barley against greenbugs. Resistant cultivars enhanced the depressive influence of a parasitoid, *Lysiphlebus testaceipes*, on greenbugs severalfold compared with that on susceptible plants.

The reason for complementary and sometimes synergistic effects of plant resistance and natural enemies is not always understood. In some instances secondary plant metabolites may be involved. Some of the chemicals are incorporated into body odors of the pest, and this body odor is detected by natural enemies to locate their hosts.

In other instances, natural enemies may be attracted directly by plant volatiles, where subsequently they find their prey or host. Moreover, resistance may prolong the susceptible host stages, giving parasitoids more time to locate and parasitize pests.

It should be mentioned, however, that some characteristics of resistant plants, either morphological or chemical, may be deleterious to natural enemies. This situation could significantly alter the ultimate utility of such cultivars.

Much research toward understanding plant-insect-natural enemy relationships, socalled tritrophic interactions, is currently underway. This research should enhance our ability to design new cultivars with greater resistance and more environmental compatibility.

CONCLUSION

Plant resistance has many advantages as a primary tactic in insect pest management strategies. Among the most important are effectiveness, selectivity against the pest, relatively long stability, compatibility with other tactics, and human and environmental safety. In addition, resistant varieties can be adopted into crop production schemes easily and economically, resulting in both short-term and long-term gains.

Although the gains of developing and using resistant plants far outweigh the disadvantages, some of the most important limitations of the approach should be mentioned. Two of these are time required for development and problems with biotypes.

The time required for the development of new resistant varieties may be as long as 15 to 20 years, as demonstrated by some wheats. Even more time may be required with woody plants. This time is exceptionally long compared with the 6 to 9 years required for insecticide registration.

However, the development of plant resistance can be reduced substantially by increasing the rate of funding for research activities. Also, new techniques in selection and breeding are being developed that are expected to shorten this time considerably. Additionally, continued developments in biotechnology are expected to significantly reduce development time.

The problem of biotypes is another worry, particularly with the use of vertical resistance, but this side effect has been much more important with pathogenic microorganisms than with insects. In most instances, entomologists and plant breeders have been able to overcome the hazards of this problem with aggressive, dynamic breeding programs.

Genetically engineered plants should make a difference here as well. Other limitations of plant resistance to insects sometimes include poor agronomic characteristics of resistant cultivars and conflicts of resistant characters between different pest species. In the latter instance, a trait resistant to one insect may be attractive to another. For example, leaf pubescence of soybean leaves is the primary mechanism for resistance to the potato leafhopper, *Empoasca fabae*.

However, the hairy surface also stimulates egg laying by the green cloverworm, *Plathypena scabra*. In instances of conflicting characters, the relative impact of one pest must be weighed against others and decisions made accordingly.

In the example, the destructive potential of the potato leafhopper is much greater than that of the green cloverworm, making resistance to the more important pest preeminent. Looking toward the near future, we generally concede that plant resistance to insects will continue to rely heavily on identification of sources of resistance and traditional plant breeding.

However, with recent successes in biotechnology, we can expect transgenic resistant plants to play an increasingly significant role.

INDEX

D

E

Q

R

U

V

W

X

Y

Z